The Chinese Labyrinth

Challenges Facing Chinese Political Development

Series Editor: Sujian Guo, Ph.D.
San Francisco State University

In an attempt to reflect the rapidly changing political environment of the People's Republic of China, editor Sujian Guo has assembled a book series to present specialized areas of research in current Chinese political studies. Incorporating theoretical, empirical, and policy research on contemporary Chinese politics both domestically and internationally, this series contemplates the Chinese past, present, and future by utilizing interdisciplinary perspectives to approach issues related to Chinese politics, economy, culture, social development, reform, the military, legal system, and foreign relations. Aimed at bringing a greater understanding of the current Chinese political climate to Western audiences, this series is focused on the emerging voices of Chinese scholars and their perspectives on the ever-changing Chinese diaspora.

Recent titles in the series are:

The Dragon's Hidden Wings: How China Rises with Its Soft Power, by Sheng Ding
"Harmonious World" and China's New Foreign Policy, by Sujian Guo and Jean-Marc F. Blanchard
China in Search of a Harmonious Society, edited by Sujian Guo and Baogang Guo
Greater China in an Era of Globalization, edited by Sujian Guo and Baogang Guo
Toward Better Governance in China, edited by Baogang Guo and Dennis Hickey
Dynamics of Local Governance in China during the Reform Era, edited by Tse-Kang Leng and Yun-han Chu
Dancing with the Dragon: China's Emergence in the Developing World, edited by Dennis Hickey and Baogang Guo
Online Chinese Nationalism and China's Bilateral Relations, edited by Simon Shen and Shaun Breslin
Multidimensional Diplomacy of Contemporary China, edited by Simon Shen and Jean-Marc F. Blanchard
Thirty Years of China-U.S. Relations: Analytical Approaches and Contemporary Issues, edited by Sujian Guo and Baogang Guo
Environmental Protection Policy and Experience in the U.S. and China's Western Regions, edited by Sujian Guo, Joel J. Kassiola, and Zhang Jijiao
China's Quest for Political Legitimacy: The New Equity-Enhancing Politics, by Baogang Guo
New Frontiers in China's Foreign Relations, edited by Allen Carlson and Ren Xiao
The Failure China's "Democratic" Reforms, by Zaijun Yuan

The Chinese Labyrinth

Exploring China's Model of Development

Edited by Baogang Guo and He Li

LEXINGTON BOOKS
Lanham • Boulder • New York • Toronto • Plymouth, UK

Published by Lexington Books
A wholly owned subsidiary of The Rowman & Littlefield Publishing Group, Inc.
4501 Forbes Boulevard, Suite 200, Lanham, Maryland 20706
http://www.lexingtonbooks.com

Estover Road, Plymouth PL6 7PY, United Kingdom

British Library Cataloguing in Publication Information Available

Library of Congress Cataloging-in-Publication Data
The Chinese labyrinth : exploring China's model of development / edited by Baogang Guo and He Li.
p. cm.
Includes index.
ISBN 978-0-7391-6575-1 (cloth : alk. paper)
1. Political development--China. 2. China--Politics and government--1976-2002. 3. China--Politics and government--2002- I. Guo, Baogang, 1960- II. Li, He, 1953-
JQ1510.C4898 2011
320.951--dc23

2011041723

The paper used in this publication meets the minimum requirements of American National Standard for Information Sciences—Permanence of Paper for Printed Library Materials, ANSI/NISO Z39.48-1992.

Printed in the United States of America

Contents

List of Figures

List of Tables

Acknowledgments

This book is a collection of papers from an international symposium, titled "China in Search of Sustainable Development, Social Harmony, and Soft Power," held between July 30 and August 1, 2010 at Endicott College, Beverly, Massachusetts. The conference was co-sponsored by the Association of Chinese Political Studies and Endicott College. We want to express our sincere thanks to the College, especially Dr. Richard Wiley for his generous support, and Dr. Fujia Lu, for his tireless efforts.

Introduction

The Chinese Labyrinth: Exploring China's Model of Development

He Li and Baogang Guo

China remains both an enigma and a reality. It has grown at an average nine percent rate each year since the 1980s, yet still has one of the weakest governance structures in the world. It is one of the oldest civilizations strongly influenced by Confucian ethics, yet has been ranked as one of the most corrupt countries in the world today. Economic liberalization has brought unprecedented prosperity to many Chinese, yet more than 100 million people still live below the official poverty line.

China's recent changes have posed many challenges to the conventional theories of political development and post-communist transition. The advocates of the "Beijing Consensus" and the "Chinese model" believe that China's successful economic reform since the 1980s has created an alternative model to the liberal model which is centered on the synchronized development of electoral democracy and a free-market economy. The new model which implies a "lopsided" development, i.e., a full market transition combined with a developmental state, according to some, may be the key to understanding China's success.[1] Some were rushing to point out that China's experience is so unique that it can neither be repeated by other developing countries, nor imitated as a model for those countries. Still others argue that there is a danger of oversimplification to make the case for Chinese exceptionalism. Guy Sorman, in his book *Empire of Lies*, asks us to regard China not as an exceptional market occurrence but as a country capable of freedom like any other.[2]

The current debate on this issue is not entirely new. The same debate also surfaced during the official Westernization Movement (1861–1894) during the late Qing period. Unlike American exceptionalism, which is based on "manifest destiny," supranational expansion, genetic interpretation, or environmental explanations, advocates of Chinese exceptionalism drew its roots more from its unique history, culture, and demographic features. Many believed that China's Confucian culture had produced a fundamentally different experience from that of the West.[3] Qing Dynasty official Zhang Zhidong (1837–1909) advocated strongly the need to maintain traditional Confucian values while applying Western modern technologies to make China rich and strong. Some contemporary scholars have questioned the notion of China being uniquely different, and argued that the peaceful nature of historical Confucianism is a myth rather than a reality. Yuang-kang Wang's study of Song Dynasty's wars with foreign powers suggested that China's behavior was ubiquitous and she followed the same principles of international relations as any other state.[4]

Is China exceptionalism a myth or reality? Will modern China, born of Confucian creeds, be culturally, economically and politically distinct from Western industrialized nations in the age of globalization? Does the Confucian culture make any qualitative difference in China's developmental path and her international behavior in dealing with other nations? Will China be something of a paradox? Will this claim of distinction be a double-edged sword that will eventually hunt China in its future development? To decipher the complex Chinese labyrinth is not an easy task. No matter how complex this Chinese labyrinth may appear to be, there are ways to understand it. A complex branching such as a maze is always multicursal with choices of path and direction. A labyrinth, however, is unicursal and has only a single, non-branching path, which ultimately leads to the center.[5] The Chinese labyrinth therefore, represents an unambiguous route to the destiny—modernity and democracy.

This edited volume is a multi-disciplinary research project and an attempt to shed some lights on these important questions. This book is based on an international symposium titled "China in Search of Social Harmony, Sustainable Development, and Soft Power." The symposium was co-sponsored by the Association of Chinese Political Studies and the Endicott College between July 30 and August 1, 2010. A group of carefully selected papers centered on the theme is compiled into this book. All papers were carefully reviewed, and all subject to rigorous post-conference revisions by the authors.

In this book, we will explore the notion of Chinese labyrinth from the following angles: the development of a new social democracy, the Chinese vision of human rights and civil society, the asymmetry between economic and political development and the puzzle it presents, and the informal politics and Chinese innovation on governance and problem solving. We will also present a number of studies detailing innovations and systems that are distinctively Chinese, including innovations at local governances, the intriguing relationship between NGOs and the state, the grievance-addressing system *(xinfang)*, and the co-existence of atheists and theists in China. Although the contributors may not reach a consensus on these issues, we want to at least raise these significant issues in a hope for more scholarly discussion and debate.

Chinese Exceptionalism: Myth or Reality?

China's rise as a leading economic and military power is among the most paramount developments in the twenty-first century. In today's global tumult, China is one of the few countries enjoying high growth rates. Since the Chinese leadership made a strategic choice to reform its economic system and to open up to the world economy in the late 1970s, China has sustained an average annual GDP growth of nine percent, the fastest in the world, implying a doubling every seven or eight years. In 2010, China surpassed Japan as the second largest economy in the world. It is now the biggest exporter and an increasingly important investor.

In the wake of the Great Recession, the world has witnessed a frantic search for new models and strategies to generate sustained development. The fiasco of neoliberal reforms in developing countries forced a belated reappraisal of investors' blind trust in the market. Over the past three decades, China achieved stunning economic growth while at the same time maintaining relative political stability. The Chinese style of development looks appealing to many developing countries. With China's rise in power, the China model could be more attractive.

China's reform strategy recently has been touted by economists, including those from the World Bank and the International Monetary Fund, as both economically and socially successful. The market reform has produced a rapidly growing middle class. The Chinese "third way"—a mixture of market and continuation of significant state influence over the economy—is acquiring normative and policy significance and has been used to challenge the intellectual pillars of the Washington Consensus—often seen as synonymous with neoliberalism and globalization—by such influential figures as Joseph Stiglitz.[6] Joshua Ramo argues that there is a new "Beijing Consensus" emerging with distinct attitudes about politics, development, and the global balance of power. He suggests that China offers hope to developing countries after the collapse of the Washington Consensus, as China provides a more equitable paradigm of development.[7]

Meanwhile, China's rise has posed many challenges to the conventional theories of political development and post-communist transition. Conventional political science models of regime transitions assign almost no adaptability to Communist party-states. Communist systems are judged to be incapable of continuous improvements in administrative organization, economic coordination, technological innovation, and international competitiveness.

The Chinese transformation has occurred so quickly that myths and misperceptions abound about the challenges and opportunities that China poses to America and the rest of the world.[8] China's economic prosperity and stability, which flourish despite its harsh authoritarian regime, have puzzled a large number of Western observers who see such regime as "out of date."[9] The China model is a subject of heated debates in the past few years. First of all, the Chinese economic "miracle" in terms of economic growth and poverty reduction has provided a new twist to the age-old debate between development and democracy. The Chinese experience seems to challenge the "democracy is good for development" camp. Though market reforms launched by Deng in the late 1970s, had tendency to contradict and weaken a communist regime, many analysts see a new model developing in China: authoritarian state capitalism that delivers the rapid growth with stability.

Second, there are two sharply contrasting view of the future of China today. The optimists believe that China could overtake the United States to become the largest economy by the mid-twenty-first century. According to a recent report by the *Economist*, China could overtake the U.S. as early as 2019.[10] In the political realm, Beijing has been studying the model of governance of other countries closely so as to avoid the downfall of other great powers, such as the former

Soviet Union. To this end, the Chinese Communist Party (CCP) has managed to change its vanguard nature into a more inclusive ruling party. The CCP is ruling mainly by the power of co-optation, not by dictatorship of the proletariat. But the power of co-optation is even stronger than the dictatorship of the proletariat, purchasing the allegiance of the peasants and workers as well as entrepreneurs and intellectuals.[11] In the foreseeable future, such strategy could spur both social stability and economic growth and not compromise the party's authority to rule China. To the surprise of many pundits, China not only has survived the domino-like collapse of the Soviet bloc but also has maintained political stability despite internal and external challenges.[12] The optimists see the authoritarian features merely as those of underdevelopment. They posit that China will become a liberal democracy as it develops.

The pessimists, on the other hand, believe that China has managed its vulnerability to crisis well so far, but there is no guarantee it will continue to do so. These have been repeated forecasts of the "imminent demise" of China over the years.[13] Despite the new assertiveness of soft authoritarianism, its long-term future remains uncertain. China's stability is heavily dependent on economic growth, yet China's high growth comes with extremely high social and environmental costs. Simultaneously, bubbles continue to grow, especially in the housing sector. Many China watchers have long questioned the sustainability of the current model of development. Some believe that the apparent contradiction, i.e. economic liberalization without political liberalization will eventually compromise China's development. As economists and strategists busily extrapolate its future growth path to predict when it will catch up to the United States, the mood in China has become somber and subdued in recent years. The Beijing leadership has started to reformulate its economic and social policies.

Third, whether the China model is a myth or reality is another topic of the debate. To begin with, sustainability is a major attribute of a model. Modernization is a long-term, dynamic, multidimensional development process in socioeconomic and political transformation. After three decades of spectacular growth, China's reform is still an unfinished business. The country is still troubled by many characteristics of underdevelopment. It is no wonder that Premier Wen Jiabao sees China's growth as "unstable, unbalanced, uncoordinated and ultimately unsustainable."[14]

Furthermore, a key tenet of the model of development is that it could be applied to other cases. Because of different initial conditions (such as size of the country, history, culture, labor supply) of China's transformation, it is not easy for other developing nations to duplicate China's success story. As Dani Rodrik observes rightly, there is simply too much diversity in the world to be shoehorned into common rules, even if those rules are somehow the product of democratic process.[15]

Finally, models of development usually contain a strategic plan. In the words of Deng Xiaoping, the Chinese reform is similar to "wading across a river by feeling for stone (*mozhe shito guohe*).[16] It has been widely acknowledged by some Western scholars that Beijing did not sequence reforms; rather, it pushed ahead where there was the least resistance.[17] According to Jiang Zemin, the Chinese reform is a process of *yushi jujin* (keeping pace with the times). Apparently the reform in China has been a gradual, adaptive process without a clear blueprint. Some scholars even argue that the overall economic transformation of China really is not a puzzle or a mystery. The Chinese style of development is almost identical to the East Asian development model.

Chapter Outlines

The Chinese success story has incited world-wide discussion on the "China model" since the mid–1990s. At the time of writing, the discussion on the China model is still very controversial. In this volume, the consistent effort is to explore the various aspects of the China model.

In the first chapter, "Rapid Economic Growth without Economic Freedom: A Puzzle Made in China," Congsheng Wu and Siyuan Zhou investigate the relationship between economic growth and economic freedom. What causes the economy to grow has been one of the most enduring questions in economics. The development economics literature indicates that economic freedom and sound legal, financial, and political institutions boost economic growth. China's phenomenal growth has been accompanied by a relatively undeveloped legal and financial system, lack of economic freedom and high corruption. China's stunning economic rise is one of the biggest stories of this generation. In just three decades since beginning to embrace market economics, China has left its desperate poverty behind to become the world's top exporting nation. However, its rapid economic growth has been accompanied by a relatively undeveloped legal and financial system, lack of economic freedom and high corruption. Its economic freedom has been constantly below the world average and has not shown any improvement over time. In fact, China was the 124th freest economy in the 2008 *Index of Economic Freedom* published by the Heritage Foundation and the *Wall Street Journal*. Author's findings reveal that China is a counterexample to the findings in law, institutions, economic freedom, and economic growth literatures. So what is the secret to China's economic miracle? Can it continue without sound legal, financial and political institutions? Congsheng Wu and Siyuan Zhou shed some light on this puzzle about China.

In chapter two, Xiaobo Hu offers a critique of paradigms that are limited to the Western history and experience as well as the made-in-China paradigms that tend to offer no insight or improvement over the theories originally developed in the West. He contends that in the studies of property rights and rent seeking and the recent development in Chinese mainland challenge the conventional wisdom of Western theories.

Hu finds out that there is a coexistence of rent seeking and surplus seeking behaviors in the reform era. Such coexistence sustains a mixed economy. While the private sector can enjoy certain freedoms and opportunities for rapid economic growth, these freedoms and opportunities are restricted to preferential policies and benefits that are often still reserved for the state sector. Surplus seeking in China's mixed economy provides strong incentives for non-state players to join in the "state club." Surplus seeking divests resources and energy from further developing the private sector.

Hu argues that the Chinese experience has enriched our understanding of comparative politics and economic development, challenged theories that are not broadly useful, and provided social scientists with a once-in-a-lifetime opportunity to explore the fundamental questions regarding human interactions that link political, economic, and social development.

Chapter three, by He Li, highlights the Chinese discourse on social democracy. Following the worldwide financial meltdown and recession, there has been a global debate on the future of democratic politics. Its focus is whether social democracy could emerge in the new form and prosper on a practical as well as an ideological level. China, too, has recently seen a resurgence of interest in European social democracy, and the emergence of the neoliberals on the one hand and the New Left on the other. Meanwhile, the Beijing leadership has started to rethink its economic and social policies.

The chapter addresses the following questions: What is social democracy? How and under what circumstances did social democracy emerge in China? What are the major arguments of the social democrats? What role has intellectual discourse on social democracy played in China's reform? Li argues that up to now there is no indication that the CCP intends to rebrand itself as a social democratic party as its counterparts in Eastern Europe did; nor will the CCP implement a multiparty system in the foreseeable future. However, the Chinese discourse on social democracy has helped the CCP adopt major elements of social democracy into its social and economic policies, without losing its identity or having to deny its socialist tradition.

Chapter four, by Jianxing Yu and Ziying He, probes the tension between governance and state-building. Governance stresses diversification, reflexive rationality, hierarchic interaction, negotiation and coordination, whereas state-building emphasizes centralization, procedural rationality, hierarchic order, control and regulation. Despite the conflict resulting from the differences between their respective essences, there is some blending between the two. On the one hand, the process of state-building is simultaneous with the process of the establishment of civil rights and democracy. On the other hand, a strong state is needed to provide the footstone for governance because of the risks associated with governance failure and the necessity of meta-governance. Such conflicts and blending construct tension and contradiction between governance and state-building, but these tensions and contradictions are precisely what make China's developmental path unique and warrant a careful study.

This chapter first makes some theoretical inquiry over the paradoxical relations between governance and state-building and then uses China as a case study to illustrate our argument that China's development model is unique precisely because of its focus on state-building in the formative years of economic reform. They believe state-building is a necessary precondition of democratic governance. However, the development of democratic governance, which China has gradually turned its attention to, can also help mitigate, if not avoid, risks associated with the former's tendency toward statism. Although there are tensions between governance and state-building, the authors believe that such tensions are unavoidable in a transitional society and can be balanced by implementing the "rule of law."

The fifth chapter, by Xinjun Gao and Baogang Guo, is based on extensive interviews in China. It examines recent developments in local-level governance reform. China has been placing strong emphasis on improving governance and operational efficiency of its governmental system. This is considered politically, economically, and socially less disruptive and better for China. Entering the twenty-first century, local-level government innovations in China have entered an active period. With institutional, theoretical, technological and cultural innovations, China has created large numbers of innovations in public service, administrative reform, political transparency, grassroots democracy, scientific policy-making, citizen participation, legislative work and helping the poor. In line with the level of innovation, including the degree to which projects were voluntary, the levels of benefits, their importance, cost-saving potential and degree of promulgation, the "China Local Innovation Award" sponsored by the China Center for Government Innovation Research in the Beijing University, through five rounds has evaluated more than 1,300 projects, accepted one hundred for final evaluations and awarded fifty "Innovation Awards." This chapter also analyzes the causes, characteristics, and sustainability of these administrative innovations and their implication for the development of a political system with Chinese characteristics.

In chapter six, Michael Kilburn and Vitaly Kozyrev examine the evolution of the Chinese approach to human rights. China has had an ambivalent relationship with the discourse of human rights. Its poor record of human rights record has been criticized worldwide and has also caused grave concern in the international community. While rights claims were made against the Kuomintang during the civil war, since its founding in 1949, the leaders of the People's Republic have privileged workers' or citizens' rights over the prevailing standards and reference points of ostensibly universal human rights enshrined in the Universal Declaration of Human Rights (UDHR). Starting in 1991, the Chinese government released a series of white papers on "Human Rights in China," which directly engaged the critics and defended its human rights record in the context of a developing "harmonious socialist society." In April 2009 the government published its first "National Human Rights Action Plan, 2009–2010" aimed at promoting and protecting human rights and improving laws and regulations upholding human rights and advancing the cause of China's human rights in accordance with the law.

Is this rhetorical strategy—as the critics claim—merely prevarication: a cynical attempt to distract the international community from serious rights violations from Tibet to Darfur; from the death penalty to freedom of expression to environmental degradation? Or does it truly represent a substantive movement to reframe and incorporate human rights in the Chinese context? Does a reanimation of the "Asian values" debate signify bluntly—as the Chinese delegate to the 1993 Vienna World Conference on Human Rights put it—that "individuals must put the state's rights before their own"? Or might the broader project to promote sustainable development and social harmony function as a counterweight to the first generation bias of Western Enlightenment notions of rights and finally provide the basis for the integration and full exercise of human rights, including the civil and political?

Authors contend that unlike the Western liberal tradition, the Chinese don't separate the individual from society and state in terms of the rights to subsistence and development. In addition, human rights are considered a function of China's fight for national independence, which is similar to the Russian concept of "sovereign democracy." The notion of sovereignty as part of human rights creates a direct challenge to the Western perception of human rights as a matter of higher priority than state sovereignty.

This chapter takes both seriously and critically China's recent approach to human rights, and suggests that the incorporation of human rights discourse into the larger project for sustainable development, social harmony, and soft power has transformative potential both for China and for the meaning of human rights itself.

The seventh chapter is Yiran Zhou's "China's Religious Policies in the Post-Mao Period: Co-existence of Atheists and Theists." The assertiveness of both the Chinese camp and Western camp in defending their claims regarding the Chinese religious status seems to make their controversy irreconcilable while putting one at a loss over how to view the contemporary Chinese religions. To gain an insight into China's state-religion relations, the author addresses the following questions: What are the root causes that divided the two camps and shaped their opposing views? What is really happening in China regarding religion and its relations with the state? Moreover, how did the Chinese management of religion evolve in recent decades? And in what trajectory would it possibly evolve in the future? To accomplish these tasks, this chapter starts with an analysis of the historical and cultural reasons behind the divergence of Chinese and Western understandings of the Chinese religions. It then explores how the state and religion interact in contemporary China by discussing the Chinese religious policies in the post-Mao period—specifically, in three eras of the party leadership with Deng Xiaoping, Jiang Zemin, and Hu Jintao successively at its core. Finally, the chapter explores the specific policies that the state might adopt in the foreseeable future, through an examination of the characters of five government-sanctioned religions (Buddhism, Taoism, Islam, Protestantism and Catholicism) and their adaptability to the state. It is concluded that the mainstream trend of the state-and-religion relations would be in the direction of mutual adaptation and accommodation, in the setting of an increasingly modernized society. In the meantime, conflicts between state and religion would emerge sporadically due to an enduring, inherent incompatibility between Communism and religion.

In the eighth chapter, entitled "China's Petition System and Its Effects on Social Stability and Regime Legitimacy," Lacey Bradley-Storey brings our attention to the petition system. In China, the petition system (*xinfang,* translated as "letters and visits") has a history several centuries long. Due to restrictions on activism and political opposition, non-democratic states frequently lack reliable communication channels between the leadership and the populace. Although expressions of dissatisfaction are often met with repression, authoritarian states sometimes solicit input from their citizens in a process known as "contacting." While these dual approaches appear paradoxical, they often work in conjunction with one another so that the central leadership can both subordinate local officials and advance regime legitimacy. *Xinfang* serves this function by enabling individuals to both report on local government malfeasance and appeal to higher authorities for redress. Despite this, there remains some measure of uncertainty regarding the *de facto* effects of *xinfang*—specifically, how does this particular contacting institution actually impact mass-elite relations? Does *xinfang*, by offering a channel for citizens to articulate their concerns and suggestions, enhance social stability and help the regime maintain legitimacy?

The author answers these questions by arguing, first, that not only does the petition system embody a complex and often conflicting mandate, but it is also a legitimating institution, meaning that it functions in a way so as to bolster (or undermine) the legitimacy of the regime. Second, the chapter argues that as a result of its conflicting mandate, the actors who participate in *xinfang*, specifically the central and local governments and petitioners themselves, have competing perceptions of the purpose and function of the system. For the central government, *xinfang* is inherently political—a tool of governance. For the local governments, *xinfang* is often considered a potential threat to the positions of local officials and to the legitimacy of local government institutions. Finally, petitioners view the purpose of *xinfang* as inherently legalistic, meaning that their participation in *xinfang* stems from a legally based claim to justice. Because *xinfang* is used for different, often-competing purposes, its ability to function in a legitimating role is necessarily hampered.

In chapter nine, "Globalization and Transformation of China's Welfare Regime," Huisheng Shou examines the impact of the Chinese integration into the world economy on China's social welfare system. Shou argues that China's welfare transformation is part of a general movement occurring in the developing world in the past decades in the new context of globalization. Globalization has induced a structural change of preferences among major social actors with regards to social protection, which in turn affects the government's policy choices. More specifically, the interaction between trade openness and low-skill based industrial structure has enabled the Chinese government to maintain a reasonably low level of welfare spending that nevertheless protects the majority of its labor force in order to maintain both market competition and sustainable development.

The author challenges two rather influential views: one is that the Maoist China was an ideal welfare state and the other is that the post-Mao China ignored the livelihood of underprivileged citizens. Instead the author finds that China's remarkable integration into the world economy changed the Chinese economic structure, hence alleviating the need to protect millions of low-skilled laborers employed by internationally-related businesses, and providing the Chinese government with more financial resources to cover more social groups. The author's insight is not limited to China as the Chinese welfare policies fit a general trend among many developing countries in the age of globalization.

The world financial crisis provided China with opportunities to demonstrate its political and economic value as a global power. This edited volume demonstrates that China slowly has developed its unique path of development which stands in sharp contrast to the liberal democracy espoused by the West. The Chinese experience demonstrates a variety of paths leading from a planned to a market economy, from an authoritarian regime to a more democratic one. There is no ideal development model for every society in the world; likewise, to emulate the development experience of other societies would be risky, considering the enduring and seminal differences across countries.

By bringing together experts of China studies, the book provides useful insights into fierce debates on China's economic, social, and political transitions. Their insightful analyses will help people have a better understanding about what is behind the great transformation in contemporary China and its implications for international politics and global economy in years to come.

Notes

1. Jonathan Anderson, "Beijing Exceptionalism," *National Interests* (March/April 2009), 23.

2. Guy Sorman, *Empire of Lies: The Truth about China in the Twenty-first Century* (Orlando, FL: Houghton Mifflin Harcourt, 2008).

3. See Christopher A. Ford, *The Mind of Expire: China's History and Modern Foreign Relations* (Louisville, KY: University Press of Kentucky, 2010); Daniel A. Bell, *Beyond Liberal Democracy: Political Thinking for an East Asian Context* (Princeton, NJ: Princeton University Press, 2006), and Baogang Guo, *China's Quest for Political Legitimacy: the New Equity-Enhancing Politics* (Lanham, MD: Lexington Books, 2010).

4. Yuan-kang Wang, *Harmony and War: Confucian Culture and Chinese Power Politics* (New York: Columbia University Press, 2010).

5. Hermann Kern, *Through the Labyrinth: Designs and Meanings over 5,000 Years (Art & Design)* (Lakewood, NJ: Prestel Publishing, 2000), Ferre Robert Edition, 23.

6. Yasheng Huang, "Internal and External Reforms: Experiences and Lessons from China," *Cato Journal* 21, no. 1 (spring–summer 2001): 62.

7. Joshua Ramo, *The Beijing Consensus* (London: Foreign Policy Centre, 2004): 65.

8. Huge volume of literature has accumulated on this subject. For some prominent work, see, Zhaohui Hong, *Zhongguo teshulun: zhongguofazhan de kunhuo he lujing* [The China Uniqueness: Dilemmas and Directions of China's Development] (New York: Cozy House, 2004); Pan Wei, ed. *Zhongguo mo shi: kie du Renmin Gongheguo de 60 nian* [China Model: A New Developmental Model from the Sixty Years of the People's Republic] (Beijing: Zhong yang bian yi chu ban she, 2009); Yongnian Zheng, *Zhongguo moshi jiangyan yu kunju* [The China Model: The Lessons and Dilemma] (Hangzhou, China: Zhejiang Renmin Chubanshe, 2010); and Zhang Weiwei□Zhongguo zhen han: yi ge "wen ming xing guo jia" de jue qi [Chinese Shock: The Rise of a Civilized Country] (Shanghai Renmin Chubanshe, 2011).

9. For details, see Suisheng Zhao, "Political Liberalization without Democratization: Pan Wei's Proposal for Political Reform," *Journal of Contemporary China*, 12, no. 35 (2003): 348–50.

10. "Dating Game: When Will China Overtake America," *The Economist*, December 16, 2010.

11. David Shambaugh, *China's Communist Party: Atrophy & Adaptation; American and European Relations with China* (Washington, D.C.: Woodrow Wilson Center Press, 2008).

12. Zhiqun Zhu, ed., *The People's Republic of China Today: Internal and External Challenges* (Singapore: World Scientific Publishing, 2010).

13. See, for example, Gordon C. Chang, *The Coming Collapse of China* (New York: Random House, 2001).

14. "China Confident in Maintaining Economic Growth: Premier," (Xinhua News Agency March 16, 2007), http://www.china.org.cn/english/2007lh/203252.htm (assessed January 2, 2010).

15. Dani Rodrik, *The Globalization Paradox: Democracy and the Future of the World Economy* (New York: W.W. Norton & Company, 2011).

16. Susan L. Shirk, *How China Opened Its Door: the Political Success of the PRC's Foreign Trade and Investment Reforms* (Washington, DC: Brookings Institution, 1994), 27.

17. Edward Friedman, "Is China a Model of Reform Success?" in Edward Friedman, ed., *National Identity and Democratic Prospects in Socialist China* (Armonk, NY: M. E. Sharpe, 1995), 200.

Chapter 1
Rapid Economic Growth without Economic Freedom: a Puzzle Made in China

Congsheng Wu and Siyuan Zhou

China's economy has grown by nearly ten percent each year for over three decades, and surpassed Japan to become the second largest economy in 2010. To the Communist party leaders, China's economic success has stemmed from the unswerving adherence to the Party's basic line. Economists, however, are challenged to understand the nature and causes of economic progress in general and China in particular.

In fact, one of the most enduring questions in economics is what causes economies to grow. The full title of Adam Smith's well-known book, *An Inquiry into the Nature and Causes of the Wealth of Nations*, published in 1776, clearly shows that the causes of prosperity are Smith's main concern. The book concludes that free markets, the protection of private property rights, and a minimal government interference in the economy lead to prosperity. Put shortly, economic freedom is conducive to economic progress.

Adam Smith's conclusions were generally accepted among economists until the twentieth century, when developments in economic theory reversed the conventional wisdom and led many economists to advocate central planning and government control as a better way of organizing economic activities, especially among less developed economies. This change is in part due to advances in economic theories and partly due to worldly events. Around the turn of the twentieth century, methods in economics began to more closely resemble the hard sciences. Economic theories have been developed through increasingly complex mathematical models. In mathematical terms, an economy's output can be depicted in a production function, where output is a function of inputs such as land, labor and capital.

The production function theory sees the economy as a machine that transforms labor, natural resources and capital into output. If output increases more rapidly, it is either because of larger amounts of inputs or because of better technology and increased efficiency. The focus on inputs, together with an acceptance of government management of the economy, led many economists to recommend government planning as the better way to create growth in less-developed countries. They argued that central planning and state control, if intelligently applied, could boost growth.

The fundamental assumption of the production function theory is that an economy's potential, defined by its resources and technology, is fully realized. To development economists, however, this assumption seems to be far-fetched. They argue that the problem of the less developed countries (LDCs) is not a lack of potential but an inability to achieve that potential. Inputs are necessary to produce output, but without the right incentives, it is too easy to combine inputs in a way that makes the final output less valuable than the original inputs.

At the end of the twentieth century, economists seemed to be turning back to the basic ideas of Adam Smith, especially after observing the collapse of most centrally planned economies around the world. In development economics, attention has therefore shifted to how and what degree economies succeed in realizing their production potential. Rather than looking only at resources and technology, development economists have started to take an interest in economic and political institutions. They are interested in two fundamental questions: How do different institutions affect economic development and growth? And how and why do "good" institutions arise?

Recent empirical work has analyzed country-level data on the gross domestic product (GDP) and various measures of legal, financial, and political institutions to uncover which institutions are associated with more rapid economic growth. For instance, La Porta et al. show that several legal variables such as the respect for the rule of law, protection of property rights, enforceability of contracts, and legal heritage have a causal relationship with levels of economic growth.[1]

Another line of empirical research focuses on the link between economic freedom and economic growth. Empirical studies along this line generally document a positive link between economic freedom and growth, using various numerical measures of economic freedom. De Haan and Sturm, for example, compare several indicators for economic freedom and conclude that these somewhat different measures show similar rankings for the countries covered.[2] They test the robustness of the relationship between freedom and growth and conclude that more economic freedom fosters economic growth.

A recent study by Wu investigates the association between the *Index of Economic Freedom*, developed by the Heritage Foundation and the *Wall Street Journal*, and the real GDP growth across countries.[3] Wu finds that countries whose economic freedom improves have faster economic growth.

China's phenomenal growth performance in the past three decades has been accompanied by a relatively undeveloped legal and financial system, lack of economic freedom and high corruption. Its economic freedom has been constantly below the world average. And it has shown little improvement over time. In fact, China ranked only 124th in the 2008 *Index of Economic Freedom*. During the period of 1995–2008, China's real GDP grew at an average annual rate of about ten percent, making China one of the fastest growing economies in the world.

Allen et al. (2005)[4] use measures from the existing literature and find that China's law and institutions, including investor protection systems, corporate governance, accounting standards, and quality of government, are significantly less developed than most of the countries. More importantly, the growth in the private sector, where applicable legal and financial mechanisms are arguably poorer than those in the state and listed sectors, is much faster than that of the other sectors. The system of alternative mechanisms and institutions plays an important role in supporting the growth in the private sector, and they are good substitutes for standard corporate governance mechanisms and financing channels.

Allen et al. thus conclude that China seems like a counterexample to the findings in law, institutions, finance and economic growth literatures. So what is the secret to China's economic miracle? Can it continue without sound legal, financial and political institutions? These issues are too broad and complicated for the current chapter to undertake. The purpose of this chapter is to shed some light on this puzzle. To this end, it explores empirically the association of economic freedom with prosperity and economic growth using country-level data. It then discusses the implications on China.

The Index of Economic Freedom

Since 1995 the Heritage Foundation and the *Wall Street Journal* have tracked the march of economic freedom around the world with the influential *Index of Economic Freedom*. The index creates ten benchmarks that gauge the economic success of most countries around the world. The Heritage Foundation describes economic freedom as the absence of government coercion or constraint on the production, distribution, or consumption of goods and services.

According to the Heritage Foundation, "economic freedom is the fundamental right of every human to control his or her own labor and property. In an economically free society, individuals are free to work, produce, consume, and invest in any way they please, with that freedom both protected by the state and unconstrained by the state. In economically free societies, governments allow labor, capital and goods to move freely, and refrain from coercion or constraint of liberty beyond the extent necessary to protect and maintain liberty itself."

Economic theory dating back to the publication of Adam Smith's *The Wealth of Nations* emphasizes the lesson that basic institutions that protect the liberty of individuals to pursue their own economic interests result in greater prosperity for the larger society. Modern scholars of political economy are rediscovering the central fact that "free institutions" are essential to sustained long-term growth.

The index of economic freedom measures ten components of economic freedom, assigning a grade in each component using a scale from 0 to 100. High scores approaching 100 represent higher levels of freedom. The higher the score on a factor is, the lower the level of government interference in the economy. The ten component scores are then averaged to give an overall economic freedom score for each country.

The ten components of economic freedom are: 1) Business freedom; 2) Trade freedom; 3) Fiscal freedom; 4) Government spending; 5) Monetary freedom; 6) Investment freedom; 7) Financial freedom; 8) Property rights; 9) Freedom from corruption; and 10) Labor freedom.

Table 1.1 presents the world average of the economic freedom index. As shown in the table, the world average hovers in a narrow range of 57–60 over the years 1995–2008. During this period, the average economic freedom improves by merely 2.6 points. The reason that economic freedom shows little improvement over time is perhaps due to the fact that the index covers far fewer countries in the early years and those that are added later on are mostly developing countries which generally have lower freedom scores. For instance, in 1995, the first year of the index, only 101 countries were covered while the number of countries included in the index increased to 157 by 2008.

Table 1.1 The Index of Economic Freedom: 1995–2008

Year	N	Mean	Median	25 percent Quintile	75 percent Quintile	Min	Max
1995	101	57.6	57.6	50.7	64.5	8.9	88.6
1996	141	57.1	58.2	49.4	66.0	8.9	90.5
1997	149	57.3	58.1	49.7	65.6	8.9	88.6
1998	155	57.2	59.1	49.6	66.1	8.9	88.0
1999	160	57.6	59.3	50.1	65.9	8.9	88.5
2000	160	58.1	59.2	50.3	65.9	8.9	89.5
2001	155	59.2	60.1	51.8	67.7	8.9	89.9
2002	157	59.2	59.1	52.5	66.5	8.9	89.4
2003	157	59.6	58.9	53.1	67.1	8.9	89.8
2004	155	59.6	58.9	53.3	66.5	8.9	90.0
2005	155	59.6	58.2	53.3	66.5	8.0	89.5
2006	157	59.9	59.1	53.6	66.4	4.0	88.6
2007	157	60.1	59.6	54.0	67.4	3.0	89.9
2008	157	60.2	60.0	54.1	68.1	3.0	89.7
Overall		58.8	59.1	52.4	66.5	3.0	90.5

Sources: Heritage Foundation, Index of Economic Freedom.

The Heritage Foundation classifies countries into five categories based on their scores in the index. Countries with very high freedom scores of 80 or more are considered as "*free*" economies. Countries with scores in the 70–79.9 range are deemed as "*mostly free.*" The next category goes to countries having scores in the 60–69.9 range, which is considered as "*moderately free.*" This is followed by "*mostly unfree*" economies whose freedom score is above 50 but below 60. At the bottom are countries with a freedom score below 50, which are referred to "*repressed.*"

In the 2008 rankings, for example, only seven nations were believed to have free economies. The next twenty-three countries were in the mostly free category. About one-third of the countries (fifty-one economies) were moderately free. Another one-third (fifty-two economies including China) were mostly not free. Twenty four economies were deemed as repressed.

The highest freedom score in the freedom index is 90.5. This honor belongs to Hong Kong for 1996. In fact, Hong Kong has been the freest economy during the entire sample period. At the other end of the ranking spectrum, the lowest economic freedom score is 3.0, which is assigned to North Korea for 2007 and 2008.

Link between Economic Freedom and Prosperity

This section investigates the association of a nation's prosperity with its economic freedom. Prosperity is measured by a nation's gross national income (GNI) per capita. The GNI and other macroeconomic data are obtained from the World Bank's *World Development Indicators* (WDI) database. GNI is gross domestic product (GDP) less net taxes on production and imports, less compensation of employees and property income payable to the rest of the world plus the corresponding items receivable from the rest of the world (in other words, GDP less primary incomes payable to non-resident units plus primary incomes receivable from non-resident units). GNI is identical to gross national product (GNP) as previously used in national accounts generally.

A country's GNI can be converted to U.S. dollars using either the market exchange rates or the purchasing power parity (PPP) implied exchange rates. The GNI data measured in current dollars are converted using the so-called Atlas method. This method uses the market exchange rates but smoothes exchange rate fluctuations by using a three-year moving average, price-adjusted conversion factor. The World Bank favors the Atlas method for comparing the relative size of economies and uses it to classify countries in low, middle and high-income categories and to set lending eligibilities in order to reduce short-term fluctuations in country classification.

Figure 1.1 depicts the link of prosperity with economic freedom for the countries that are covered by both the Heritage Foundation and the World Bank's WDI database. In the figure, prosperity is measured by a country's arithmetic average market-based GNI per capita, in natural logarithm, from 1995 to 2008. Economic freedom is the average freedom score for each country during the same period.

The purchasing power parity (PPP) conversion factors take into account differences in the relative prices of goods and services, particularly non-tradables, and therefore provide a better overall measure of the real value of output produced by an economy relative to other economies. The GNI (PPP) data are measured in current international dollars which, in principle, have the same purchasing power as a dollar spent on GNI in the U.S. economy. Many of the currencies from developing countries are either fixed or managed by their governments. These currencies are typically undervalued relative to the PPP exchange rates. As a result, the GNI statistic converted using the market exchange rate substantially underestimates the economic performance of many developing countries. The World Bank favors this measure for accurate measurement of poverty and well-being. In Figure 1.2, we use the PPP-based GNI per capita for a country's prosperity.

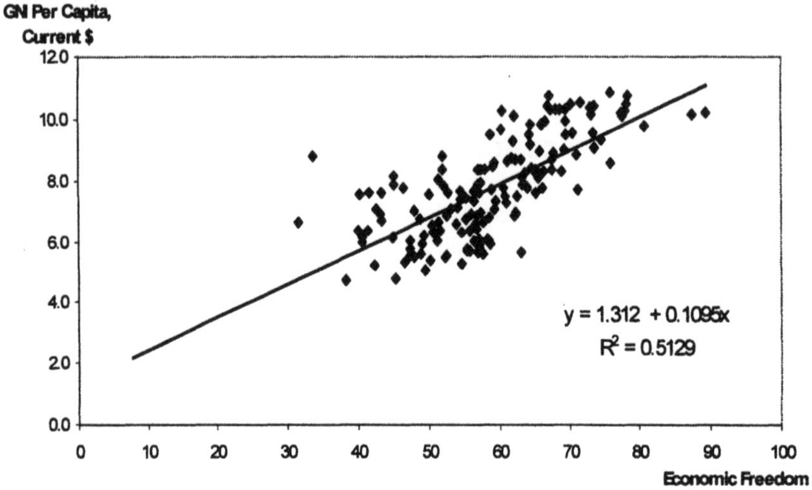

Figure 1.1 Economic Freedom and Prosperity

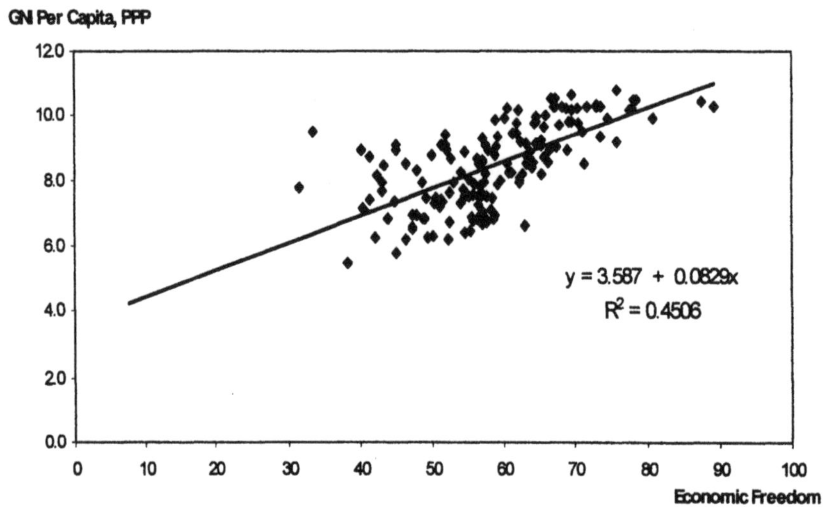

Figure 1.2 Economic Freedom and Prosperity (PPP)

As can be seen from both figures, there is a clear and positive link of prosperity with economic freedom. We also add the trend line in the two figures, and the cross-country regression results where prosperity (the natural logarithm of GNP per capital) is regressed on the average economic freedom index. The coefficient estimate of economic freedom is positive and statistically significant.

In order to use the rich time series and cross-sectional data, we run the following regression:

$$\text{Prosperity}_{it} = \alpha + \beta^{*}\text{Economic Freedom}_{it} + \varepsilon_{it}$$

We use the ordinary least squares (OLS) method to run the regression and present the results in Table 1.2. In the first two regressions, the dependent variable is the natural logarithm of the market-based GNI per capita while it is replaced by the PPP-based GNI per capita in the last two regressions.

As can be seen from the table, when economic freedom is the only independent variable, its coefficient estimate is positive and statistically significant at the 1 percent level. The result is consistent with the notion that economic prosperity is positively associated with economic freedom. When the year dummies are added as independent variables, the coefficient of the freedom variable remains basically unchanged.

It should be noted that the regression results do not necessarily imply that economic freedom leads to economic prosperity. GNI per capita, in current dollar, is converted using the Atlas method, which uses the market exchange rates but smoothes exchange rate fluctuations by using a three-year moving average, price-adjusted conversion factor. GNI per capita, PPP, is converted using the purchasing power parity exchange rate. Economic freedom is the overall freedom score. China dummy equals one for China and zero for all other countries.

Table 1.2 Regression Results of Economic Prosperity and Economic Freedom

	Ln (GNI Per Capita, Current Dollar)		Ln (GNI Per Capita, PPP)	
	(1)	(2)	(4)	(5)
Intercept	1.525 [10.38]***	1.431 [7.81]***	3.814 [31.18]***	3.670 [23.96]***
Economic Freedom	0.1056 [43.39]***	0.1049 [43.26]***	0.079 [38.95]***	0.0782 [38.54]***
Year Dummies	No	Yes	No	Yes
F-value	1882.7	139.8	1517.3	111.0
Adjusted R^2	0.487	0.495	0.434	0.438

*** represents statistical significance at 1 percent level

Economic Freedom and Economic Growth

The empirical literature on economic freedom and growth is relatively recent. There were only a few empirical studies until the late 1990s, after which there has been an explosion of interest on this issue. In general these studies use a measure of economic growth as the dependent variable and a measure of economic freedom as part of a set of explanatory variables. The majority of previous studies regress economic growth rates on the levels of economic freedom. More recent studies show that the change in economic freedom, rather than its level, is robustly related to economic growth. Gwartney, Lawson and Holcombe (1999)[5], for instance, find strong evidence in favor of the effects of changes in economic freedom on growth.

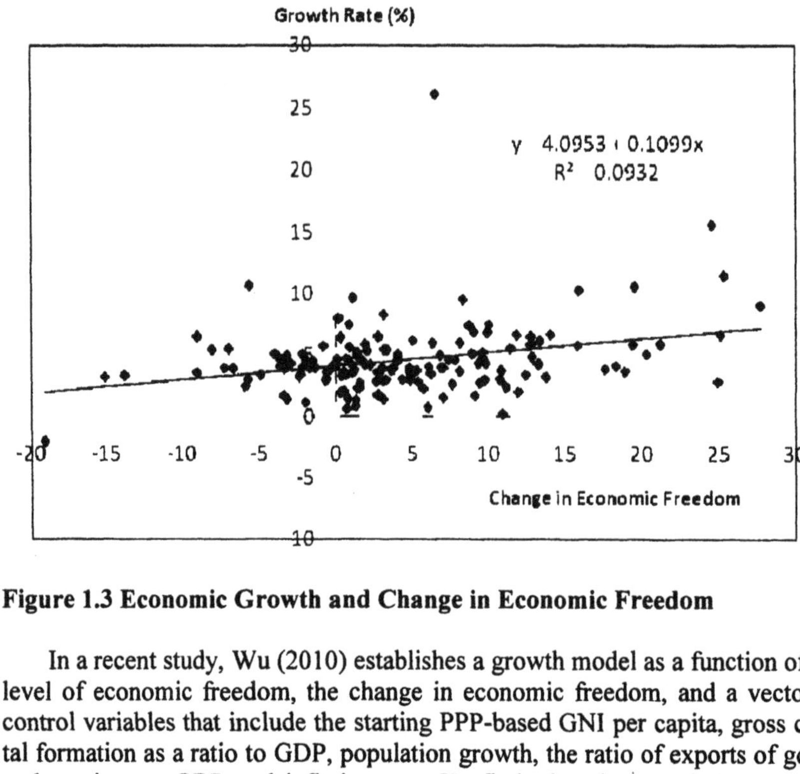

Figure 1.3 Economic Growth and Change in Economic Freedom

In a recent study, Wu (2010) establishes a growth model as a function of the level of economic freedom, the change in economic freedom, and a vector of control variables that include the starting PPP-based GNI per capita, gross capital formation as a ratio to GDP, population growth, the ratio of exports of goods and services to GDP and inflation rate. He finds that the correlation between economic growth and the change in economic freedom is significantly positive. The level of economic freedom, however, is insignificant once the control variables are included as explanatory variables.

The positive relationship between economic growth and the change in economic freedom can be illustrated in Figure 1.3. The vertical axis in the figure is the arithmetic average annual growth rate in real GDP for a country over the 1995–2008 period. The horizontal axis represents the difference between the 2008 economic freedom score and the starting score (in 1995 or the year the coverage is initiated) for the country.

The slope of the trend line in Figure 1.3 is 0.10. This number implies that when the economic freedom score improves by 10 points over the 1995–2008 period, the average annual GDP growth will increase by 1 percent.

China's Economic Indicators

Table 1.3 presents China's main economic indicators from 1995 to 2008. Data are obtained from the World Bank's *World Development Indicators* (WDI) database. The GDP data shown here measured in current U.S. dollars are converted using annual, market exchange rates. China's annual real GDP growth rate is between 8 percent and 13 percent, with an average of around 10 percent over our sample period. Its GDP reached $4,326 billion in current dollars in 2008, making it the third largest economy behind the United States and Japan. China is projected to overtake Japan to be the second largest economy by 2010.

Table 1.3 China's Main Macroeconomic Indicators

Year	GDP (current US$ bn)	Real GDP growth (%)	GNI (Current US$ bn)	GNI, PPP (Current Int'l $ bn)	GNI per capita (Current US$)	GNI per capital, PPP (Current Int'l $)
1995	728	11	644	1,784	530	1,480
1996	856	10	788	2,003	650	1,650
1997	953	9	919	2,233	750	1,810
1998	1,019	8	982	2,422	790	1,950
1999	1,083	8	1,062	2,651	850	2,110
2000	1,198	8	1,169	2,940	930	2,330
2001	1,325	8	1,273	3,253	1,000	2,560
2002	1,454	9	1,407	3,627	1,100	2,830
2003	1,641	10	1,631	4,097	1,270	3,180
2004	1,932	10	1,938	4,654	1,500	3,590
2005	2,236	10	2,273	5,340	1,740	4,100
2006	2,658	12	2,639	6,153	2,010	4,690
2007	3,382	13	3,180	7,154	2,410	5,430
2008	4,326	9	3,899	7,984	2,940	6,020

Source: The World Bank's World Development Indicators (WDI).

The Chinese *yuan* had been fixed at RMB 8.28 per U.S. dollar from 1995 up to July 2005, when the Chinese government revalued its currency by 2 percent. After the revaluation, the *yuan* had risen steadily to 6.83 per dollar by the end of 2008.

Despite the steady appreciation of the *yuan*, most economists and especially international institutions such as the World Bank and the International Monetary Fund (IMF) believe that the *yuan* is still significantly undervalued against the dollar. Consequently, the GNI figure converted using the market exchange rates will substantially underestimate the economic performance of China. For example, when the PPP approach is used, China's GNI per capita was $6,020 in 2008, compared to only $2,940 under the Atlas method used by the World Bank.

China's Economic Freedom

Despite its rapid economic growth, China's transition to greater economic freedom has been sluggish over the life of the *Index of Economic Freedom*. Table 1.4 and Figure 1.4 show that China's overall freedom score is below the world average every year, fluctuating within a very narrow range of 51.3 to 56.4. The freedom score is 53.1 in the most recent year of the period, making its economy the 124th freest in the 2008 ranking.

Efforts to embrace market principles have been made from time to time, but overall progress has been modest. Rapid development of coastal cities has resulted in increasing disparities in economic freedom and standards of living across the country. Foreign investment is controlled and regulated, and the judicial system is highly vulnerable to political influence. The state maintains tight control of the financial sector and directly or indirectly owns all banks.

China has liberalized parts of its economy to a notable degree since the early 1980s. It joined the World Trade Organization (WTO) in 2001, and its industrial and manufacturing sector is now second in size only to that of the United States. At the same time, however, China remains a one-party state in which the Communist Party maintains tight control of political expression, speech, religion, and assembly. Any social group that can organize on a large scale is deemed a threat, as are many individual dissidents. The government is struggling to manage environmental degradation, demographic pressure, and the world's largest-ever migration from rural to urban areas, all of which contribute to social unrest.

Business Freedom. The overall freedom to establish and run a business is constrained by China's regulatory environment. Starting a business takes about the world average of thirty-five days, but obtaining a business license requires more than the world average of eighteen procedures and two hundred and eighteen days. China lacks legal and regulatory transparency. China's grade in this category remained flat at around fifty-five for most of the years, but dropped slightly in the last three years of our sample period.

Trade freedom. China's trade freedom has improved substantially after it joined the WTO in 2001. China's weighted average tariff rate was 3.9 percent in 2008. Despite lower non-tariff barriers pursuant to WTO requirements, import and export bans and restrictions, import and export licensing, non-transparent tariff classifications, complex regulations and standards, subsidies, state trading in certain goods, services market restrictions, issues involving the protection of intellectual property rights, and inconsistent and corruption-prone customs administration add to the cost of trade.

Fiscal freedom. China has a high income tax rate and a moderate corporate tax rate. The top income tax rate is 45 percent, and the top corporate tax rate is 25 percent. The government encourages new-technology businesses with a reduced corporate rate of 15 percent. Other taxes include a value-added tax (VAT)

Table 1.4 Index of Economic Freedom for China

	1995	1996	1997	1998	1999	2000	2001	2002	2003	2004	2005	2006	2007	2008
Business Freedom	55	55	55	55	55	55	55	55	55	55	55	43.1	46.9	50.3
Trade Freedom	20.0	20.0	30.0	34.0	38.2	42.6	46.0	48.6	50.6	51.4	54.4	68.0	68.0	70.2
Fiscal Freedom	70.6	70.7	70.4	70.5	70.5	70.4	70.4	70.3	66.9	66.4	67.9	70.0	66.6	66.4
Government Spending	93.7	94.6	95.4	95.9	95.1	90.3	94.1	92.3	90.2	88.4	86.0	86.0	87.0	89.7
Monetary Freedom	68.4	61.5	62.7	68.2	75.2	84.0	84.1	87.6	85.8	86.4	84.8	79.4	75.5	76.5
Investment Freedom	50	50	50	50	50	50	30	30	30	30	30	30	30	30
Financial Freedom	50	50	50	50	50	50	30	30	30	30	30	30	30	30
Property Rights	30	30	30	30	30	30	30	30	30	30	30	30	20	20
Freedom from Corruption	30	30	22	24	29	35	34	31	35	35	34	34	32	33
Labor Freedom	-	-	-	-	-	-	-	-	-	-	65.0	65.2	64.2	64.8
Overall Score	52.0	51.3	1.7	53.1	4.8	56.4	2.6	52.8	52.6	2.5	53.7	53.6	52.0	53.1
World Average	57.6	57.1	57.5	57.2	57.6	58.1	59.2	59.2	59.6	59.6	59.6	59.9	60.1	60.2
China's Rank	71	97	107	105	104	98	114	117	120	124	113	118	133	124

Sources: Heritage Foundation, Index of Economic Freedom.

and a real estate tax. As of October 2008, individual income tax was no longer paid on interest on bank deposits. In 2008, overall tax revenue as a percentage of GDP was 18.3 percent.

Government spending. Government expenditures, including consumption and transfer payments, are low. In the most recent year, central government spending equaled 19.9 percent of GDP. State ownership of enterprises persists in most sectors. Mergers have been more frequent than divestments. The first anti-monopoly law was enacted in August 2008.

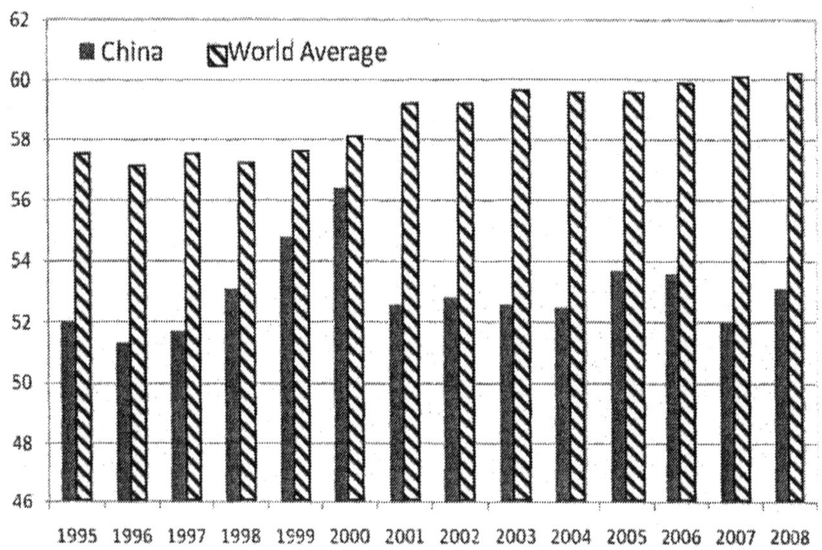

Figure 1.4 China's Economic Freedom vs. World Average: 1995–2008

Monetary freedom. Inflation has been moderate since 1996. The market determines the prices of most traded products, but the government maintains prices for petroleum, electricity, pharmaceuticals, coal, agricultural products, and other "essential" goods. Subsidies allow state-owned enterprises to produce and sell goods to wholesalers and retailers at artificially low prices. Fifteen points were deducted from China's monetary freedom score to adjust for measures that distort domestic prices.

Investment freedom. The score for this category dropped by 20 points to 30 in 2001 from 50 in 2000, and remained at that level ever since. China's Foreign Investment Catalogue delineates sectors in which foreign investment is encouraged, permitted, restricted, and prohibited, as well as such specific restrictions as caps on foreign ownership and permissible types of investment. Investors face regulatory non-transparency, complex and inconsistently enforced laws and regulations, weak protection of intellectual property rights, corruption, industrial policies protecting local firms, and a legal system that cannot guarantee the sanctity of contracts. Foreign investors may access foreign exchange for current account transactions like repatriating profits, but capital account transactions are tightly regulated. Chinese law prohibits nationalization of foreign investment except under "special" circumstances.

Financial freedom. Similar to investment freedom, the financial freedom score dropped by 20 points to 30 after China joined WTO in 2001. China's complex financial system is tightly controlled by the government. The China Banking Regulatory Commission supervised roughly 5,600 financial institutions in 2008. China has only two private banks; four state-owned banks account for over 50 percent of total assets. The state directs the allocation of credit, and the big four state banks lend primarily to state-owned enterprises. Since joining the WTO, China has gradually removed barriers to foreign banks, but cumbersome regulations remain. Foreign banks account for only about 2 percent of total assets. Foreign participation in capital markets remains limited. Expanding access to financial services still remains a challenge.

Property rights. China's judicial system is weak, and many companies resort to arbitration. Local officials can ignore court decision with impunity. All land is state-owned, but individuals and firms may own and transfer long-term leases (subject to many restrictions) as well as structures and personal property. Intellectual property rights are not enforced effectively. Copyrights, patents, brand names, trademarks, and trade secrets are routinely stolen.

Freedom from corruption. Freedom from corruption is among the lowest categories in the freedom index, ranging from 22 to 35. Corruption is perceived as widespread in China. China ranked 72nd out of 179 countries in Transparency International's Corruption Perceptions Index for 2008. Corruption affects banking, finance, government procurement, and construction most severely and there is a lack of independent investigative bodies and courts.

Labor freedom. China's labor regulations hinder overall employment and productivity growth. The non-salary cost of employing a worker is high. Dismissing an employee may require prior consultation with the local labor bureau and labor union.

Discussions and Conclusions

What causes the economy to grow has been one of the most enduring questions in economics. The production function theory treats the economy as a production machine that transforms land, labor and capital to output. Economy grows as inputs are increased and technology is advanced. This classic theory assumes that an economy's potential, defined by its resources and technology, is fully realized. But the problem with the less developed countries is not a lack of potential but an inability to achieve that potential. Inputs are necessary to produce output, but without the right incentives, it is too easy to combine inputs in a way that makes the final output less valuable than the original inputs.

In search for the causes of economic growth, economists have recently begun to turn back to Adam Smith's basic idea. Smith made the case that free markets, the protection of private property rights, and a minimal government presence in the economy lead to prosperity. In such a setting, individuals pursue their own interests and are led as if by an invisible hand to do what is the best not only for themselves but also for the whole society.

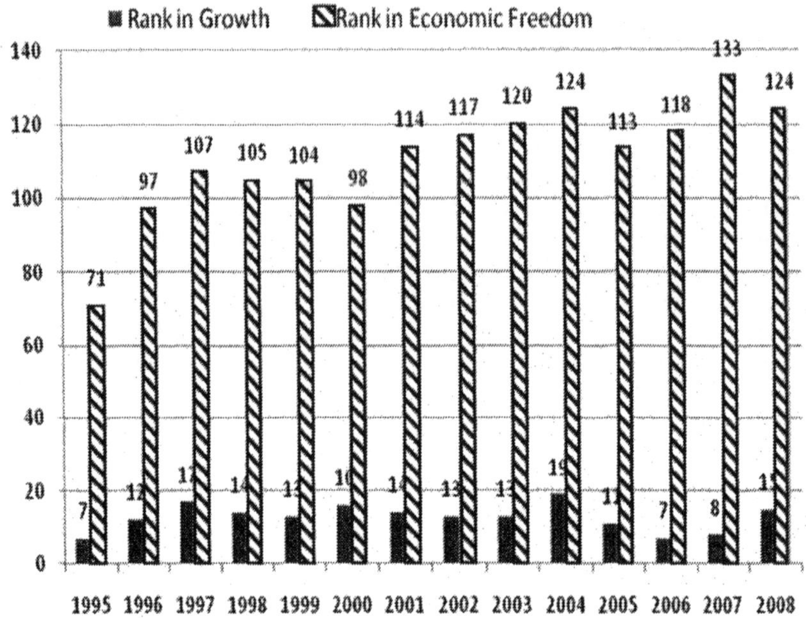

Figure 1.5 China's Rank in Growth and Economic Freedom

Recent empirical studies have found that the respect for the rule of law, protection of property rights, enforceability of contracts, and legal heritage have a causal relationship with levels of economic growth. Empirical research that attempts to investigate the relationship between economic freedom and economic growth generally documents a positive link between the two.

Nevertheless, China's phenomenal growth performance has been accompanied by a relatively undeveloped legal and financial system and high corruption. In terms of economic freedom, China's score has been constantly below the world average. Moreover, it has shown little improvement over time. China's freedom score lies within a very narrow range of 51.3 to 56.4, barely above the "repressed" category. China's economic freedom ranking is below 100 most of the years. In fact, China ranked only 124th in the *2008 Index of Economic Freedom* compiled by the Heritage Foundation and went down to 140th in 2010 in the same index.[6]

China's low economic freedom ranking is in sharp contrast to its amazing economic performance. China's growth rate is on top 10 for three years, on top 15 for ten years, and on top 20 each year from 1995 to 2008. China's average annual growth rate of 9.64 percent makes China the seventh fastest growing economy overall among the 153 countries covered by both the *Index of Economic Freedom* and the World Bank's WDI database.

Given the size of its economy and the prolonged period of close to double-digit growth, China indeed is a notable counterexample to the findings in law, institutions, economic freedom and economic growth literatures.

Notes

1. Lopez-De-Silanes La Porta, A. Shleifer and R.W. Vishny, "Legal Determinants of External Finance," *The Journal of Finance* 52, no. 3 (1997), 1131–1150; R. La Porta, F. Lopez-De-Silanes, A. Shleifer, and R.W., Vishny, "Law and Finance," *The Journal of Political Economy* 106, no. 6 (1998), 1113–1155.

2. J. De Hann and J. E.Sturm, "On the relationship between economic freedom and economic growth," *European Journal of Political Economy* 16 (2000), 215–241.

3. Congsheng Wu, "Economic Freedom, Growth and China," *Chinese Economy*, 2010, forthcoming.

4. F. Allen, J. Qian and M. Qian, "Law, Finance, and Economic Growth in China," *Journal of Financial Economics* 77, no. 1 (2005), 57–116.

5. J Gwartney, R. Lawson and R. Holcombe, "Economic freedom and the environment for economic growth," *Journal of Theoretical and Institutional Economics* 155 (1999), 643–663.

6. *Index of Economic Freedom*, 2008 and 2010, Heritage Foundation, available from: http://www.heritage.org.

Chapter 2
Beyond the China Paradigms: Comparative Studies of Property Rights and Rent-Seeking Politics

Xiaobo Hu

The issues raised by the calls for China paradigms or models are not new but they capture the constant progress of new scholarships in, among other fields, the study of comparative politics. If you take the two extremes among debates over paradigms, you may have on one end such arguments as "China is China is China . . . ." that overemphasizes the uniqueness of the Chinese history, culture, institutions, or current policies. On the other end, you may have arguments initiated by David Easton or Jerry Hugh that all societies or systems proceed through the same process of input and output. In this perspective, one single theory or paradigm should be enough to help understand the political behaviors of human beings from different societies—understanding one paradigm should enable one to understand all the rest.[1] Other arguments could be found lying between these two extremes.

More recently, the academic debate regarding a China paradigm comes more from inside China than from the outside, following the initial policy discussion of the "Beijing Consensus" by Joshua Ramo.[2] Short of arguing that the China paradigm is unique, the Beijing Consensus was presented by Ramo as an alternative economic development model to the end-of-history "free market" model, or the so-called Washington Consensus, promoted by the United States and such major international organizations as the IMF and the World Bank. By Beijing Consensus, Ramo emphasizes the "commitment to innovation and constant experimentation" and sustainable economic development based on equitable distribution of wealth—"equitable, peaceful high-quality growth."[3]

Through the "Beijing Consensus" Ramo tries to present a paradigm that is "making a path for other nations around the world who are trying to figure out not simply how to develop their countries, but also how to fit into the international order in a way that allows them to be truly independent, to protect their way of life and political choices in a world with a single massively powerful centre of gravity."[4]

Early this year, Chinese universities in both Beijing and Shanghai created forums to engage more scholars in such debate. Once again this debate brings back some of the old questions addressed by the scholars mentioned in the previous paragraphs. However, in order to move beyond this seemingly eternal loop of paradigm debates, we need to bring in two new perspectives. First, in *The New Asian Hemisphere: the Irresistible Shift of Global Power to the East*, Kishore Mahbubani points out with overwhelming evidence that the "shift" is in fact a return to the "normal" as Asia, particularly China and India, in the past 2,000 years was dominant in the world economy until some 150 years ago.[5] Development paradigms or models in the past one hundred years are ignorant of this fact. Second, in his more recent works, Francis Fukuyama has to revise his belief in "the end of history" and admits that the world is still open to different paths to development.[6] Indeed, even in the West, democratization took different journeys.[7] Both Mahbubani and Fukuyama have exposed the limited or skewed perspectives some of us continue to hold on in face of the growing globalization.

With the insights of previous scholarships, I will apply my new research findings on property rights and rent seeking to address the scholarly and empirical challenges that China's rise has presented to our existing theories and paradigms. In doing so, this chapter offers a critique of both the paradigms that are limited to the Western history and experience as well as the made-in-China paradigms that tend not to offer insights to refine the theories originally developed in the West. The Chinese experience has enriched our understanding of comparative politics and economic development, challenged theories that are not broadly useful, and provided social scientists with a once-in-a-lifetime opportunity to explore the fundamental questions regarding human interactions that link political, economic, and social development.

The China Debate and Beyond

Before we examine the insights from Mahbubani and Fukuyama, it is useful to provide a short summary of the debates among the Chinese scholars regarding the China paradigm.[8] There are three major issues in the debates and they concern the recent rapid development of China and the directions of China's future development. Specifically, the Chinese scholars addressed whether there is a China model, if so what major features the China model encompasses, and what future the China model faces. To different degrees all these issues are related to the relationships between the state and the economy, between the government and the market, and between different policy priorities.

If we incorporate all these questions, the development models can be categorized in accordance with the ownership systems and the degrees of government regulation, as one scholar points out.[9] Along the line of ownership systems, there are state ownership systems versus private ownership systems; while along the line of government regulation, there is the planned economy versus the *laissez-faire* economy. In this case, there are at least four mega blocks of models (see Table 2.1).[10]

Among all the participants in the debates, one group of scholars believes that China is a socialist market economy, because the state still holds the deciding share of the leading companies in various industries in China. A second group argues that China has essentially become a market economy after the three decades of reforms. Although China is different from the United States, this group continues, the Chinese government no longer makes mandatory economic plans for industries, nor can it control the economy as it wishes. It is only able to promote the economic development through its fiscal policies and market regulations like most other market economies.

Table 2.1 Development Models

		Government Regulation	
		High	Low
Ownership	Predominantly State	*The Planned Economy*	*Market Socialism*
	Predominantly Private	*State Capitalism*	*The Market Economy*

A third group of Chinese scholars argues that China has transformed itself from the Planned Economy to a Market Socialist Economy and then to a State Capitalist Economy in the last 30 years. They view the Chinese economy as predominately a market-based, competitive economy. However, as it is different from a "typical" market economy, i.e. that in the U.S., they recognize the important roles that the Chinese government has played in promoting the economic development. Although the size of the Chinese government has shrunk tremendously–perhaps it is less than half the size three decades ago—it is still very active in promoting the country's economic development and regulating the economy for that purpose.

The debates are much more heartening than described above. However, what the Chinese government is doing today is similar to what the many governments in East Asia have been doing, including those in Singapore, South Korea, and Japan. The governments in these countries, which we refer to as the Developmental States, play critical roles in promoting the economic development for the entire country, increasing GDP, attracting investment, fostering the education, alleviating poverty, and so on.

In addition, most of the debates tend to be confined to the experience of China in the past thirty years. To this limit, the broader historical perspectives that Kishore Mahbubani and Francis Fukuyama have provided might be useful to further the discussion of development models.

In the preface of his 2008 book, Mahbubani cautions that his new book might offend some of his old friends in the West. Indeed, his arguments might be too combative to Western readers, as one reviewer put it. "His offering is more like a bucket of cold water than a gentle tap on the door with a soothing cup of tea" to the West. Mahbubani has struck a strong tone to separate new Asian development from the Western models.

In reference to the recent rise of China, contrary to the well-accepted prospect that the 21st Century is the Pacific Century, Mahbubani argues that it is not that the gravity of universe has shifted from the West to the East, but that the

Table 2.2 Economic Development: Share of World GDP, 1-2001

	1	1000	1500	1600	1700	1820	1870	1950	2001
Western Europe	10.8	8.7	17.8	19.8	21.9	23.0	33.0	26.2	20.3
Eastern Europe	1.9	2.2	2.7	2.8	3.1	3.6	4.5	3.5	2.0
Russia	1.5	2.4	3.4	3.5	4.4	5.4	7.5	9.6	3.6
U.S.	-	-	0.3	0.2	0.1	1.8	8.8	27.3	21.4
Japan	1.2	2.7	3.1	2.9	4.1	3.0	2.3	3.0	7.1
China	**26.1**	**22.7**	**24.9**	**29.0**	**22.3**	**32.9**	**17.1**	**4.5**	**12.3**

Source: Angus Maddison, *The World Economy: Historical Statistics* (OECD, 2003), 261.

gravity has *returned* to its normalcy. He bases his argument on the historical development of the world economy since *Anno Domini* (see Table 2.2).[11]

However, different from the calls for a China paradigm, Mahbubani finds the reasons for the rise of China less China-characteristic. He believes that the following seven features contribute to China's rise. They are: free market economics, science and technology, meritocracy, pragmatism, a culture of peace, the rule of law, and education. Given his historical view, it is not surprising that Mahbubani does not believe that democratic institutions make a difference to economic development. Instead, he criticizes the West as moving towards a selfish and incompetent defense of its own interests. He views that Western leaders have succumbed to competitive populism and structural short-termism, as they drift away from meritocracy and science and technology.[12]

Interestingly, according to Mahbubani, a combat author as described by some of his Western counterparts, the seven pillars of wisdom for China's success were also the pillars for success in the West. In fact, they have always been considered as wisdom for success in any development models. It seems, while he argues that the global center has returned from the West to the East irresistibly, Mahbubani does not see the fundamental ingredients of the China model as unique to other successful stories, the East or the West.

In another incident, the recent shift in Francis Fukuyama is worth noticing. After having claimed the end of history about two decades ago, Francis Fukuyama has to revisit and revise his Neo-Conservative themes regarding the model of development. In his recent writings Fukuyama exhibits conflicting thoughts regarding the end of history. On one hand, he shies away from celebrating the American model of economic development, world dominance, or financial management, admitting "a certain vision of capitalism has collapsed."[13] On the other hand, he still considers that "the modern liberal state is . . . the end of history" and "the Chinese political system . . . is in the long run unstable . . . [even though] they can move faster than a democracy and cut through interest groups."[14]

One of the biggest problems of Fukuyama is that he approaches complex issues with a broad brush on a big canvas. Everything he discusses sounds interesting but he can hardly get it right. As Avery Goldstein once pointed out, the forces at play in China's rise are simply too complex to permit any easy predictions.[15] Systematic studies of various major factors instead of politicized claims are needed in order to comprehend what are really behind the various developments, the East or the West.

In the debates over development models, most if not all of these scholars have focused on macro and policy analysis. However, any sound policy analysis should be based on solid, basic academic research regarding the interactions among individuals and groups and between individuals and institutions.

Along increasing globalization in the past thirty years, China's reform has brought in a great deal of new information and new knowledge to social sciences. This has presented challenges to our theories and paradigms, and this has also presented significant opportunities for us to test, refine and further develop the existing concepts, theories and paradigms. In the following, I will focus on two areas of comparative studies, i.e., political economy of property rights and rent-seeking politics. The purpose of this discussion is two-folded. On one hand, I will demonstrate how limited the existing Western theories are in analyzing China's development. On the other hand, I will demonstrate how China's development has further developed the existing theories, making them more globally relevant. The Chinese development does not alienate itself from the rich body of social sciences, but enrich them, which could also make the Chinese experience more universal. An open perspective on "made-in-China" models could benefit all countries around the world.

Comparative Political Economy of Property Rights

Formal, secure property rights of individuals have been considered as the foundation for Western economic development. Transformation of property rights then became the core of post-communist transition; hence, naturally, theory of property rights assumes the core of transition theories. However, in face of the Chinese experience with an unprecedented speed of growth, conventional wisdom could not provide a coherent explanation.

In this section, I will demonstrate studies of China's transition have generated at least three new findings that could help further our understanding of a general theory of property rights as well as revisit some of the conventional wisdom regarding Western economic history. First, new China studies raise the possibility that informal property rights could also produce efficiency and rapid economic development. Second, China's economic growth has been relatively steady while its property rights system has gone through a process of informalization and then formalization. Third, during this process, different parts of the property rights were separated and then re-united but in different hands, which reveals a process of privatization not yet discussed in much of the existing literature.[16]

In neo-classical literature, writers widely subscribe to the idea that institutions of formal and well-defined property rights provide a necessary precondition to economic prosperity. In a properly functioning capitalist market economy, the well-defined and well-protected private property rights are set up to reduce transaction costs, and to prevent shirking and make the owner the true residual claimant. In this system, according to neo-classical economics, the "wedge" of true private property blocks the infinite regress of inefficiency and shirking that characterized the old socialist economic system. This is because the true property owners have the power and incentives to stop losses and encourage profitability. As advised by this theory, the socialist economy should transfer its properties into private hands and such a transfer should take place "overnight." This has been the mainstream of property rights theories in the Western literature.[17]

Contrary to the predictions of the neo-classical economics, the steady and rapid economic growth in China has largely resulted from a "vaguely defined" property rights system.[18] Two theories have been developed in an attempt to explain the relationship between such a practice and rapid economic development in China as well as why property rights were not clearly defined (though credibly enforced). First, the cooperative culture theory argues that economic development can be initiated through cooperative culture, even in the absence of formal or well-defined property rights. Weitzman and Xu attributed the Chinese rural development generated by the township-village enterprises (TVEs) to λ, a cooperative culture whereby the TVEs operate.[19] This explanation goes beyond neoclassic traditions by incorporating cultural factors that are important to economic development.

Ambiguity theory is another explanation that tries to tackle the problems puzzled by many scholars. It emphasizes the ambiguity of Chinese property rights in transition, and argues that the Chinese non-state firms have successfully taken an ambiguous form of property rights in order to minimize transaction costs and uncertainties in the market place.[20] In the form of ambiguous property rights, the owners have to fight for the "control rights." According to the ambiguity theory, the owners choose this form of rights when they have to operate in a "gray market" and when a second player could be included so as to reduce the high transaction costs and high uncertainties in the market place. The consequent property rights are therefore ambiguous, because there are no "prenuptial" agreements or binding rules as to who will be in control in various *ex post* contingencies and owners have to fight for control under different circumstance.[21]

Further studies of China's privatization detect a process of informalization and then formalization of the property rights in China's economic growth. Indeed, such a process of informalization and formalization separates the three essential parts of the property rights—i.e., the user rights, the extractor rights, and the seller rights—into different hands and then gets them reunited in the hands of private owners.[22]

Different from the conventional wisdom that views privatization as a process of creating well-defined private property rights, transformation of China's property rights has gone through a process of informalization and then formalization of the property rights. During the Chinese transition, while part of the property rights was not formally recognized for a period of time, the process of gradual emergence of *de facto* separation of extractor rights from the state ownership as well as the gradual emergence of this not-legally-recognized private extractor rights is considered as *informalization of property rights*. This informalization started gradually as soon as the Chinese government launched its post-Mao reform in the late 1970s and early 1980s, and accelerated in 1992. The year of 1997 started the process of formalization of property rights, impelled by roughly the same groups of people.[23] This process is well demonstrated through major economic reform programs and policies as depicted in Figure 2.1. Such a process of informalization and formalization offers important cases to investigate in detailed interactions between individuals and institutions as well as changes of property rights.

Transformation of different parts of the property rights is a process of selecting and reselecting different forms of property rights. From the perspective of political economy, such process is advanced by different political alignments

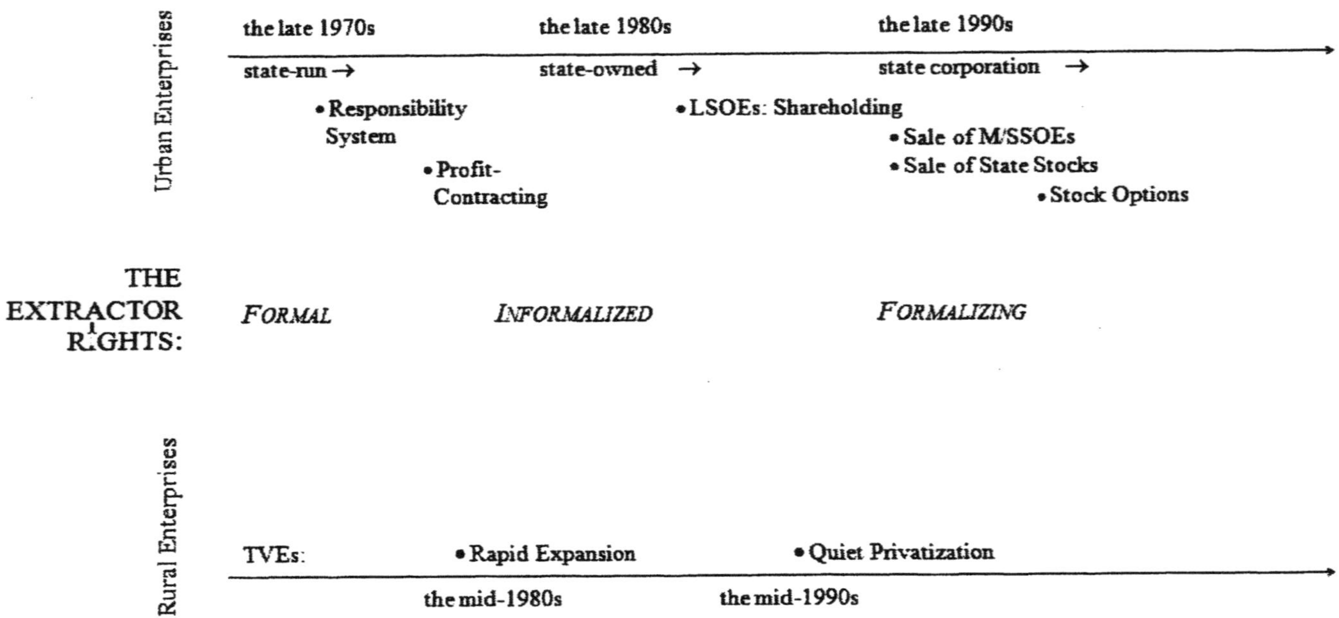

Note: LSOEs refers to large-sized state-owned enterprises, M/SSOEs medium- to small-sized state-owned enterprises, and TVEs township and village enterprises.

Figure 2.1 Transformation of Property Rights in China: Piece-Meal Privatization

at different periods of time. Studying informalization and formalization of property rights has yielded a better understanding of how as well as why economic transition in China has taken the current form. In China, transformation of the user rights, extractor rights, and seller rights reflects the development of the vested interests, such as leaders and bureaucrats in the central and local government, directors and mangers of the state-owned enterprises, and private owners. It reveals how and why piece-meal transition has taken place in China. Though at a different pace or through a different path, other post-communist countries may share similar political mechanisms of transition.[24]

The new social experiments in China in the past thirty years do not separate China from the rest of the world. Instead they contribute to the knowledge of human behaviors and global development. Indeed these social experiments in China were inspired by experience and knowledge foreign to China while the Chinese were trying to sort out the relationship between the state and the economy and to solve their own development problems. In addition, theoretical findings in the China studies may allow us to reexamine the roles of informal property rights or other institutions as well as the process of privatization in other countries.

Comparative Political Economy of Rent Seeking

Many of the theories and much knowledge in social sciences from abroad have provided tremendous insights into problem-solving in China. Others may have caused difficulties and confusions in applying to the Chinese cases. Theories in the West are not immune of shortcomings or defects, and there is always room for further improvement. The early introduction of rent-seeking theories to the Chinese academics resulted in many confusions in China.[25] Some of the confusions were original in the concepts of rent-seeking theories. For instance, there has been no consensus on a single definition of rent.[26]

In this section, I will examine how application of rent-seeking theory in China studies has broadened the original theory. In addition, the new findings through China studies may help us further explore in the market economy what we didn't think would exist there. Particularly, surplus and surplus seeking were thought only possibly existing in the planned economy, but through analysis of the Chinese cases in transition we may realize that they also take place every day in the market economy like that of the United States.

Rent Seeking versus Surplus Seeking

Government restrictions upon economic activities "give rise to rents of a variety of forms, and people often compete for the rents. Sometimes, such competition is perfectly legal," according to Anne Krueger as she began her seminal article on rent-seeking society.[27] As long as there is government regulation, there is rent. Government regulation creates rents.

The exploration of rent seeking builds upon a premise that the government increases the rents (or surplus) of a favored group at the expense of the buyers of the group's products or services. In a market economy, rents created by the government are similar to monopoly rents created by business monopoly. A monopoly rent can be created through a business gaining monopoly in the market and then limiting its supply in order to artificially increase the price from equilibrium (P_e) to a monopoly level (P_m), thus creating a rent, that is, $P_m abP_e$ in Figure 2.2. The rents that the government can help provide are a prize worth seeking, thus involving various parties in rent-seeking activities.

Anne Krueger first elaborated the theory of rent seeking, and Robert Tollison further defined rent as a return in excess of a resource owner's opportunity cost—it is a payment to the resource owner above the amount his or her resources could command in their next best alternative use.[28] The theory of rent seeking explores how people compete for artificially contrived transfers.

In most cases, the rent when created goes to producers. For instance, Organization of Petroleum Exporting Countries (OPEC) creates a monopoly rent by limiting the daily production of crude oil. Provided the demand stays constant, the oil price rises in accordance to where OPEC sets its production limit. Then the rent in the form of extra profits goes to the OPEC producers. Indeed the producer and consumer may share contrasting interests, and each may work to place pressure on the government in the opposite directions.

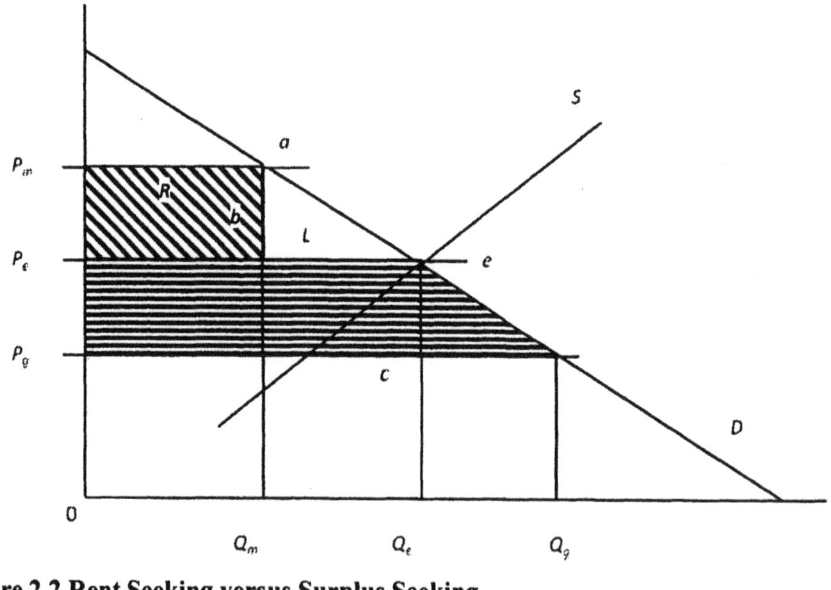

Figure 2.2 Rent Seeking versus Surplus Seeking

Sam Peltzman extended the discussion of rent seeking by including a vote-maximizing politician who supplies regulation, in other words, whose job is to create rents.[29] It is understood that the main beneficiaries of regulation are the regulated firms, although that regulation also prevents natural monopoly from taking place. According to George Stigler, regulation brings price to a level somewhere between the pure monopoly and pure competition prices.[30] Consumer interest groups can also "buy votes" through their campaign contributions. In this sense, the vote-maximizing politician's job is to juggle how much of a rent to be rewarded to the regulated firms, and how much of a loss she should help the consumers to prevent.[31]

However, there are some fundamental differences between rent seeking in a market economy and surplus seeking in a planned economy. Current literature has failed to recognize the significance of such differences.

Prior to its economic reform in the late 1970s, China was characterized by shortage of goods and services and central planning or rationing.[32] Rationing of the goods and services in shortage by the government may aim at equitable distribution. These two features, i.e. the centrally controlled supply of goods at fixed prices *below* market clearance and high demand for these goods, however, create a contrived surplus (P_eecP_g) somewhat comparable to the rent generated in competitive market exchanges (see Figure 2.2). When K. K. Fung first studied this, he realized that, different from the rent, the surplus resulted from the direct control over the price.[33] Hence the surplus-seeking activities center on control over goods and their distribution, rather than the market share.[34]

It is essential to note that the contrived surplus emerges from an artificially lowered money price (P_g) rather than from a market-clearing price (P_e). For example, if the U.S. Congress adopts Lindsey Graham and Charles Schumer's punitive seventeen-point-five-percent tariff on imports of Chinese textile, the tariff will increase the U.S. consumer prices of the textile products made in China from the market-clearing level, which will consequently increase the consumer prices of the textile made domestically as the demand shifts from Chinese textile to domestic textile. The gap between the pre-tariff, market-clearing price and the higher price as a result of the punitive tariff represents the rent. Rent benefits target producers, but not individual consumers. On the other hand, in China before the economic opening-up, the gap between the lowered prices (P_g) in the state-run stores and the prices of similar products in the black market (P_e) represented the surplus.

Indeed, the state rationing distorted the market price by artificially lowering it downwards. However, such a practice is supposed to benefit consumers rather than producers. In some cases, this is true. For instance, according to Robert H. Bates, artificially lowered price for agricultural products benefits urbanites in many African countries.[35] This was also true in China when only people with urban household registration could receive various coupons—e.g., for cloths, rice and meat—and access to other rationed goods and services.

In contrast to rent seeking, surplus seeking differs in the following three areas. First, when output is kept below the competitive market level, a contrived rent is created and rent seeking follows. For instance, rent is created through license on market entry or tariff. Krueger's initial article provides a perfect example of how tariffs create rents and how different businesses seek the rent;[36] the same applies to business license and the different ways to ensure a business license. Take coal as another example. Tariffs on import of coal would limit domestic coal supply, which in turn would increase the coal price; therefore companies would seek the entry to capture the price difference.

On the other hand, surplus is created through government control over prices. Specifically, the government lowers the selling price below the market clearing level. Many of the producer goods were under direct control of the government in China before the post-Mao economic reform. Again, take coal as an example. The price for coal was kept at about forty-nine *yuan* per ton by the government even until the late 1980s when the "black" market price for coal had already reached as high as one hundred and fifty *yuan* per ton. Surplus-seeking activities thus involve physical control over or distribution of the products.

While the focus of rent seeking is on market shares, the focus of surplus seeking is on government relations. While rent seeking could improve efficiency, surplus seeking divests investment from productivity to bureaucratic activity.

Second, surplus is initially transferred to distributors or government officials who control the goods and services in ration, but the distributors or government officials are not necessarily the final consumers of the goods or services. Nor can the distributors or government agencies legitimately cash in and materialize the profits that are presented in form of surplus. Nonetheless, they always trade the privileged access to the goods and services in ration for other economic or non-monetary returns. In this sense, the officials are not necessarily interested in efficiency in distribution or whether all the products can be sold out.

Third, surplus is also created when the government lowers the price of the good or service to zero. In a sense, these goods and services can be priceless. For instance, free public education renders tremendous efforts being devoted to surplus seeking activities. Such surplus seeking activities take on different forms in different countries. In the same vein, some goods and services cannot be auctioned off. For instance, the positional goods and *guanxi* cannot be easily estimated in monetary terms. Positional goods are either scarce in some absolute or socially imposed sense or subject to congestion or crowding through more extensive use.[37] They constitute a very important part of the surplus. Surplus seeking in this case takes on very different meaning and dynamics than rent seeking. For instance, competition to gain preferential access to rationed goods and services promotes exchange of favors. Indeed, only those well-positioned individuals have favors to exchange. Those who possess positional goods are sought in exchange of surplus. Those who are in control of goods and services in shortage or ration have a favorable position in surplus seeking or exchange of favors. Exchange of favors also promotes special bond and particularistic relationship among a small circle of friends. Personal *guanxi* or loyalty is therefore strengthened.

In case of "priceless" goods and services, the value of what has been exchanged must be different to different traders, more of a contextual and psychological nature. This creates an instant sense of indebtedness, from one party to another. Such contextual and psychological indebtedness can lead to intimate personal bond or reciprocal exchanges that may continue beyond the initial exchange. An exchange is considered incomplete if the buyer cannot pay up to or the seller cannot charge what the rationed goods are worth. Surplus seeking could lead to a long-term reciprocal relationship.

According to János Kornai, a planned economy systematically produces chronic shortage of all commodities, either because central planning has set over-ambitious production targets, or because incentives for enterprises to grow to meet unmet demand produce a voracious demand for inputs. Hence there is continual pressure to expand capacity—for capital, intermediate and consumer goods' production—but the lack of slack resources adds to the excess demand and produces a self-generating vicious cycle of shortage.[38]

What Kornai does not realize is that surplus creation also generates sustained shortage by artificially lowering the selling price, thus resulting in a shift in demand for goods and services from Q_e to Q_g, an artificially increased demand for more goods and services. Although, because of government corruption, many may still have to pay for the surplus in order to obtain the goods and services rationed, those who have access at low or no cost tend to over-consume the products. This over-consumption leads to further shortage in supply of goods and services that are rationed. Examination of surplus seeking in the planned economy provides a better understanding of the economics of shortage.

Coexistence of Rent Seeking and Surplus Seeking

In the past thirty or so years, China's economic system has experienced tremendous transformation. As a result, central planning has been largely replaced by market competition. Central price control over industrial and agricultural goods came to an end in the early 1990s. Contrived surplus created by traditional price control is diminishing.

On the other hand, the development of the market economy and transformation of government functions in order to meet the demand of an expanding market give rise to rent and rent seeking activities. The government has changed from running the economy through central plans to managing the economy largely by market regulations. In many areas, the government has substituted price control with control over market entry. In particular, entry restrictions are placed on non-state players.

However, regardless of diminishing traditional price control, surplus still exists "whenever a fully developed market based on pure exchanges is absent."[39] Competition for such surplus continually constitutes surplus seeking. For instance, systematic undervaluation of state assets in privatization generates lucrative surplus for potential buyers. A most recent example is the management buyout (MBO) of the public firms in China. In these MBOs, individual managers purchase the state shares from their own companies. It is estimated that all state shares have been sold below the market clearing price to the private managers, and in seventy-seven percent of the MBO cases the state shares were sold even below their book value.[40] Surplus seeking in this area leads to serious stripping of the state assets.

Let's return to coal again for a moment. Even until the late 1990s and the early 2000s, Tim Wright's recent work notices, the price of coal for power plants, which were mostly state-owned, was set at between fifteen percent and twenty percent below the market clearing level.[41]

As it is moving away from sole control over the selling price, the government still can manipulate the transaction costs in favor of targeted groups. For instance, the government offers minimum waiting time when some firms seek export license. It can also help cut down the red tape while a firm applies for and proceeds in, for instance, construction projects. By so doing, the government maintains surplus by offering "free" or low-priced goods and services, and thus surplus seeking activities.

Such exploration of surplus and surplus seeking may help extend our discussion to additional human interactions, therefore further expand the application of rent-seeking theories. Serious research needs to be conducted in these areas in order to understand the nature of exchange of values and extended application of rent-seeking theories.

In a mixed economy, competition for low transaction costs constitutes surplus seeking while competition for market entry rent seeking (see Figure 2.2). Surplus seeking consists of competition for goods and services that cannot be auctioned off.

In a post-planned economy that is developing competitive market mechanisms, there still exist surplus and surplus seeking while the government starts to create rents by regulating the newly emerged market. The coexistence of rent seeking and surplus seeking may yield the following complications. First, surplus seeking in China's mixed economy provides strong incentives for non-state players to join in the "state club." As discussed above, the focus of surplus seeking is on getting the "red cap." Even in the mixed economy, the state still has many policies favorable to state-owned or state-controlled businesses. For instance, the state banks provide preferential loans to the state sector.

Second, surplus seeking divests resources and energy from further developing the private sector. When private businesses engage in surplus seeking or pursue the "state club" membership, they face greater opportunity costs in the private sector. Since the surplus does not necessarily go to the producers or consumers as discussed above, private players outside of the state chain of distribution are indeed presented with an incentive and an opportunity to capture this surplus.

Third, coexistence of surplus and rent seeking sustains a mixed economy. While the private sector can enjoy certain freedom and opportunities for rapid economic growth, it is also restricted to preferential policies and benefits that are often still reserved for the state sector. In this sense, any rational private business would feel compelled to invest in the state sector. By investing in the state sector, the private sector in effect helps sustain a mixed economy. It becomes a mixed economy wherein the state and private businesses hold shares in the same company, and wherein the state sector continues to operate along the growing private sector.

Although the government opens up a competitive market, surplus seeking has not been eliminated, nor has it been replaced by rent seeking. Examination of surplus and surplus seeking in China's development enriches the discussion of rent seeking and makes rent-seeking theory more relevant to the China case. This helps build a more generalizable rent-seeking theory. Furthermore, in the discussion of surplus and surplus seeking in China, there is always a relevant and legitimate theoretical question to ask, that is, whether we could also find similar surplus and surplus seeking in the market economies. If so, the China experience is more relevant to global knowledge and universal human interactions.

Conclusions

The purpose of this chapter is to offer a critique of both Western paradigms that are limited to their own history and experience as well as the made-in-China paradigms that tend not to offer insights to refine the theories originally developed in the West. The Chinese experience has enriched our general understanding of comparative politics and economic development, challenged theories that are not broadly useful, and provided social scientists with a great opportunity to explore the fundamental questions regarding human interactions that link political, economic, and social development.

In the studies of property rights and privatization, the new development in China challenges the conventional wisdom of Western theories. This challenge, instead of drawing China away from comparative studies, helps to further develop the existing theories and make them more useful in providing a better understanding of development in China and other countries.

This is the same in the studies of rent seeking as we find out that China's development offers rich information to studying general human interactions under various political and economic environments. It provides crucial insights to the politics behind the economics of shortage. It raises probing questions of whether surplus and surplus seeking also exist in a predominantly market economy.

All this contributes to the debates over development models, although these are but two areas of studies, property rights and rent seeking. In many other areas of studies, we may also find comparative analyses that are insightful to both the Chinese experience and that of the rest of the world. Solid basic academic research regarding the interactions among individuals and groups and between individuals and institutions provides necessary foundation to any sound policy analysis and advice. This should be the premise of a "China paradigm" or the "Beijing Consensus."

Acknowledgement

*A draft of this chapter was presented at a conference on "From Revolution to Reforms: Characterizing Made-in-China Transition Paradigms," June 16–17, 2011, University of Saint Joseph, Macau, China. The author would like to acknowledge the financial support for the presentation as well as constructive comments received from the conference. Special thanks to Emilie Tran.

Notes

1. For example, David Easton, *A System Analysis of Political Life* (New York: Wiley, 1965); and Jerry Hough, *The Soviet Union and Social Science Theory* (Cambridge: Harvard University Press, 1977).

2. Joshua Ramo, "The Beijing Consensus," Foreign Policy Centre, London, May 2004.

3. Joshua Ramo, *op cit.*, 4.

4. Joshua Ramo, *op cit.*, 3.

5. See this work of his, published in 2008 by PublicAffairs.

6 See his *American at the Crossroads: Democracy, Power, and the Neoconservative Legacy* (New Haven: Yale University Press, 2006) and "The Fall of American, Inc.," in *Newsweek*, October 13, 2008.

7. See Barrington Moore, Jr., *Social Origins of Dictatorship and Democracy* (Boston: Beacon Press, 1966).

8. This summary highlights predominantly the inputs from a Tsinghua forum, "Centennial Tsinghua Forum," April 20, 2011, at Tsinghua University, Beijing, China, and another forum organized by Fudan University Institute of Advanced Studies in Social Sciences and University of Sydney China Studies Centre, March 29, 2011, at University of Sydney, Sydney, Australia.

9. Similar categorization was discussed by Guo Sujian.

10. We could further divide countries into various sub-sets within each mega block in accordance with the scale of state versus private ownership and the degree of government regulations.

11. Mahbubani elaborated it in more detail in his interview with CNN International, March 2009.

12. See Kishore Mahbubani, *The New Asian Hemisphere: the Irresistible Shift of Global Power to the East* (New York: PublicAffairs, 2008).

13. See Francis Fukuyama, "The Fall of America, Inc.," in *Newsweek*, October 3, 2008, http://www.newsweek.com/2008/10/03/the-fall-of-america-inc.html (accessed May 27, 2011).

14. See "From 'End of History' Author, a Look at the Beginning and Middle," in *The New York Times*, March 8, 2011 http://www.nytimes.com/2011/03/08/ (accessed May 27, 2011).

15. See Avery Goldstein, "Parsing China's Rise: International Circumstances and National Attributes," in *China's Ascent: Power, Security and the Future of International Politics*, eds. by Robert S. Ross and Zhu Feng (Ithaca, NY: Cornell University Press, 2008).

16. Discussion in this section draws from various writings of mine published and unpublished.

17. Xiaobo Hu and Gang Lin, eds., *Transition towards Post-Deng China* (Singapore: Singapore University Press, 2001), 17.

18. See Martin Weitzman and Chenggang Xu, "Chinese Township-Village Enterprises as Vaguely Defined Cooperatives," *Journal of Comparative Economics*, no. 18 (1994): 121–145; and Victor Nee and Sijin Su, "Institutions, Social Ties, and Credible Commitment: Local Corporatism in China," in John McMillan and Barry Naughton, eds., *Reforming Asian Economies: The Growth of Market Institutions* (Ann Arbor: University of Michigan Press, 1996), 111-134.

19. Xiaobo Hu and Gang Lin, eds., *op cit.*, 17.

20. David D. Li, "A Theory of Ambiguous Property Rights in Transition Economies: The Case of the Chinese Non-State Sector," *Journal of Comparative Economics*, no. 23 (1996): 1–19.

21. Xiaobo Hu and Gang Lin, eds., *op cit.*, 18.

22. For detailed discussion, see Xiaobo Hu (2001) in Hu and Lin, eds.

23. Xiaobo Hu and Gang Lin, eds., *op cit.*, 20.

24. Xiaobo Hu, "The State and the Private Sector in a New Property Rights System," in Gang Lin and Xiaobo Hu, eds., *China after Jiang* (Stanford: Stanford University Press, 2003), 69–89.

25. In China, Rent seeking has been widely misunderstood as corruption.

26. Discussion in this section draws from various writings of mine published and unpublished.

27. Anne O. Krueger, "The Political Economy of the Rent-Seeking Society," *American Economic Review*, no. 64 (June 1974), 291–303.

28. Robert D. Tollison, "Rent Seeking: A Survey," *Kyklos* 35 (1982): 575–576.

29. Sam Peltzman, "Towards a More General Theory of Regulation?" *Journal of Law and Economics*, no. 19 (August 1976): 211–240.

30. George J. Stigler, "The Theory of Economic Regulation," *Bell Journal of Economics and Management Science*, 2 (Spring 1971): 137–146.

31. While rents are created, social loss is also rendered by the resultant shortage in supply, that is, a shift from Q_e to Q_m in Figure 2.2. The loss that results is the triangle *abe*, which deserves systematic discussion in a different chapter.

32. Xiaobo Hu, "Decentralization Reform in Post-Mao China: A Framework of Choice," *Issues & Studies* 32 (September 1996): 41–68.

33. K. K. Fung, "Surplus Seeking and Rent Seeking through Back-Door deals in Mainland China," *American Journal of Economics and Sociology* 46, no. 3 (1987): 299–317.

34. See Dorothy J. Solinger, *Chinese Business under Socialism: the Politics of Domestic Commerce in Contemporary China* (Berkeley: University of California Press, 1984).

35. Robert H. Bates, *Essays on the Political Economy of Rural Africa* (Berkeley: University of California Press, 1983).

36. Anne O. Krueger, *op cit.*, 291–303.

37. Fred Hirsch, *Social Limits to Growth* (Cambridge: Harvard University Press, 1976), 27.

38. Janos Kornai, *Economics of Shortage* (New York: North-Holland Publishing Company, 1990).

39. K. K. Fung, *op cit.*, 299–317.

40. Xiaobo Hu and Minglong Yao, "Path Dependence and Insider Privatization: Management Buyout of the Public Firms in China," ms, 2007.

41. See Tim Wright's chapter in Ngo and Wu, eds., 2008.

Chapter 3
The Chinese Discourse on Social Democracy

He Li

The relationship between capitalism and democracy dominates the political theory of the last two centuries.[1] Marxism ran into trouble as time passed, many of Marx's predications failed to come true. Fukuyama claimed that the fall of communism marked "the end of history." Henceforth, the world would belong to liberal capitalism. There was no alternative and we could all march forward in unison towards a future shaped by peace, democracy, and free markets.[2] However, twenty years after the fall of the Berlin Wall, this assertion looks threadbare. Meanwhile, social democracy has not only come to power in many countries, it has succeeded beyond the wildest dreams of its founders.[3]

Chinese intellectuals of the twenty-first century could be primarily grouped into two camps: the liberals and the new-leftists. Discourse of social democracy is very important because it provides a potential alternative to the seemingly inevitable dilemma between the New Left and nationalists on the one hand and the liberals on the other. In the desperate search for a Chinese road to modernity, social democracy has been the subject of intense reflection and debates.

China's reform, which started with the repudiation of egalitarianism and the encouragement to "get rich first," has resulted in spectacular economic growth along with rampant income disparity, pervasive official corruption, growing ethnic tensions, and worsening environment degradation. The current global financial crisis has badly dented the American model of free-wheeling capitalism and profoundly changed many people's view of appropriate roles of state and market. Many Chinese scholars share a declining faith in liberal capitalism. Meanwhile, they are obviously impressed with the sustainable economic development of Western Europe and look upon the Swedish system as a possible model. A large number of Chinese intellectuals are increasingly interested in the European-style social democracy in spite of the ongoing financial crisis in the Euro-Zone.

As Hans Hendrischke contends, "the debate about social democracy marks an important breakthrough in China's ideological discourse. Never before in the history of the People's Republic of China have such broad and unorthodox views on major political questions been allowed a public airing."[4] Over the past thirty years, social democracy has regained public attention and become part of public discourse in China. In a 2009 study, social democracy was listed as one of the major schools of social thought in China.[5] It was confirmed by another study published in 2010.[6] When one searches for "*shehui minzhu zhuyi*" (social democracy in Chinese) in Baidu.com (a top search engine in China), one can get over 628,000 results. Clearly, any attempt to evaluate the intellectual discourse in China is incomplete without understanding of place of social democracy in it.

L. T. Hobhouse holds that great changes are not caused by ideas alone, but they are not affected without ideas.[7] Current Chinese social and economic policy is a revised edition of social democracy. Naturally, it is impossible to understand China's dramatic transformation without understanding the intellectual discourse since the late 1970s. The key to understanding the Chinese quest for modernity lies in an appreciation of the interrelatedness and interplay of different schools of thought.[8] This chapter explores the emergence of discussion on social democracy in China. In addition, it examines the relationship between social democracy and other schools of political thought in China. The study will address following research questions: What is social democracy? How and under what circumstances did social democracy emerge in China? What are the major arguments of the social democrats? What role has intellectual discourse on social democracy played in China's reform?

What is Social Democracy?

Anyone who writes about social democracy confronts an interpretive problem at the outset: what does the term mean? Actually, it is not easy to define social democracy. The scholarly work laid down on the topic of social democracy is plentiful to say the least and often incoherent. Many simply refer social democracy to all forms of socialism that follow an electoral, reformist or evolutionary path to socialism, rather than a revolutionary one. Neither Eduard Bernstein (1850–1932), the founder of social democracy, nor the democratic socialists after him had a very clear definition. In fact, social democracy is a rather complex system of ideas which includes many concepts such as freedom, solidarity, equality, and social justice. Social democracy comes in various national, political, and ideological forms. In this study, social democracy is defined as a political ideology that advocates a peaceful, evolutionary transition of society from capitalism to socialism through democratic means such as election; and promotes equality, freedom, and well-being of the citizens via state regulation and welfare system.

The Chinese translation of "social democracy" is "*shehui minzhu zhuyi*" and that of "democratic socialism" is *minzhu shehui zhuyi*. Two terms, "*shehui minzhu zhuyi*" and *minzhu shehui zhuyi*, are interchangeable in China. It is necessary to distinguish social democracy from democratic socialism in the historical context. The former developed in the early twentieth century as a moderate branch of international socialism and the latter as a major leftist force in the West. By contrast, most of the political parties transformed from communist parties in the former Soviet bloc countries have chosen the term "democratic socialism."[9] In general, both of them advocate a policy in favor of social justice and equity, as well as a democratic transition from capitalism to socialism.

One of the key founders of contemporary social democracy was Eduard Bernstein. *The Prerequisites for Socialism and the Tasks of Social Democracy* (1899) was Bernstein's most significant work and was principally concerned with refuting Marx's predictions about the imminent demise of capitalism.[10] His observations about capitalism led him to believe that it was not leading to an increasing concentration of wealth, but rather was becoming increasingly complex and adaptable. Bernstein believed that socialism would be achieved through capitalism, not through capitalism's destruction. It is due to the fact that rights were gradually won by workers, their cause for grievance would be diminished, and consequently, so too would the foundation of revolution.

In the late nineteenth century, "revisionist" was used to describe social democrat writers such as Eduard Bernstein who sought to revise Karl Marx's ideas about the transition to socialism and asserted that revolution through force was not necessary to achieve a socialist society. The views of Bernstein gave rise to reformist theory, which asserts that socialism can be achieved through gradual peaceful reforms from within a capitalist system.

Many Chinese people may have heard the names of Eduard Bernstein and Karl Kautsky (1854–1938), forerunners of social democracy, because they were associated with "revisionism" and denounced by the Chinese media frequently prior to the late 1970s. However, their knowledge of these figures' ideas does not go beyond the sound bite. The exposure to less prominent scholars is far more restricted. They certainly do not recognize foreign names like Antony Giddens and Henry George,[11] and have, of course, read none of their writings, not even the most famous.

Spread of Social Democracy in China

The Chinese discussion of social democracy can be traced back to the Republican period.[12] During much of that period, the Chinese intelligentsia looked to the Western ideas for a source of wealth and power which would lead China to modernity. Sun Yat-Sen, the founding father of the Republic of China (ROC), was deeply impressed with the writings of Henry George to adopt the single tax. He called for "equalization of land rights" and "restriction of capital."[13] Sun's scheme of *Tianxia weigong*[14] embraces the idea of equality, social justice, and great harmony (*da tong*).[15] *Sanmin zhuyi* ("Three Principles of the People") developed by Sun represents a form of social democracy.[16] *Sanmin zhuyi* considers the people to be the collective ownership of the state, and public interests are above the rulers' own self interest.

Jiang Kanghu (1883–1954) advocated socialism and organized the Chinese Socialist Party in Shanghai in November 1911. The party rapidly grew to 400,000 members, but it was dissolved by the Yuan Shikai government in 1913. After visiting the Soviet Union in 1921–22, Jiang returned to China once more to try to establish socialism there. He revived the Chinese Socialist Party in

1924, which he reorganized in 1925 into the Social Democratic Party, giving it a platform similar to those of the Western European social democratic organizations. However, with the communist victory in 1949, social democracy lost its political base in China and Maoism dominated.

Total denial of social democracy was China's official policy for many years. Denunciation of social democracy went hand in hand with the critique of revisionism of the Soviet Communist Party. Social democratic parties were traditionally regarded as allies of the bourgeoisie. The Chinese routinely described the social democrats in the West as "modern revisionists" and "traitors" in much of the 1960s and the 1970s. In the early 1960s, Mao Zedong and the Chinese Communist Party (CCP) revived the term *revisionism* to attack Nikita Khrushchev and the Soviet Union over various ideological and political issues, as part of the Sino-Soviet split.

In the wake of the market reforms launched by Deng Xiaoping in 1978, the Marxist ideology became a severe constraint on the development of social sciences in China once it was adopted as the state ideology or dogma.[17] Research on social democracy began in the mid-1980s and led to numerous articles and book publications.[18] Within the context of mainland China, authors were extremely cautious to make openly dissenting statements. Instead, they had to rely on quotes, often from foreign sources, to present their views. In this way they could make indirect statements on sensitive issues, provided they refrained from any overt personal judgment. This was the way in which the topic of social democracy was introduced.[19] In 1986, Deng Xiaoping told Gösta Ingvar Carlsson, the president of the Swedish Social Democratic Party, "We are all leftists."[20] Starting from the early 1980s, the CCP established party-to-party relationships with social democratic parties throughout the world. Additionally, ambassadors from European countries to China were invited to give talks on social democratic models of their home countries at a variety of Chinese universities and think tanks. Large numbers of Chinese delegations were now visiting Europe to find out more about social democracy in practice.

However, the image of social democracy was tarnished by Mikhail Gorbachev when he described *perestroika* as building a "new, humane, and democratic socialism." From the Chinese perspective, the Gorbachev's reform has essentially embarked on a social democratic reform course. A major conclusion in the CCP's analysis of the collapse of communist rule in the Soviet Union was that flirting with social democracy was to be avoided at all costs, for otherwise China would become as unstable as Russia.

In recent years the concept of social democracy has gained its political and intellectual momentum worldwide. The Third Ways, or the renewal of social democracy, has become a focus of ideological debate in Europe and the United States. The policies implemented by Tony Blair, Bill Clinton and Barack Obama are considered a revised edition of democratic socialism. The Western scholars produced a literature that has affected thinking about social democracy and their ideas have been quickly echoed in China.[21] By the late 1980s, it was generally accepted that market economy was not only here to stay, but also an invaluable tool for producing growth and wealth.

In the first decade of the millennium, market failure and growing income inequality have become a major concern. Neither orthodox Marxism nor laissez-faire economics is able to cope with such challenges. The reason that social democracy has risen as an attractive alternative is its ideological neutrality and thus political practicability. As Xu Youyu noted, for many people, "Liberalism is too Westernized and irrelevant to China's national condition; China's reality is Marxism-Leninism. If liberalism is at the far ideal end, then social democracy is somewhere between it and the reality."[22]

Since the beginning of the twenty-first century, the Chinese debate on the direction and strategy of reforms has been intensifying. The writings of Bernstein and Karl Kautsky were reexamined. One of the most passionate calls came from Xie Tao, a former vice president of People's University in Beijing, who suggested that China follow what he described as a Sweden's model of "socialist democracy." Writing in *Yanhuang Chunqiu* in February 2007, Mr. Xie warned that unless the party embraced democracy, it was headed for defeat. Wen Jiabao, the prime minister, largely endorsed such thinking, though in more cautious language, when he held his interview with the *Financial Times* in 2009, Wen states that "without the successful political restructuring, one can't ensure success in our economic restructuring. The goal in our political restructuring endeavor is to promote socialist democracy, and better ensure people's rights to democratic election, democratic decision making, democratic management, and democratic supervision."[23] Xie's article has created a storm in China and has since rekindled the domestic debate on social democracy.[24]

The Chinese social democrats have quite a few things in common. First, they are mostly scholars or reform-minded cadres who joined the CCP prior to the victory of the Communist Revolution in 1949. Many of them have originally been Marxists. They are "critical intellectuals." In Western parlance, they could be called public intellectuals, intellectuals who speak out publicly on political issues. Second, these intellectuals have a penchant for social justice and income equality. Some of them, such as Qin Hui and Cao Siyuan, could be considered simultaneously liberals and socialist democrats.[25] Third, to disseminate their ideas they publish papers and columns in newspapers, write blogs, give public lectures, hold seminars, and submit policy suggestions to the governmental decision makers. But those public intellectuals are not organized politically.[26] They are not linked with political organizations or non-governmental organizations abroad, thus denying the authorities any pretext to silence them. For instance, *Yanhuang Chunqiu*, their leading voice, is officially registered.[27] The last but not the least, they are strong supporters of the reform. In the words of Xie Tao, China did not collapse in the event of tremendous changes in the Soviet Union and Eastern Europe. This credit should go to Deng Xiaoping, for launching reform and opening-up policies prior to the upheaval.[28]

Intellectual Discourse on Social Democracy

There is an unprecedented tendency to regard the ideas of social democracy as a source for inspiration and of solutions for the problems in China. Some establishment intellectuals, as well as liberal intellectuals, have argued that social democracy should not be rejected in the first place because "scientific socialism" was originally known as social democracy; that by definition social democracy means socialism plus democracy, two of the fully legitimate goals for the official ideology; that social democracy has proven to be the best method for the developed capitalist world to achieve socialism; and that social democracy has been effectively adapted to the changing environment of the world.[29]

From time to time, reform-minded Chinese scholars raise the issue of possibly transferring to the European-style social democracy. Zhang Rulun called for us to follow the "third path" between capitalism and socialism: He stressed that political democracy and economic democracy must work as a pair, like the two wheels of a cart and the two wings of a bird. Without economic democracy, political democracy will lose its fundamental meaning; without political democracy, economic democracy could not be guaranteed.[30]

There have been major efforts to distinguish radical Marxism from later writings of Marx and Engels. Xin Ziling pointed out that Marx and Engels made major revisions to their earlier theory when they wrote the third volume of *Capital* and many other works; they endorsed stock ownership as a way of realizing public ownership.[31] According to him, Marx and Engels in their later years were democratic socialists and initiators of "peaceful transition to socialism." In his view, democratic socialism is the orthodox of Marxism.[32] Engels' ideas about "peaceful evolution" were fully developed in the preface to Karl Marx's *The Class Struggles in France* (1895), which was considered the "political will of Engels."[33] Xie quoted Engels: "History showed that we have also been wrong. The point of view that we held in 1848 was only a fantasy; history did more than that: it has not only eliminated our confusion of the time, but has also completely changed the condition for class struggles. Violent revolution advocated by the Communist Manifesto has long gone out of date."[34]

In his article Zhang Qiuyuan quoted Engels, "Thus great stress is laid on the dictum that communism is not a mere party doctrine of the working-class, but a theory compassing the emancipation of society at large, including the capitalist class, from its present narrow conditions. This is true enough in the abstract, but absolutely useless, and sometimes worse, in practice."[35] Zhang continued to argue that, in his view, Marx and Engels realized some of their ideas were unpractical and made three major revisions of their thinking: (1) abandon violent revolution; (2) democratic republic is good for the working class and there is no need for the dictatorship of the proletariat; (3) social democracy should be implemented.[36]

Current social democratic discussion is dominated by three themes: democratic constitutionalism, deep but incremental political reform, and the Swedish model of social democracy.

Democratic Constitutionalism

Democratic constitutionalism is of central concern for social democrats. Right in the beginning of the adoption of open door policy, Chinese scholars were committed to looking for the path of economic and societal development suitable to China. Many of them call for adoption of a competitive electoral system and a multi-party system. Some of them decided to focus on specific subfields of law in order to substantially promote the rule of law in China.

The central theme of Xie's paper "The Social Democractic Model and China's Future" was constitutional government (*xianzheng*). In the words of Xie Tao "Only democratic constitutionalism can provide fundamental solutions to the Party's corruption problem. Only democratic socialism can save China."[37] Cao Ciyuan, a key proponent of constitutional and political reform, notes that there was competition between social democracy with constitutional government and totalitarian socialism under dictatorship in the twentieth century. Constitutional government was the key to the success of the Swedish sustained economic development.[38] In a similar vein, Li Rui, a former secretary to Mao Zedong, has openly called for the adoption of the Scandinavian-style democratic socialism. Li said he agreed with the late patriarch Deng Xiaoping that most party members were not even sure what socialism meant. "Yet we can be sure of one thing," Li wrote recently, "Socialism cannot do without democracy, and it cannot do without rule of law."[39] There is a growing consensus among the Chinese intellectuals that the CCP's only way out is through implementing constitutional democracy.

Social democrats firmly believe only constitutional democracy can fundamentally solve the problem of corruption in the ruling party. Xie Tao says, "There are now inner-party deliberations on the separation of the powers (the separation of decision-making, supervision and implementation: the Party Congress and the Standing Committee to exercise decision-making power, the Party Central Committee to exercise executive power, and the Central Discipline Commission to exercise the power of supervision), and on the democratization of the leadership system, in order to achieve a breakthrough in the reform of the political system and in some local experimental areas. From absolute rejection to combining the exploration of the separation of the three powers with its practical form is a major breakthrough in the political reform of the guiding ideology." He pointed out: "As the ruling party, the Communist Party must make fundamental changes in its method of operation." Then he said, "From reform of the system of leadership by the ruling party to reform of the country's political system, this two-step strategy may well be a constitutional path with Chinese characteristics."[40]

Today, political power in the PRC is at the hands of the CCP, which in practice forbids formation of competing political parties. The CCP claims that apart from the Communist Party, eight so-called democratic but nominal parties are allowed to take part in the advisory body, the Chinese People's Political Consultative Conference (CPPCC). The CCP has over 70 million members, while the eight democratic parties combined have a membership of 600,000.

Given the latter's relatively tiny size; it is hard for them to play the role of checks and balances, and provide consultancy service for the CCP.[41] Wan Gang, Chairman of *Zhigongdang* (China Zhi Gong Party), is the only minister (Science and Technology) in at least three decades who is not a member of the Communist Party.[42] This lack of broad-based and well-organized political opposition in the PRC makes it doubtful that a multi-party political system could develop in the near future. Nevertheless, the scholars who embrace social democracy are becoming increasingly vocal in their calls for deep political reform to adopt a real multiparty political system and liberal constitutional democracy. Li Rui even called the CCP to change its name to the Chinese Social Democratic Party and join the Socialist International.[43]

Incremental Democracy

The Chinese social democrats believe that China's road to democracy should take the form of gradual reform. Most of them are firmly convinced that the existing system could be made to work peacefully within. Li Zehou and Liu Zaifu, two well-known scholars involved in the pro-democracy protests in the Tiananmen Square in 1989, have grown disenchanted with the cause of radical reform. Instead, they argued a country could achieve democracy only after economic progress, personal freedom, and social justice.[44] Li acknowledged that he was influenced by the works of Eduard Bernstein.[45]

Such an idea was echoed by other scholars such as Xie Tao. Xie said that the Chinese problem can be described by three words: haste, wait, push. One cannot be hasty; but one cannot wait either; so one has to push forward. The Communist Party is heading in the right direction towards constitutional democracy in small steps. It is impossible to take big steps, and those slow steps will result in many small steps that turn out to be big changes twenty or thirty years later.[46] Xie Tao did not mention multiparty systems explicitly. But he scorned the party's continuing reverence for a "utopian" ideal of communism and warned that: "Political reform cannot be delayed any longer. Seeking to retain the Maoist political system whilst pursuing only economic reform will lead to a bureaucratic capitalism of the kind presided over by Chiang Kai-shek and *Guomindang* (the nationalists), as they headed towards defeat."[47]

Generally speaking, the Chinese scholars prefer a way of progressiveness. Yu Keping, deputy director of the Compilation and Translation Bureau of the Central Committee of the CCP and a professor at Peking University, is one of the most important Chinese thinkers supporting an incremental transition to democracy. Yu constructs a theory of "incremental democracy" and "incremental reform," maintaining that democracy should be achieved progressively. Yu mapped five possible roads for the democratic evolution of Chinese governance since the Reform, that is, from monistic governance towards pluralistic governance; from centralization towards decentralization; from rule of man towards rule of law; from regulatory government towards service government; and from intra-party democracy towards social democracy.[48]

Yu holds that it would be a grave mistake to assume that China only needs intra-Party democracy, instead of a truer people's democracy (*renmin minzhu)* or social democracy (*shehui minzhu*), both of which would include grassroots and general democratic elections.[49] For Yu, intra-Party democracy and people's democracy are complementary. The former is top-down or inside-out and the latter is bottom-up, but ideally they can meet in the middle. Similarly, Wang Changjiang, professor and chairman of the Department of Party Building at the Central Party School (CPS), claimed that promotion of intra-Party democracy need not be at the expense of social democracy. In Wang's words, "social democracy should not wait."[50]

Swedish Model of Social Democracy

A growing number of the Chinese scholars agree that China should model itself politically and economically on Sweden, which is viewed as more genuinely socialist than China. They are fascinated with the sustained social and economic development in Western European countries. There is a consensus among them that in the Nordic countries the welfare state has been extraordinarily successful in eliminating poverty.

Sweden is a rare case where socialism has prevailed to dominate the politics and society of a Western developed democracy. Swedish socialism has been channeled through the Social Democratic Workers' Party (SAP, commonly called the Swedish Social Democratic Party), which has ruled the country almost continuously since the breakthrough of democracy after the First World War until 2007. It should be stressed that Sweden has a multiparty democracy with one dominant party and the SAP has a profound experience of cooperation with other political parties, both to the left and to the right. There are several examples of one party achieving dominance over a country (the LDP in Japan, the PRI in Mexico, the KMT in Taiwan, and the PAP in Singapore) all with their unique characteristics, but in none of these cases have the dominance been as long as in Sweden. Furthermore, no other socialist democratic party has had the same influence over a stable and democratic country.

The SAP has not only been dominant but also implemented socialist policies alongside capitalism. The SAP has given the issue of equality top priority, at least for the last decade, and molded it to their ideological package. Both parliament and cabinet has a 50 percent women representation and the Swedish society is generally viewed as one of the most equal, in particular the labor market. Sweden is today the most democratized country in the world with a long period of stability: no wars for 200 years, and social changes managed without revolution. During the Social Democratic rule, Sweden has become one of the richest countries in the world with one of the widest networks of general welfare.[51]

As Xiao Liang proposed that one notion the economic basis of the socialist superstructure should be taxation, rather than public ownership. As the economy grows, the sources of taxation will grow and thus also the power of the state. With this power the state can correct unjust economic distribution and create a socialist market economy with market features and social justice and equality.[52] This scenario is more or less a blueprint of the Swedish model of so-called "cradle-to-grave" welfare capitalism. It should be noted that in recent decades, social democrats in Sweden have implemented significant neo-liberal policies to the extent that many believe the "Swedish model" to be dead and buried.

The welfare policy of social democratic regimes became a major area for which the state could play a positive role reversing the traditional Marxist view of the bourgeoisie state as a tool of suppression. In 2004, Xie Tao published a paper at *Yanhuang Chunqiu*, in which he advocated Sweden's Social Democratic Party as a model for China.[53] In 2007, Xie Tao once again raised the subject in a lengthy essay in the same journal under the headline "The Social Democratic Model and China's Future." In the paper, Xie cites Sweden as a model for a largely egalitarian society with adequate welfare benefits as well as full protection of the rights of workers and farmers.

Some scholarly works deal with how social democratic parties under changing economic and social conditions have managed to broaden their popular support, even among the rural population and the self-employed. The main reason was seen as their flexibility in responding to changes without insisting on dogmatic positions.[54] The inquiry of the Swedish social democracy is likely to increase in the future. From the Chinese perspective, the study of the Swedish social democracy is necessary in order to learn how to reform society and change the party from a revolutionary party to a ruling party. In the aftermath of the global financial meltdown, a growing number of Chinese scholars began to advocate using active state-initiated programs to ameliorate or remove the injustices inflicted by the unbridled market.

As Yongnian Zheng noted that in the Chinese social fabric, apart from a minority of market worshippers (market fundamentalists) or state worshippers (state fundamentalists), most people have little difficulty in accepting a balance as emphasized by the European model between the three forces [state, society, and market], especially a balance between market forces and social forces. However, Zheng stressed that the most contentious aspect of social democracy in China is the "democracy" part, or to put it more plainly the question of a multiparty system.[55]

Critique from the Left and the Right

Social democracy attracted a great deal of scholarly attention and quite a bit of criticism as well. Since the early 1990s, the Chinese intellectuals became deeply divided, with neo-leftists supporting Maoism and nationalism, and rightists favoring classical liberalism.[56] Democratic socialism draws criticism from both the liberal and New Left camps. Without any doubt, democratic socialism and liberalism bear a strong resemblance to each other on the subject of democracy, especially when they both advocate liberty and constitutional democracy. In history, it is liberalism that first came into being in the West and provided a "platform" for social democracy to ascend to rectify the problems that grew out of unbridled capitalism. According to Qin Hui, there is a strong "overlapping consensus" between liberalism and social democracy in contemporary China, and the differences between liberals and social democrats have not yet become an issue.[57]

The obvious similarities between liberals and social democrats, however, should not lead us to ignore their differences. In fact, social democrats differ from liberals in several ways. First, social democrats claim diversity in the origin of their theory, which derives its key doctrines from Marx, Engels as well as Lassalle and Bernstein. The liberals consider classical liberalism their unequivocal theoretical root. Liberals, like Xu Youyu, insist that any social democratic solution to China's problems can only be considered within a liberal-democratic constitutional framework. Liberalism, in his word, is an "inescapable stage in China's democracy." Second, while the liberals lay emphasis on individual liberty, social democrats seek to balance liberty with equality. Third, social democrats are basically champions of the welfare state. However, a strong state is slammed by the liberals.

Xie's essay was fiercely attacked by the Old Left. One basic line of attack was associating Xie Tao with Gorbachev and implicitly with the ensuing chaotic tendencies in Russia. In a Cultural Revolution style they fitted Xie with caps such as "revisionist," "capitalist roader," and "serving foreign interests." There were a dozen criticism meetings during which Xie was accused of subverting the Communist Party, socialism, the state constitution and the Party constitution. They argue that the Chinese workers have lost their rights gradually and that division between the superrich and the rest has grown dramatically since the beginning of the twenty-first century. This is a real threat to China's "harmonious society" and could lead to chaos, even revolution.

The New Leftists disagree with social democracy as well. They assert the Hu-Wen administration has moved too far to the right, betraying socialism and interests of the working class. *Utopia*, a prominent website of the New Left, has a special column to vilify almost every influential paper published by *Yanhuang Chunqiu*.[58] New Leftists associate growing inequality and official corruption in today's China with the market-oriented reform. They don't think the social democracy is the right answer to the challenges China faces today. Zhang Shuhua's work on Gorbachev's reform concludes that social democratic reform under Gorbachev is the root cause for the implosion of the former Soviet Union.[59]

The heavy cost of the welfare state is another major concern of the New Left circle. Pan Wei, a leading New Left scholar, maintains that social democrats are socialist in the economy and democratic in politics. Yet they are not interested in explaining how a welfare state could be practical among the radically different demography of 1.3 billion, and simply proclaim that the adoption of a competitive electoral system would allow for the building of a "welfare state." Welfare is attractive to the Chinese, but surely not the Nordic kind of taxation.[60]

Some studies by New Left scholars even argue the great (ongoing) recession in West has proved China's model superior to the Anglo-Saxon development model. They consider that state socialist countries had been more successful in meeting people's basic needs (nutrition, health care, education, housing, and pensions) and improving women's conditions than capitalist countries with similar levels of economic development. Another argument of the New Left camp was that socialism offers the best hope for humanity to avoid global ecological catastrophes and to build harmonious relationships between human beings and our environment.[61] As one New Left scholar came to the conclusion that democratic socialism and capitalism can only harm China, only socialism can save China.[62]

To the surprise of many people, including Xie Tao himself, Xie's paper on social democracy was not banned nor censored by the Chinese authorities. Three months after Xie's essay, *Renmin Ribao* (People's Daily), the primary mouthpiece of the CCP, published a response to a reader's inquiry about Xie's essay. *Renmin Ribao* dismissed the European version of democracy as unsuitable for China. Nevertheless, it stated that social democracy "contains some merits that China could learn."[63] The central government communicated the following about Xie's essay: it will not be disseminated; it will not be republished; it will not be criticized; it will not be argued over with the media. However, individuals are entitled to express their views.[64] It should be added there are some common grounds between social democracy and orthodox Marxism. First, they are all committed to building a socialist society. Second, they all emphasize the role of the party as a main political actor in such process. In summary, social democracy is something of a hybrid. It shares with liberalism a commitment to liberty, democracy, and market economy. But in public policy, social democrats believe in the virtue of collective actions for collective good.

Social Democracy with Chinese Characteristics

The Chinese leadership has been searching for an ideological justification for China's emerging economic and political reforms. For this purpose, social democracy might be appropriate, because it is embedded in an international workers' movement and does not require the abandonment of the notion of socialism.[65] In China, the policy stream consists primarily of intellectual elites including scholars in universities and research institutions, and policy analysts inside and outside governmental systems.[66] Prior to June 4, 1989, the reform was supported by the Chinese intellectuals wholeheartedly. Their attitudes helped promote the public acceptance of the market reform and open-door policy launched by Deng in 1978. It has become common for Chinese officials to present advanced working drafts of new theoretical and policy positions to meetings of domestic and sometimes foreign experts for feedback. Such presentations often give a good indication of the direction in which policy is heading. Though the Chinese authorities expressed a reservation towards social democracy discussions on multiparty system and competitive election, they are more tolerant of the different interpretations of social democracy.

With the spread of social democracy, the Beijing leadership has started to rethink its economic and social policies. In the words of Xie Tao, the reform and open-up policies since 1978 really belonged to democratic socialism, but in order to avoid being called "revisionist," the reformers referred to them as the road of "socialism with Chinese characteristics." Xie believes that the constitutional amendment to include the "theory of Three Represents" and the protection of private property marked the beginning of democratic socialism in China.[67]

Contrary to the expectation that tight political control and the censorship in combination make political discourse on democratic transition irrelevant in China, Beijing has adapted its political ideology to the rapidly changing Chinese society and economy. Many of the ideas that were previously identified with social democracy have found their way into "socialism with Chinese characteristics."[68] Bernstein once said that revisionism means reformism, when this theoretical concept is translated into political language. In a similar way, the Chinese authorities coined a new catch phrase: "changing with time" [*yushi jujin* in Chinese] to justify their policy change. Xie states that since the start of the reform launched by Deng Xiaoping, "China has stepped onto the path of democratic socialism."[69] It is true that the spread of social democracy could be a challenge for the party-state. However, so far, the Chinese approach on social democracy has generated some positive effects on China's transition.

First of all, the vast changes unleashed by economic reform and spread of social democratic ideas led Beijing to reject the twin pillars of orthodox Marxism—class struggle and historical materialism—and openly replace them with *xiaokang society*, which aims at a "basically well-off" middle-class-oriented society, and harmonious society.[70] The concept of the dictatorship of the proletariat was quietly replaced by "Three Represents," which indicates an attempt to reform one-party rule by making it more inclusive.[71] In fact, the proletariat practically disappeared from the official discourse and class struggle was replaced by "harmonious society." An opinion piece by Professor Wang Changjiang, published on May 3, 2010 by *Xuexi shibao* [Study Times], a weekly paper run by the Central Party School, contends that "staying in power firmly is the core interests of the Party." It should be added that Wang Changjiang works at the Central Party School, a prominent think tank, and is known to have close ties with senior leaders of the CCP.[72] The Marxist view of democracy as a "bourgeois" facade for class rule was abandoned, and democracy was proclaimed essential for socialist ideals. Wen Jiabao argued that socialists should welcome the ideas associated with liberal thinking in the West. "Democracy, rule of law, freedom, human rights, equality and fraternity do not belong solely to capitalism."[73]

Indeed, the conservatives are correct when they claim to see in the "Three Represents" rationales for a major revision of the Communist Party doctrine. Willy Wo-Lap Lam reported that this revision to the party doctrine has resulted in one of the hottest fads in Chinese elite circles: studying the structure and philosophy of European social democratic parties. Apart from the economic advantages of facilitating growth and social stability, one frequently perceived political advantage of the transformation would be that, having shed the "communist" label, a Chinese-style, at least nominally social democratic party could become less of a target for Western criticism and political sabotage.[74] "Three Represents" is just an example of revision of traditional Marxist ideas such as class struggle, surplus value, and the dictatorship of the proletariat. If this is not a betrayal of Marxism, it is at least a Bernstein type of revisionism that the CCP once spent a great deal of time and energy to condemn.

Second, the Swedish welfare state struck a responsive chord among liberal intellectuals and perhaps even the central party leadership itself. In the name of "scientific development," a new politics of equity is replacing the politics of efficiency. Hu's catch phrase, "harmonious society," has become the ideological umbrella under which China has taken the first steps toward developing a redistributive welfare program. Concerns over efficiency of the Deng-Jiang era (1978-2002) were gradually replaced with concerns over equity. When being interviewed by Fareed Zakaria in 2008, Premier Wen Jiabao, answering the question concerning the China's model of development, argued that the complete formulation of China's economic policy is to give full play to the basic role of market forces in allocating resources, but under the macro-economic guidance and regulation of the government. In other words, both hands (visible and invisible) need to be given full play.[75] Yongnian Zheng noted that Hu Jintao's theories of "scientific development" and politics based on human beings [*yi ren wei ben*] owed much to the European social democratic tradition.[76]

By the late 1990s, China had begun to introduce a broadly based system of social insurance to cover unemployment, old age pensions and other areas, such as combining market economy with social and regional income equality. Beijing's efforts to focus more on equality—including protecting the environment, providing better social services and addressing income inequality—began in earnest with the adoption of the 11th Five-Year Plan in 2006. These policy initiatives help boost the regime's legitimacy. As one public opinion survey of 4,029 people across China by the *Remin Ribao* (People Daily) in 2010 reveals that on the question "What should be the priority for income distribution system in 2010: equity or efficiency, or both?" 50.8 percent respondents believed that equity should be given priority.[77]

Third, as social democrats in Western Europe did in the past two centuries, over the past three decades the CCP has been undertaking "incremental changes," drifting away from the Marxist ideology. The Chinese leadership is in favor of a mixed economy, which is in many ways capitalistic, but explicitly defends governmental provision of certain social services. Increasingly, social democrats in China have adopted the goal of state regulation, but not state ownership, of business and industry as sufficient to further economic growth and equitable income. In a similar vein, the Chinese government privatized much of SOEs and provided a growing though insufficient public goods and services for the Chinese citizens. I share the view of Suisheng Zhao that although some CCP leaders have considered the feasibility of transforming the CCP into a social democratic party, they certainly are not ready to see, coincident with the transformation, a lifting of the ban on forming new political parties. The CCP wants to transform itself into a social-democratic party by establishing a democratic socialism where single party rule prevails despite changes in other areas.[78]

Road Ahead

In spite of the limited public attention it has received in official Chinese media, social democracy has played a central role in the contemporary Chinese ideological discourse.[79] Liberalism favors individual liberty and political freedom, economic equality has never been the principal goal of liberalism, yet without it there is no real democracy for the people as a whole.[80] Nowadays for the majority of the Chinese people, economic equality is more vital than political democracy. The Chinese leadership has recognized the limited role of the self-regulated market in health care provision and demonstrated its willingness to be the main guarantor of social services of the residents.

The social democrats' ideal state is one in which people enjoy both liberty and equality. This has made social democracy more attractive than liberalism in the twenty-first century. While China has carried out direct elections of people's deputies to county-level people's congresses for two decades, there is no timetable for the introduction of popular election at the provincial and national level. In fact, most authors in party journals insist that democracy can be functionally consistent with single-party rule. Meanwhile, they all agree that it is necessary to enliven intellectual life and creativity, and curtail official corruption.

Before the ongoing financial meltdown, the Chinese liberal scholars in general supported globalization and favored the American model; in the words of Li Zhenzhi, "globalization is Americanization." In light of the current global crisis, the hold of liberal thinking has considerably diminished and debates on social democracy heat up. In short, the Chinese discourse on social democracy has gone a long way but is far from over. Up to now there is no indication that the CCP intends to rebrand itself as a social democratic party as its counterparts in Eastern Europe did; nor will the CCP implement multiparty system in the foreseeable future. However, the Chinese discourse on social democracy has helped the CCP adopt major elements of social democracy into its social and economic policies, without losing its identity or having to deny its socialist tradition.

Acknowledgement

This study is supported by a faculty development grant from Merrimack College. Author would like to thank Dorothy J. Solinger, Curtis Martin, Richard Levy, Shaohua Hu, Yu-kyung Yeo, Baogang Guo, Victoria Zhuang for their valuable comments on earlier versions of this chapter.

Notes

1. Gabriel Almond, "Capitalism and Democracy," *PS: Political Science and Politics* 24, no. 3 (September, 1991): 467–474.

2. Francis Fukuyama, "The End of History?" *National Interest*, 16 (1989): 3–18.

3. Tony Judt, *Ill Fares the Land* (New York: Penguin Press, 2010), 220.

4. Hans Hendrischke, "The Chinese Discourse on Social Democracy," in Maurice Brosseau Suzanne Pepper and Tsang Shu-ki eds., *China Review, 1996* (Hong Kong: The Chinese University Press, 1996), 96.

5. Xiao Gongqin,"*Dangdai Zhongguo liuda shehui sichao de lishi yanbian yu weilai zhanwang,*" ["Evolution and Future Development of Six Major Social Thoughts in Contemporary China"] *Leaders*, no. 29 (August 2009).

6. Ma Licheng, *Jiaofeng: Dandaizhongguo de bazhong sichao* [Crossing Swords: Eight Schools of Thought in Contemporary China], Tongzhougongjin, no. 1, 2010 available at http://www.chinaelections.org/newsinfo.asp?newsid=165595 (accessed August 8, 2010).

7. Leonard Trelawny Hobhouse, *Liberalism* (New York: Oxford University Press, 1964), 21.

8. Edmund Fung, *The Intellectual Foundations of Chinese Modernity: Cultural and Political Thought in the Republican Era* (Cambridge: Cambridge University Press, 2010).

9. For detailed discussion on the topic, see Chongyi Feng, "The Third Way: the Question of Equity as a Bone of Contention between Intellectual Currents," *Contemporary Chinese Thought* 34, no. 4 (Summer 2003): 75–94.

10. Eduard Bernstein, edited by Henry Tudor, *The Preconditions of Socialism* [The Prerequisites for Socialism and the Tasks of Social Democracy] (Cambridge: Cambridge University Press, 1993).

11. Antony Giddens is the author of several books on social democracy. Some of his works were translated into Chinese. Henry George promoted the Single Tax Movement, which sought a form of democratic socialism.

12. For a more detailed discussion on the subject, see Edmund Fung, "State Building, Capitalist Development, and Social Justice Social Democracy in China's Modern Transformation, 1921–1949," *Modern China* 31, no. 3 (July 2005): 318–352.

13. Henry George (1839–1897) is an American reformer that was perceived as a socialist at the time. Edmund Fung, *The Intellectual Foundations of Chinese Modernity: Cultural and Political Thought in the Republican Era* (Cambridge: Cambridge University Press, 2010), 210.

14. *Tianxia weigong* can be literally translated into global oneness or community ownership of the public sphere.

15. Baogang Guo, *China's Quest for Political Legitimacy: the New Equity-Enhancing Politic* (Lanham, MD: Lexington Books, 2010), 7.

16. Edmund Fung, *The Intellectual Foundations of Chinese Modernity: Cultural and Political Thought in the Republican Era* (Cambridge: Cambridge University Press, 2010), 225.

17. Dorothy Solinger, *China's Transition from Socialism: Statist Legacies and Market Reforms, 1980–1990* (Armonk, NY: M.E. Sharpe, 1993) and Bill Brugger and David Kelly, *Chinese Marxism in the Post-Mao Era* (Stanford, CA: Stanford University Press, 1990).

18. For example, see Yuanping Qiu, Shangjin Chai, and Deshan Lin eds., *Dang dai she hui min zhu zhu yi yu "di san tiao dao lu,"* [Contemporary Social Democracy and the 'Third Way'] (Beijing: Dang dai shi jie chu ban she, 2004).

19. Hans Hendrischke, "The Chinese Discourse on Social Democracy," in Maurice Brosseau Suzanne Pepper and Tsang Shu-ki, eds., *China Review, 1996* (Hong Kong: The Chinese University Press, 1996), 98–99.

20. Gao Feng, "Ruidian shihui minzhu dang yu shehui minzhu zhuyi" [Swedish Social Democratic Party and Social Democracy], http://www.chinareform.net/ (accessed August 8, 2010).

21. Anthony Giddens, *The Third Way and its Critics* (Cambridge: Polity Press, 2000) and Anthony Giddens, *The Third Way: The Renewal of Social Democracy* (Cambridge: Polity Press, 1998).

22. Xu Youyu, "Zi you zhu yi hai shi she hui ming zhu zhu yi? Qian yi wei ai zhong guo xiang zheng yuan li," ["Liberalism or Social Democracy?—Preliminary Analysis on China's Constitutional Principles in Future"], in Feng Chongyi and Zhu Xueqin, eds., *Xian zheng yu zhong guo, Zhong guo zi you zhu yi lun cong zhi yi* [Constitutionalism and China, Book Series on Chinese Liberalism vol. 1] (Hong Kong: Hong Kong Press for Social Sciences Ltd, 2004), 198.

23. Daniel W. Drezner, "Chinese Premier Endorses Adam Smith," *Financial Times,* February, 2, 2009.

24. Xie Tao, "Minzhu shehuizhuyi yu Zhongguo qiantu," ["The Model of Democratic Socialism and China's Future"] *Yanhuang Chunqiu*, no. 2 (February 2007): 1–8. *Yanhuang Chunqiu* is a monthly backed by reformist party elders. The early version of the essay, entitled "Zi you min zhu she hui zhu yin neng jiu zhong guo," ["Only Democratic Socialism Can Save China"], was published as the preface to Xin Ziling, *Hong tai yang de yun luo: qian qiu gong zui Mao Zedong* [The Fall of Red Sun: The Merits and Sins of Mao Zedong] (Hong Kong: Shuzuofang, 2007).

25. Cao Siyuan, one of the most famous scholars on constitutional law in China, has contributed tremendous amount of time to push forward the progress of constitutionality and social democracy. In the early 1980s, he successfully lobbied the National People's Congress (NPC), the Chinese legislature, to pass PRC's first law of bankruptcy.

26. There are several websites on social democracy. For details, see http://dscn8.info/index.php.

27. Established in 1991, *Yanhuang Chunqiu* is an influential journal. It has published articles dealing with critical issues such as democracy, constitutional governance, as well as critical reviews of important but sometimes sensitive events and leaders including Zhao Zhiyang and Hu Yaobang.

28. Xie Tao, "Preface," in Xin Ziling, *Hong tai yang de yun luo: qian qiu gong zui Mao Zedong* [The Fall of Red Sun: The Merits and Sins of Mao Zedong] (Hong Kong: Shuzuofang, 2007), xx.

29. Chongyi Feng, "The Third Way: the Question of Equity as a Bone of Contention between Intellectual Currents," *Contemporary Chinese Thought* 34, no. 4 (Summer 2003): 84–85.

30. Zhang Rulun, "Disantiao daolu," ["The Third Way"] in Li Shitao, ed., *Zhishifenzi lichang—ziyouzhuyi zhizheng yu Zhongguo sixiangjie de fenhua* [The Positions of the Intellectuals—Debate on Liberalism and the Scission among the Chinese Intelligentsia] (Changchun, Shidai wenyi chubanshe, 2000), 343.

31. Xin Ziling, *Hong tai yang de yun luo: qian qiu gong zui Mao Zedong* [The Fall of Red Sun: The Merits and Sins of Mao Zedong] (Hong Kong: Shuzuofang, 2007), 770–771.

32. Xie Tao, "Preface," to Xin Ziling, *Hong tai yang de yun luo: qian qiu gong zui Mao Zedong* [The Fall of Red Sun: The Merits and Sins of Mao Zedong] (Hong Kong: Shuzuofang, 2007), xxii.

33. Xin Ziling argues that Engels passed away four months after he wrote these words. Therefore, it should be treated as his "political will." New Left scholars contend that there is no such a thing like "political will" of Engels.

34. Xie Tao, "Minzhu shehuizhuyi yu Zhongguo qiantu," ["The Model of Democratic Socialism and China's Future"] *Yanhuang Chunqiu*, no. 2 (February, 2007).

35. Friedrich Engels, "Preface to the English Edition," in *The Condition of the Working Class in England*, in *Marx Engels On Britain* (London: Penguin Books, 1987), 38

36. Zhang Qiuyuan, "Engesi de hua geiwou de qishi," [New Thinking from the Writings of Engels"] http://new.21ccom.net/articles/gsbh/article_2010072914396.html (accessed August 8, 2010).

37. Xie Tao, "Minzhu shehuizhuyi yu Zhongguo qiantu," ["The Model of Democratic Socialism and China's Future"] *Yanhuang Chunqiu*, no. 2 (February 2007).

38. Cao Siyuan, "Ruidian jingyan: xianzheng baohu le minzhu shehui zhuyi," ["*Swedish Experience*: The Constitutional Protection of Democratic Socialism"] *Yanhuang Chunqiu*, no. 8 (August 2009).

39. *Wenzhai Bao*, February 17, 2007.

40. Xie Tao, "Preface," in Xin Ziling, *Hong tai yang de yun luo: qian qiu gong zui Mao Zedong* [The Fall of Red Sun: The Merits and Sins of Mao Zedong] (Hong Kong: Shuzuofang, 2007), xxxv–xxxvi.

41. Gao Fang, "Bainianlai kexue shehui zhuyi yu minshu shehui guanxi de yianbian," ["Evolution of Relationship between Scientific Socialism and Democratic Socialism"] in Tianyu Cao, ed., *She hui zhu yi hai shi she hui min zhu zhu yi?: Zhongguo gai ge zhong de "min zhu she hui zhu yi" si chao* [Socialism or Democratic Socialism? Democratic Socialism during the Chinese Reform Era] (Hong Kong: Dafeng Chubanshe 2008), 277.

42. Wan Gang is the first cabinet minister from a non-Communist party since the late 1970s when China launched its economic reform and opening-up drive.

43. Li Rui, "Preface," in Xin Ziling, *Hong tai yang de yun luo: qian qiu gong zui Mao Zedong* [The Fall of Red Sun: The Merits and Sins of Mao Zedong] (Hong Kong: Shuzuofang, 2007), viii.

44. Li Zehou and Liu Zaifu, *Gaobie geming: huiwang ershishiji Zhongguo* [Farewell to Revolution: Looking Back on Twentieth-century China] (Hong Kong: Tiandi Book Company, 1997).

45. For an overview of Li Zehou's philosophical system, see Gu Xin, "Hegelianism and Chinese Intellectual Discourse: A Study of Li Zehou," *Journal of Contemporary China* 8 (Winter/Spring 1995): 1–27.

46. "Xie Tao Speaks At Hong Kong University," September 22, 2007, http://www.zonaeuropa.com/200709.brief.htm (accessed August 8, 2010).

47. Xie Tao, "Minzhu shehuizhuyi yu Zhongguo qiantu," ["The Model of Democratic Socialism and China's Future"] *Yanhuang Chunqiu*, no. 2 (February, 2007).

48. Yu Ke-ping, "Incremental Democracy: The Political Implication of the 'Three Rounds Two Votes' in the Township Executive Elections," ["Zengliang Minzhu: "Sanlun Liangpiao Zhi" Zhenzhang Xuanju de Zhengzhixue Yiyi"] *Marxism & Reality* [Makesi Zhuyi yu Xianshi], 3 (2000): 27–28.

49. Yu Keping, "*Xuyao liqing youguan minzhu de jige guanxi,*" ["The Necessity to Clarify Several Conceptual Factors Concerning Democracy"], *Beijing ribao* [Beijing Daily], March 16, 2009. Also see http://theory.people.com.cn/GB/49150/49152/8965735.html (accessed August 8, 2010).

50. Wang Changjiang, "*Zhuoli tuijin dang zhizheng de gaige chuangxi,n,*" [Promoting Reforms and Innovation in the Party], *Jiefang ribao* [Liberation Daily], September 28, 2009.

51. For detailed discussion on the Swedish model, see Henrik Simonsen, *Toward a "One-Party Democracy"?—Prospects for a Future Democratic PRC with Reference to Swedish Democratic Experience*, http://nccur.lib.nccu.edu.tw/handle/140.119/34906 (accessed August 8, 2010).

52. Xiao Liang, "lilun de tupo yu gege de tupo" ["Theoretical Breakthrough and Reform Breakthrough"], *caijin wenti yanjiu* [Financial and Economic Studies], no. 11, 2007. Quoted in Wang Yanlai, *China's Economic Development and Democratization* (Ashgate, 2003), 171.

53. Xie Tao, "Ruidian moshi: Shehuiminzhudang de yizhong tansuo," ["The Swedish Model: Exploring the Social Democratic Party"] *Yanhuang Chunqiu*, no. 1 (January 2004).

54. Yuanping Qiu, Shangjin Chai, and Deshan Lin, eds., *Dangdai shehui minzhu zhuyi yu 'disan tiao daolu'* [Contemporary Social Democracy and the 'Third Way'] (Beijing: Dangdai Shijie Chubanshe, 2004).

55. Yongnian Zheng, "China Shows Increasing Interest in Social Democracy Despite Resistance to Multiparty System," *Lianhe zaobao*, October 16, 2007, http://www.zaobao.com/special/forum/pages5/forum_zp071016a.html (accessed August 8, 2010).

56. For a recent review of the topic, see Joseph Fewsmith, *China since Tiananmen*, 2nd edition (Cambridge: Cambridge University Press, 2008) and He Li, "Debating China's Economic Reform: Liberals vs. New Leftists," *Journal of Chinese Political Science* 15, no.1 (March 2010): 1–23.

57. See Qin Hui, "Ziyou zhuyi, shehui minzhu zhuyi yu dangdai zhongguo 'wenti,'" ["Liberalism, Social Democracy and Issues in Contemporary China"] *Zhanlüe yu guanli* [Strategy and Management], no. 5 (2000): 83–91.

58. For details, see http://www.wyzxsx.com/Article/Special/zaoyaoxin/Index.html (accessed August 8, 2010).

59. Zhang Suhua, "Sulian jietie shi minzhu shehui zhuyi de bochan," ["Bankruptcy of Democratic Socialism Is the Cause of the Breakdown of the Soviet Union"] in Tianyu Cao ed. She hui zhu yi hai shi she hui min zhu zhu yi?: Zhongguo gai ge zhong de "min zhu she hui zhu yi" si chao (Hong Kong: Dafeng Chubanshe 2008), 129–140.

60. Pan Wei, "Western System versus Chinese System," *EAI Background Brief*, no. 530, East Asian Institute, National University of Singapore (May 20, 2010).

61. Minqi Li, "After Neoliberalism: Empire, Social Democracy, or Socialism?" *Monthly Review* 55, no. 8 (2004): 21–36.

62. Wu Bing (pseudonym), "Minzhu shehui zhuyi jiuzhi ziben zhuyi," ["Democratic Socialism is Capitalism"], the paper was initially published at maoflag.net, the English translation of the paper is available at http://www.wengewang.org/read.php?tid=14959&uid=1645 (accessed August 8, 2010).

63. "How to Evaluate Social Democracy?" *Renmin Ribao* (People's Daily), May 10, 2007.

64. Ma Licheng, "Jiaofeng: Dandaizhongguo de bazhong sichao," [Crossing Swords: Eight Schools of Thought in Contemporary China], *Tongzhougongjin*, no. 1, 2010, http://www.chinaelections.org/newsinfo.asp?newsid=165595 (accessed August 8, 2010).

65. Hans Hendrischke, "The Chinese Discourse on Social Democracy," in Maurice Brosseau Suzanne Pepper and Tsang Shu-ki, eds., *China Review, 1996* (Hong Kong: The Chinese University Press, 1996), 96.

66. Xufeng Zhu, "The Influence of Think Tanks in the Chinese Policy Process: Different Ways and Mechanisms," *Asian Survey* 49, no. 2 (March/April 2009): 333–357.

67. Xie Tao, "Preface," in Xin Ziling, *Hong tai yang de yun luo: qian qiu gong zui Mao Zedong* [The Fall of Red Sun: The Merits and Sins of Mao Zedong] (Hong Kong: Shuzuofang, 2007), xx.

68. Hans Hendrischke, "The Chinese Discourse on Social Democracy," in Maurice Brosseau Suzanne Pepper and Tsang Shu-ki, eds., *China Review, 1996* (Hong Kong: The Chinese University Press, 1996), 97.

69. Xie Tao, "Minzhu shehuizhuyi yu Zhongguo qiantu," ["The Model of Democratic Socialism and China's Future"] *Yanhuang Chunqiu,* no. 2 (February 2007).

70. Harmonious Society is a socio-economic vision that is said to be the ultimate end result of Chinese leader Hu Jintao's signature ideology of the scientific development outlook.

71. The CCP claims that apart from the Communist Party, eight so-called democratic but nominal parties are allowed to take part in the advisory body, the Chinese People's Political Consultative Conference.

72. Cheng Li, "Intra-Party Democracy in China: Should We Take It Seriously?" *China Leadership Monitor*, no. 30 (Fall 2009), 7, http://www.hoover.org/ (accessed August 8, 2010).

73. Quoted in Joseph Kahn, "In China, Talk of Democracy Is Simply That," *New York Times*, April 20, 2007.

74. Suisheng Zhao, "Political Liberalization without Democratization: Pan Wei's Proposal for Political Reform," *Journal of Contemporary China* 12, no. 35 (2003): 351.

75. "We Should Join Hands, China's Prime Minister Speaks out in His First Interview with a Western Publication in Years," Available at *www.newsweek.com/2008/09/28/we-should-join-hands.html* (accessed August 8, 2010).

76. Yongnian Zheng, "China Shows Increasing Interest in Social Democracy despite Resistance to Multiparty System," *Lianhe zaobao*, October, 16, 2007, http://www.zaobao.com/special/forum/pages5/forum_zp071016a.html (accessed August 8, 2010).

77. Available at http://voting.people.com.cn/vote_show/index.php?qid=9783 (accessed August 8, 2010).

78. Suisheng Zhao, "Political Liberalization without Democratization: Pan Wei's Proposal for Political Reform," *Journal of Contemporary China* 12, no. 35 (2003): 351.

79. Hans Hendrischke, "The Chinese Discourse on Social Democracy," in Maurice Brosseau Suzanne Pepper and Tsang Shu-ki, eds., *China Review, 1996* (Hong Kong: The Chinese University Press, 1996), 118.

80. Edmund Fung, *The Intellectual Foundations of Chinese Modernity: Cultural and Political Thought in the Republican Era* (Cambridge: Cambridge University Press, 2010), 247.

Chapter 4
The Tension between Governance and State-Building

Jianxing Yu and Ziying He

As a reaction to various types of statism prevailing in the middle of the 20th century, neoliberal reforms were carried through in Western democracies one after another during the late 20th century. Furthermore, the post-communist states in the former Soviet Union and Eastern Europe had also been experiencing transitions towards the liberalist state model, and likewise the Newly Industrializing Countries (NICs) in East and Southeast Asia. After the 1997–98 Asian Financial Crisis, the "developmental state," which up to that point had been seen as the basis of the "Asian Miracle," was increasingly regarded as the root of Asian crisis. Meanwhile, the whole world has been overwhelmed by a revolution of "from government to governance." Heywood points out that all these pointed towards an inevitable trend of "de-statization" or a "rolling back" of the state and decentralization of state power in favor of the market and civil society.[1]

Unfortunately, "de-statization" or "rolling back" not only failed to deal with both old and new social and economic issues faced by western democracies, it also contributed little to the newly emerged democracies, and led this second group to suffer from becoming weak or failed states during the process of privatization and democratization.

In such context, "state-building" is an issue of worldwide significance and has once again become a central theme in both academic and practical discourses. B. Jessop, for instance, revealed the importance of meta-governance and state-building, and indicated the contemporary necessity of reimagining, redesigning and rebuilding of state.[2] Francis Fukuyama also argues that "state-building is one of the most important issues for the world community because weak or failed states are the sources of many of the world's most serious problems, from poverty to AIDS to drugs to terrorism."[3] In light of the political conflicts and instabilities confronted by new democracies, many scholars advocate "democratic sequencing"—putting off democracy until the rule of law and a well-functioning state are in place. In this view, the state-building is a precondition for democratization and marketization.[4]

However, the shift from privatization to governance and state-building should not be understood as the rise and fall of statism and liberalism. To the contrary, it only indicates that a one-track approach favoring one over the other is inadequate in explaining various practices of governance today. This has been one of the most important topics of debate with respect to contemporary discussions of theories related to state-building, governance and the role of the state in governance.

This chapter will first make some theoretical inquiry over the paradoxical relations between governance and state-building and then uses China as a case study to illustrate our argument that China's development model is unique precisely because of its focus on state-building in the formative years of economic reform. We share the view that state-building is a necessary precondition of democratic governance. However, the development of the democratic governance, which China has growingly turned its attention to, can also help mitigate, if not avoid, risks associated with the former's tendency towards statism. There is a tension between governance and state-building, it is concluded that such tension is necessary and that it should be balanced vis-à-vis the "rule of law."

The Rise of Governance and Meta-Governance

The concept of Governance appeared in the late 1980s. G. Stoker summarizes five propositions of governance which could be seen as the essence of governance:

> Governance refers to a set of institutions and actors that are drawn from but also beyond government; Governance identifies the blurring of boundaries and responsibilities for tackling social and economic issues; Governance identifies the power dependence involved in the relationships between institutions involved in collective action; Governance is about autonomous self-governing networks of actors; Governance recognizes the capacity to get things done which does not rest on the power of government to command or use its authority.[5]

The rise of governance is a double reflection on and a replacement of both market-failure and state-failure. The theoretical underpinnings of its ideals are "evidently constructed both from the supposed virtues of markets and third-sector alternatives to the state, as well as from a belief in the virtue of competition, choice, and multiagency collaboration."[6] In the 1980s, Wolf points out that market-failure or state-failure was inevitable, and "it is neither a choice between perfect markets and imperfect governments nor one between imperfect markets and perfect governments. Instead, it is a choice between imperfect markets and imperfect governments, as well as imperfect combinations between them."[7] Nowadays the advantages of the state's hierarchical regulation and the market's anarchic coordination "are lost in a world that is characterized by increasingly dense, extended, and rapidly changing patterns of reciprocal interdependence, and by increasingly frequent, but ephemeral, interactions across all types of pre-established boundaries, intra- and inter-organizational, intra- and inter-sectoral, intra- and international."[8]

Compared with the anarchy of exchange (i.e. the market mechanism) or the hierarchy of control (i.e. the state), governance emphasizes self-organization, a horizontal network and partnership, and "refers to mechanisms and strategies of coordination in the face of complex reciprocal interdependence among operationally autonomous actors, organizations, and functional systems."[9] It stresses negotiations and reflections of inter-organizations, interpersonal networks, inter-forces and inter-mechanisms. Negotiation and reflection means the diversification and dispersal of forces involved in governance. In other words, governance expresses our expectations to achieve collective objectives and interests without the imperative forces of state. And the objectives of destatization and liberalization pursued by governance led it to be closely associated with the civil society movements of the 1970s and 1980s, which in turn contributed to a decentralization of state power and the rise of the market and civil society, which sought a kind of "polycentric governance" through the networking, partnering and self-organizing governance practiced by liberalized market forces and civil society organizations.

However, it seems increasingly difficult to achieve governance objectives in the real world, especially in most developing countries. As argued by Fukuyama, "the dominant trend in world politics for the past generations has been, after all, the critique of 'big government' and the attempt to move activities from the state sector to private markets or to civil society."[10] In his view, during the liberalization process, which aimed to build a new market economy, whether in developing countries in Asia, Africa and Latin-America or in transitional countries in the former Soviet Union and Eastern Europe, inappropriate forms of decentralization resulted in weak or failed states and in some cases, even anarchy, which in turn evoked a set of serious troubles in global governance. He therefore argues that state-building might be more important than governance, and building a strong state might be more urgent than the introduction of governance from the Western context to developing and transitional countries.

Essentially, governance itself requires state-building or rebuilding. In his definition to governance, Stoker regards government or the state as a key actor in governance. Another crucial governance theorist, Kooiman, also points out that governance is a type of interaction among the state, the market and civil society, that it is a fixed institutional arrangement "in terms of handling the growing diversity, dynamics and complexity of societal issues."[11] To date, the state remains the only public institution that can mobilize social resources and provide public goods for society with the necessary levels of efficiency and breadth. And state leaders remain the main operators in the various processes of decision-making, implementation and assessment of public policy. It is true that governance is a very politicizing concept, one that is used to represent the ideas about the changing roles of state, the developments that itself desires, and the relationships among the state, market and civil society as well as the method of power exercise.[12] In short, governance expresses the demands of a society that is willing to have dialogues, share values, responsibilities and authorities with the state, and participate in the processes of state-building or state-rebuilding positively (rather than resisting state or government negatively).

Nevertheless, the role of the state in the governance system is not on the same footing as the other involved forces. Jessop argues that governance was just as prone to failure as market-failure and state-failure.[13] He introduced a new concept, "meta-governance", which is "a reflexive and responsive process through which situated actors aim to combine, facilitate, shape and direct particular forms of governance in accordance with a specific standard for what is to be considered as 'good governance'."[14]

Among the pluralistic authorities of the governance system, the state should play a major role in meta-governance, but "meta-governance should not be confused with some super-ordinate level of government in control of all governance arrangements."[15] In meta-governance, the state plays active institutional and strategic roles as follows:

> To design, establish and maintain the general rules and regulations by which all governance forces should strictly abide;
>
> To establish a platform for negotiation and dialogue, and to organize an open, just, transparent and effective decision and policymaking network;
>
> To build information exchange and feedback mechanisms, and to encourage all governance forces to correct their own pursuits and governance practices reflexively;
>
> To set up the learning networks among governance actors, organize open investigation platforms, and among different governance forces, promote an understanding of the differences among their own practical rationalities and cognitive methods;
>
> To serve as a "court of appeals" and organize a "jury" that mediates through collective negotiation when there are controversies about shared objectives, conflicts of interest, or other disputes among different governance forces;
>
> To manage networks as well as the coordination channels among multifarious forms, forces and mechanisms strategically, and to make the state itself act as the balance point for effective coordination among them, and so forth.

That the state should assume a positive role in meta-governance does not mean that the state is going to eliminate other forces of governance and other modes of coordination or that the state should take care of everything. On the contrary, what meta-governance requires from the state is the development of systems and structures designed to improve the performance of polycentric governance. If the state wants to play such roles in governance and meta-governance, it has to dethrone its own supremacy, reflexively decentralize its power to civil society and the market, and build partnerships with them. In so many words, the state must be redesigned, reimagined and rebuilt for the sake of governance and meta-governance.

Paradoxical Relations between State-Building and Governance

This chapter is a dialectical inquiry into the paradoxical relationship between state-building and governance, in which state-building aims to enhance centralization of state power and state capacity whilst governance aims at decentralization. However, western experiences also demonstrate that democracy and rule of law in the process of state-building have safeguarded state-building from becoming statism. Democratic state-building is a process of protecting civil rights and establishing the rule of law, thus providing the rules of game for the development of civil society and its struggle against the state with regards to centralization and decentralization. Although tensions and conflicts between governance and state-building exist, the rule of law can help achieve a balance between the two tasks.

In this sense, the goal of state-building, based on the experience of East Asian developmental and transitional countries, is to build a strong state, which makes possible the consolidation of democracy and the implementation of governance. The role of a strong state in these countries has been prominent in the absence of Western-type matured civil society and market institutions. But experience also shows that such a strong state can also become a fetter for democracy and governance. This study argues that the favorable condition for governance in developing and transitional countries (e.g. China) is the reconstruction of the state rather than the dismantlement of a strong state. That is to say, state reconstruction should be carried out according to the level of development of civil society and market, and the proper roles and responsibilities of the state should be redefined, on the basis of the rule of law, and some roles and responsibilities of the state (i.e. power) should be transferred to society and market, rather than a total retreat of the state from society and market.

State-building means to (a) build an independent, sovereign nation-state ruled by the central political authority within a defined territory, (b) set up the state's legitimate monopoly of violence over the society, and (c) construct effective state institutions, organizations and apparatuses in the fields of security, public administration, taxation, social control, macro-economic regulation, protection of civil rights, creation of legal systems, and public goods provision, and thereby intensify the state's strength and promote the state capacities within the proper scope of state functions.

Modern state-building originated in Western Europe.[16] A. Giddens divided the developments of modern states into three phases: the traditional state, the absolutist state and the nation-state.[17] According to Giddens, modern national states with powerful militaries, highly centralized governments, and violent proclivities combined these factors to initiate the new epoch of modern capitalist states. Following Weber's ideal-typical definition to the modern state, Zheng summarizes the attributions of the process of centralization of absolutist states to modern state-building, "the absorption of smaller and weaker political units into larger and stronger political structures; a strengthened ability to rule over a unified territorial; the application of a more unitary, centralized and calculable rule by a single, sovereign head."[18]

In fact, Marx distinctly revealed the historical achievements and the essence of centralization of modern state-building in *The Civil War in France* before Weber and Giddens. Marx wrote, "The centralized State power, with its ubiquitous organs . . . originates from the days of absolute monarchy . . . . Still, its development remained clogged by all manner of mediaeval rubbish, seigniorial rights, local privileges, municipal and guild monopolies and provincial constitutions. The gigantic broom of the French Revolution . . . swept away all of these relics of bygone times, thus clearing simultaneously the social soil of its last hindrances to the superstructure of the modern State."[19] The state theorist argues that this remarkable passage of Marx was nowhere better expressed, because modern states were closely intertwined with the state apparatus of the monarchy and given the importance of bourgeois revolutions in modern state-building.[20]

With respect to modern capitalist state-building, centralized absolutist states created a unified national market and their powerful military forces guaranteed the unified interests of national bourgeois, who in turn became increasingly stronger. They then conquered state power through the bourgeois revolutions and seized political authority, replacing the kings of feudalist dynasties. Thus, the absolutist state gradually transformed to the modern capitalist nation-democracy state. Accordingly, there are two basic characters of modern states: first, it is a nation-state, meaning that the organizational form of modern states is based on national sovereignty; second, it is a democracy-state, meaning that the institutional system of the modern state is based on political legitimacy.

The processes of nation-state-building and democracy-state-building in the West were essentially simultaneous. In general, "Both the rule of law and liberal democracy, draw a borderline preventing the central state's authority from coerce first by putting it under a set of transparent and universal rules, and secondly by ensuring that the exercise of power reflects the popular will."[21] At the state level, Dillon's Rule and the Home Rule charter work in tandem to maintain state supremacy over local government while at the same time give local government autonomy in handling local affairs innovatively.

Comparatively, there is serious disequilibrium between the two processes in most developing countries. The former is more easily accepted than the latter between the two major Western "state products:" nationalism and democratism. The demand of nation-state-building usually overwhelms that of democracy-state-building in late developing countries given urgent historical missions of national independence and renaissance. However, this disequilibrium is not one with an insurmountable intrinsic nature.

It is the disintegration, unceasing conflicts (political, martial and ethnic conflicts) and impoverishment in most contemporary developing countries that shapes the real context in which state-building is advocated by scholars. For instance, after his examination of failed experiences of Africa, C. Anthony argues that there was no modernization without basic state-building.[22] Taking Japan between 1950s and 1980s as example, Ravina describes the sequence from state-building to economic growth and then to democratic transformation as well as its consolidation.[23] In their opinions, building a stronger state is the precondition of building a richer nation, stating that "economic development has a strong endogenous effect on democratization,"[24] and then a more democratic state will subsequently emerges in developing countries.[25] This type of theory is usually labeled "democratic sequentialism."

This theory generally attributed the success of NICs in East Asia to the strong "developmental state," with industrialization as its priority objective, sustainable economic development as its primary goal, markets dominated and controlled by the state severely, powerful intervention over national economy by governments, and deliberate state projects formulated by state elites based on their own strategic rationality.[26] The state-centered theorist Skocpol argues that it was the absolutely autonomic and centralized state that ensured the economic miracle of East Asian economies. Similarly, the Chinese state is also regarded by some scholars as a "socialist developmental state" because of the remarkable economic statism it practiced in the process of developing a functional market economy in the 1990s.

When the Asian Financial Crisis broke out in the late 1990s, however, "the developmental state" became the target of various reflections and critiques. Neoliberalists argued that the real roots of crisis were attributable to excessive government intervention and the insufficient deregulation in the financial sectors. Contrarily, supporters of the developmental state argued that the crisis was caused by excessive liberalization and deregulation. As a matter of fact, these countries not only had problems associated with pursuing rapid financial system liberalization and high capital mobility sans adequate state supervision and regulation, they also had rigid exchange systems. It was a comprehensive moral crisis as well as the opacity of cooperative management and financial transactions that conduced to the Asian Financial Crisis.[27] Subsequently, the developmental state was requested to shift its attitudes with respect to civil society, promote and activate the society's governance abilities, facilitate hierarchies, guide the political participation of citizens, and realize the aims of decentralization and democratization.

However, the process of decentralization and democratization in developmental states does not mean that they should transform themselves into powerless states. Rather, it means a new type of transformation of state power should take place: old authoritarian power should be weakened on the one hand, and the "fundamental abilities" of the state should be strengthened on the other, namely "the ability of the state to penetrate society, organize social relations, and implement policies through a process of negotiation and cooperation in society."[28] The core challenge for democracy promotion in countries moving away from authoritarianism is to diminish or counterbalance an overly strong state.[29]

So it can be seen from the above discussion that there is not only some conflict but also some blend between state-building and governance. The conflict is remarkable. In terms of their own intrinsic characteristics, state-building emphasizes stability, order and regulation, thus demonstrating characteristics of rigidity, hierarchy control and procedural rationality; however, governance stresses diversification, negotiation and coordination, thereby demonstrating features of flexibility, hierarchic interaction and reflexive rationality.

In terms of their own institutional objectives, state-building is state-centered, whether in the building of the organizational form or institutional system or intervention over social and economic fields. Even though there is also decentralization and democratization in the process of state-building, the development of market forces and organizations in civil society is still dependent on the support of a powerful state. Comparatively, governance emphasizes the diversification and decentralization of authority, aims to deconstruct the absolute authority of the state and dethrone the state's supreme sovereignty as one of the aspects of modernity, and requires that the state alter its "method of rule" as well as share the resources of authority and power with the society equally (and therefore carries some postmodern implications). It definitely proposes an idea of polycentric governance, which forces the state's sovereignty to open up to individuals and non-governmental organizations, including the authority of public administration of government.

However, there is some sort of mix in most aspects of governance and state-building. Because of the risks of governance failure, meta-governance as "the governance of governance" is crucial and only the state can be competent in this role. Contrary to arguments that governance is completely negative to state-building, in the new political realities, how governance is conceived can create a new pathway for evaluating the state's ability and for readjusting the relation between the state and society. In state-building, Fukuyama suggests that "the problem for many countries was that in the process of reducing state scope they either decreased state strength or generated demands for new types of state capabilities that were either weak or nonexistent."[30] So, these countries were trapped into the "governance crisis." Accordingly, Fukuyama argues that the urgent affair was state-building in order to overcome their crisis. In a word, good governance must be based on a strong state, even if, in the carrying out a liberalist reformation, the strong state is more effective than a weak one.[31]

Likewise, state-building does not mean the suppression of the development of governance. From England's "The Citizen's Charter" to France's "the Declaration of Human Rights" to America's "the Bill of Rights," all have demonstrated that the process of modern state-building was also the process of establishing and developing civil rights and democracy. It is only under the protection of the state that a powerful civil society can grow up.[32] Thus, a civil society based on civil rights is also helpful to modern nation-democracy state-building because it can prevent the rise of a modern state that was born out of the absolutist state, i.e., from a "dictatorship" and "aggrieving public lives." There can be and in fact there have been positive relations between the state and civil society, centralization and decentralization, state powers and civil rights. As argued by Skocpol, the process of the great transformation of modern society is "the coincidence of political with social transformation."[33] Hobsbawm also argues that modern society was derived from the "dual revolution:" Industrial Revolution and French Revolution.[34] In sum, there are three processes in "the great transformation" of the modern world: the building of a modern market economy, a modern state and a modern civil society. In western history, the three processes were mutually articulated but not accomplished synchronously. It shows that there is no antinomy necessarily between modern state-building and modern civil society building.

Keeping the Tension between Governance and State-building

It is only through a dialectic relationship between governance and state-building that one can find a way to overcome the abstract opposition between liberalism and statism, and thereby pave a way to reshape the relationship between the state and society along with improving governance systems.

After examining the implications of post-Fordism, the rise of governance and globalization for contemporary capitalist states, Jessop points out that the old boundary of state power was retreating and the state needed to give these powers back to society, while the new boundary was expanding and the state needed to strengthen abilities and powers in new fields. In other words, the state had to give up its traditional powers in old interventional fields if it wanted to obtain new powers in new fields.[35] Fukuyama emphasizes that "what is most urgent for the majority of developing countries is to increase the basic strength of their state institutions" after his review of most "failed states" and "powerless states."[36] Both Jessop and Fukuyama emphasize the dual needs of centralization and decentralization of state power. On the one hand, the state not only needed to continuingly act as night watchman for free market, but it also needed to make use of welfare policies in order to realize social justice. Furthermore, in the drastic process of globalization, the state gets involved in nearly all important policy fields at both regional and global levels and faces a number of new transnational problems of coordination and regulation. On the other hand, if the state does not improve the structures of governance, it will be unable to effectively fulfill the old and new functions mentioned above. "As the state becomes overloaded with demands on its national and local administrative capacities, it continues to delegate and disperse regulatory and distributive powers to quasi-public corporations, trade associations, professional organizations, social service corporations, labor unions, chambers of commerce, scientific associations, and many other private non-profit organizations."[37]

As noted previously, a zero-sum game between the centralization and decentralization of the state is not inevitable. Centralization can be realized through decentralization, and decentralization is helpful to centralization. In an increasingly complicated society, the state has to centralize its powers in some key functions and new regulatory fields. As P. Aucoin said, "this paradox of a simultaneous centralization and decentralization in government structures has constituted a central feature of the new public management."[38] However, lacking an advanced civil society or market forces, the state will become an all-powerful government because there are no competent agents to whom the state could delegate its authorities and powers even if it wanted to do so. As public affairs are becoming increasingly complicated, a state may be unable to deal with them effectively and promptly because of its limited resources. Consequently, old problems will languish unsolved while new problems emerge and grow more serious. In the worst case scenario, such a situation might cause general social discontentment and disappointment towards the state and government, whereby the state might in turn lose social support and political legitimacy, which could ultimately lead to a powerless state or failed state.

This certainly does not suggest that there is no conflict between the state and the civil society or no contradictions between governance and state-building. On the one hand, in terms of the "authoritative pluralism" essence of governance and the "centralization" essence of state-building, there are contradictions between them all the time. On the other hand, in terms of the "centralization" and "decentralization" aspects of state-building, the state might not necessarily reach agreements with the civil society with respect to which fields the state should centralize or decentralize its powers and authorities. In other words, the tensions between governance and state-building originate from the complexities and difficulties faced when the state and the civil society try to reach agreements on issues of centralization and decentralization.

It is necessary to keep such tensions between the state and the civil society. The state will engulf the civil society and asphyxiate market forces. Without such tensions, the state will become seemingly more powerful but nevertheless weak in many areas. For example, if the state does not regulate the market forces and the civil society rationally, it will become a smaller but weaker state. The question is how to keep and balance the necessary tensions between them? The key lies in the establishment of the rule of law. "In all Western democracies, administration is bound by law."[39] As mentioned above, the Constitution of the United States defined the relation between federal government and state government distinctly and established the borders of administrative powers of governments through the protection of civil rights. Sequentially, the state passed through the Dillon's Rule and Home Rule to define the relation between state government and local government.[40] These laws established the baseline between centralization and decentralization of state power. Western experiences indicate that it's difficult to establish and keep the balance and interaction between governance and state-building without the rule of law.

The Case of China

The process of Chinese modern state-building and development of governance system provides a lively case for the examination of the dialectic of balancing tensions between governance and state-building.

At the end of the 19th century, the Qing Dynasty was forced to start its state-building, including reforming taxation, opening free trade, embarking in mine, railway and marine enterprises in terms of economics, as well as reforming education and the merit and promotion system in terms of politics. However, the Qing Dynasty failed ultimately because it was an absolute monarchy. The success of the Revolution of 1911 and the establishment of the Republic of China in 1912 started the process of modern state-building. The establishment of the People's Republic of China in 1949 symbolizes the completion of nation-state-building. From then on, a Leninist party-state system was formed which exhibited the characters of high-level centralization in political, economic and social fields. The state controlled by the Chinese Communist Party (CCP) set out to build a modern China. Unfortunately, in the period of "Cultural Revolution" (1966–1976), the mass movement not only seriously interrupted the process of economic development, but also badly undermined and even substantially destroyed the state apparatus and government system.

In the year of 1978, China started her great "Reform and Opening Up", which was the prelude to the building or rebuilding of Chinese state. Marketization and democratization were the two major themes in China's political and economic development in the 1980s.

To accommodate marketization, the Chinese state decentralized power massively, yielding power to the market and local government via a roll back, principally, from economic fields. First, the state reformed the agricultural production system, and carried out the household responsibility system. Second, the state encouraged the development of private enterprises, and allowed individuals to become rich legally. Third, the state started to reform state-owned enterprises (the SOEs) with the aim of "separating government from enterprises" in order to increase their productivity. Fourth, the state began the "tax instead of profit" reform, whereby enterprises were required to pay only income taxes in lieu of whole profits. Subsequently, in 1987, the state also introduced the contract responsibility system to expand the decision-making power of the SOEs. Fifth, the state started the fiscal system reform referred to as "cooking in separate kitchens," by reducing subsidies to local governments, canceling the rigid fiscal targets of local governments, and permitting local governments' budget revenue autonomy.[41] As the result, a great deal of private entrepreneurs rose rapidly in China, and the market competition capacities of the SOEs also increased notably. Therefore, newly rising market forces grew and are growing in strength gradually and have made and are making important contributions to China's rapid economic growth.

Along with the market-oriented economic transformation, the CCP also started a new process of state-building. Seeking for a more rational and efficient bureaucratic system suited to the new economic system, the Chinese state carried out bureaucratic restructurings twice, first in 1982 and second in 1988. Following the currents of reform in the 1980s, these restructurings were designed to accommodate the decentralization of administrative powers.

Political reform and democracy-state-building, as the political support to marketization and economic decentralization, was another goal of state-building. The CCP defined clearly the goal of political system reform as "separating the Party from the government." Therefore, the Party started reforms of the central collective leadership system, the cadre and personnel system, the socialist legal system, and so on. The political reform of "separating the party from the government" led to increased political liberalization in the process of democracy-state-building. The elites in intellectual circles advised the Chinese state to learn from Western democratic institutions, and advocated decentralization, liberalization, democratization and individualism. Under these political, economic and cultural conditions, there was a rapid and unprecedented expansion of organizations in civil society as the government rolled back from most spheres of production, business, civil affairs, culture, arts and academics, and transferred its regulatory responsibility to civil organizations. "By 1989, there were 1,600 national non-governmental organizations and more than 200,000 local ones."[42] Seen from the process of political and economic transformation in the 1980s, there was an interaction and a blending of the development of governance system and state-building. Of course, the democratization in this period mainly focused on the readjustment of the Party-state system through "democracy within the Party." The "checks and balance" and "multi-party system" were still regarded by the leadership as being contrary to socialism. And the rapid growths of organizations in civil society were mainly alternatives in the functional fields from which the state had rolled back.

Unfortunately, the fallout associated with the Tiananmen Event in 1989 dealt the process of democracy-state-building a setback. In the 1990s, the CCP no longer permitted the discourses of democratization in public. Democracy-state-building was laid aside, and the party-state enhanced its control over civil society and monopoly of political power. Meanwhile, the Chinese state carried through reforms with aim of improving state capacities via centralization, which in turn contributed more to the Chinese "economic miracle."

Because of the Tiananmen Event in 1989, marketization reforms suffered heavily from opposing, conservative forces inside the CCP. Facing this situation, Deng Xiaoping made his famous speech during his tour of Southern China in 1992. He said that whether an economy was more market-based vs. planned was not the difference between socialism and capitalism and that the CCP and the government must advance the market reform firmly. In 1997, the Fifteenth Party Congress formally legitimized the market economy as China's basic economic system. In terms of institutional construction, the CCP began to attach more importance to state-building and emphasize the centralization and macroeconomic regulation, showing strong implications of economic statism. In 1994, following the radical fiscal decentralization of the 1980s, the state undertook the "revenue-division system" reform to adjust the central government's decreasing fiscal capacities. The new system divided total tax revenues into three parts: central, local and shared, and it set up two separate institutions, the central tax bureau and the local tax bureau. As a result, the central government's fiscal capacities were greatly improved, and the proportion of total taxes shared by the central government increased year by year. Furthermore, Premier Zhu Rongji initiated a new bureaucratic reform in 1998. He restructured the ministries and bureaus in State Council entirely, reduced by half their number of civil servants, and established a "State Economic and Trade Commission", which is analogous to Japan's Ministry of International Trade and Industry (MITI) as the highest center of decision-making with respect to economic reform. As a result, the efficiency of the state increased remarkably. Simultaneously, the macroeconomic management capacity of the central government was strengthened greatly.

Between 1997 and 1998, China had also encountered troubles resembling those felt by some developed Asian states during the Asian Financial Crisis. Under such pressures, the Chinese state undertook a number of radical measures to reform its financial system, hoping to strengthen the state's macro-regulation over the market economy and improve the capacity of the state financial sectors to cope with global financial risks. Firstly, the Chinese state reconstructed the People's Bank of China to build up a new banking system, one that was analogous with the US Federal Reserve system. It began to function in 1999. Subsequently, the People's Bank of China, as the central bank, was able to supersede political interventions by local governments, gradually expanding its autonomy and finally became a powerful instrument for the state's indirect management of economy. Secondly, in 1998, the CCP Central Committee established the Financial Work Committee and Financial Discipline Committee. And in the same year, the Chinese state established the China Securities Regulatory Committee and the China Insurance Regulatory Committee in order to strengthen the state's regulation over financial systems by establishing the state's vertical guide and control. Thirdly, "serious measures were introduced into non-bank financial institutions aimed at curbing illegal behavior in this sector", such as the bankruptcy of Guangdong International Trust and Investment Corporation and China Education, Science and Technology Trust and Investment Corporation, as well as the closure of twenty-one urban credit cooperatives and eighteen rural credit cooperatives.[43] It was these measures of centralization, with strong implications of state-building that helped the Chinese state overcome the negative impacts resulting from the Asian Financial Crisis. These economic transformations and institutional developments are construed by some scholars as "rebuilding the leviathan state," and they argue that "the reconstitution of the Chinese state thus has fundamental implications for the expansion of liberty and democracy."[44]

In the 1990s, although these state-building measures had positive effects on rapid and sustained economic growth in China, they also carried some negative effects as well, including a state monopoly of power with respect to the management and direction of economic restructuring[45] in tandem with a close state-business nexus.[46] To some extent, a lot of economic and social troubles in contemporary China were closely related to negative effects. At the same time, similar to its emergent economic centralization, the state expanded its guidance and supervision over the civil society while the Party intensified its monopoly of political power. Although the Fifteenth Party Congress formulated the strategy of "rule by law," it was still very different in nature from "rule of law." It was thus evident that there was stronger tension between the state-building and the development of governance system in the 1990s.

In the beginning of the 21st century, the Hu Jintao leadership formulated the new development strategies of "the Scientific Outlook on Development" and "Building a Harmonious Socialistic Society", and readjusted the Party-state's previous attitudes and measures with respect to state-building and the development of the governance system. First, after the Asia Financial Crisis, the Chinese state began to reshape the relations between the central and local governments in order to seek a balance between centralization and decentralization. With 1994's Tax Sharing System in hand, the Chinese state increased the proportion shared by the central government in 2001. As a result, the central government shared 50 percent of the total revenue in 2002, and the proportion rose to 60 percent in 2003.[47] The central government's ability to increase its revenues was thereby strengthened. The total revenue was increased from 1,600 billion *yuan* in 2001 to 3,900 billion *yuan* in 2006, and the average proportion shared by the central government reached 53.84 percent between 2001 and 2005.[48] Additionally, since 2003, the State Council canceled many local "Economic Development Zones" and took the powers in land and resources administration back from local governments. Furthermore, the "Outline of the Eleventh Five-Year Plan" definitively stipulated five major areas supported by central government investment, namely, "new countryside construction," public service, resource and environmental development, an "independent innovation system" and provisions for infrastructure. Thus, the demarcation of affairs between the central and local was made clearer than before.

Secondly, the relationship between the state and the market has experienced constant adjustment since China joined the WTO in 2001, and since becoming more deeply integrated in the global economy. In 2003, via a new round of reforms dedicated to restructuring the bureaucracy, the State Council established the State-owned Assets Supervision and Administration Commission and the China Banking Regulatory Commission. It also created the Ministry of Commerce and transformed the State Development and Planning Commission into the National Development and Reform Commission. Its aim was to accommodate development of the market economy. However, as Burns found, despite the new bureaucratic restructuring, "the CCP continues to maintain control over the *bianzhi* system because of its importance for Party patronage and social stability. Fundamentally conflicted, the CCP needs both to maintain official positions . . . and to cut positions for the sake of the economy."[49] The conflict between these two needs resulted in no substantial improvements in governmental efficiency, transparency and responsibility. Along with the bureaucratic restructuring, the state's market-control mode has been transitioning from direct to indirect regulation, including the promulgation of the Administrative License Law of the People's Republic of China in July 1, 2004. According to this law, those who can be effectively regulated by the market competition mechanism are not required to apply for administrative licenses.

However, rent-seeking is still common in administrative license system given the lack of democratic supervision and transparency.

Third, the state changed its unfriendly attitude towards civil society organizations. Thus, civil organizations once again entered a new period of rapid expansion. By the end of September 2009, the total number of civil organizations registered with the Ministry of Civil Affairs exceeded 412,000, including 228,000 social groups, 183,000 non-profit and non-governmental organizations, and 1,692 foundations.[50] In fact, unregistered civil organizations outnumber registered ones. However, the most important fact was that although these civil organizations became more and more significant to Chinese political and economic development and played more and more important roles in the management of public affairs, they did not yet acquire independence from the state. To some extent, this situation was the real description of the peculiar development pathway of Chinese civil society.

In the Seventeenth Party Congress held in October 2007, the Party proposed that China should further improve the development of market economic system, reform the state administration system, expand social democracy, improve democracy at the ground level, and reinforce the construction of social organizations. These proposals indicate that China has been trying to improve the balancing of state-building and development of the governance system by restructuring how the state, market, and civil society relate to each other. The process of implementing "the Scientific Outlook on Development" further can also be described as a process for restructuring the state–market–civil society relationship and improving the development of the governance system. However, tension between state-building and governance will no doubt persist. In terms of governance, the roles of civil society as one of the most important actors in the governance system must be strengthened urgently and the "separating the party from the government" is still the major challenge facing the construction of a "democracy-state under the rule of law."

Based on lessons from transitional states like Russia, some Chinese scholars argue that the Chinese state also needs to be rebuilt. During this process, it is argued, the state has to pay more attention to building jurisdiction sectors than building administrative ones.[51] Undoubtedly, building a good jurisdiction system as one part of state-building or rebuilding can provide a legitimatized, procedural and institutionalized platform for inter-organizational negotiation and reflection among, interpersonal networks, inter-governments and between the state and society. However, whether "separating the Party from the government" and "rule by law" or "building a good jurisdiction system" is in essence not at all about the "rule of law." In the Leninist party-state system, because the constitution and laws are always the concretion of the will of the party means that they are subordinated to the absolutist authority of the party. Accordingly, the tension between governance and state-building is finally revealed, following long-term, rapid economic growth, as the tension between the Party and the rule of law.

The case of China clearly indicates that (a) state-building is the precondition of the development of the governance system, and the aim of good governance can hardly be achieved without a strong and effective state; (b) there are interactions between state-building and governance that, in spite of their substantial conflicts, result on the one hand in the improvement of state capacities and contribute more to economic growth and the development of civil society, while on the other hand, the growth of civil society contributes to democratic state-building; (c) however, the strong state gradually becomes the main obstacle to good governance because of the absence of the rule of law, while the Party-state system constrains the improvement of efficiency, transparency and responsibility of government; and (d) it remains a question of how the Chinese state can realize its desired goals of changing "from authoritarian government to governance" and democratization without weakening state capacities.

Conclusions

This article has developed some ideas about governance and state-building, with a view towards demonstrating the necessary tension between them. The state has to play a major role in governance and meta-governance given the risks of market-failure, state-failure and governance-failure. Therefore, state-building or rebuilding is crucial for governance. Furthermore, the urgent business facing most developing countries is state-building precisely because a weak or powerless state is the root of their serious troubles. The objectives of governance are hard to achieve without a strong and effective state. As a consequence, the state would also get into trouble when dealing with the old and new issues in the field of Public Management without the cooperation of other forces involved in governance, such as market forces and civil society organizations, because of the increasing complexity of contemporary society and limited resources of state itself. But this does not mean there are no contradictions and conflicts between state-building and governance. The former emphasizes the centralization of state power, whereas the latter requests the state to dethrone its own supremacy over society and decentralize its power to market forces and civil society organizations. In our opinion, it is the conflict between centralization and decentralization that creates the necessary tension between governance and state-building. It is necessary to keep such tension through rule of law in order to realize various social, political and economic values and aims of human society, especially for developing countries.

Acknowledgement

This paper was published by *Journal of Chinese Political Studies* 16, no. 1 (March 2011): 1-17. The editors wish to thank the journal's editor for granting permission to include it in this book.

Notes

1. A. Heywood, *Politics*, 2nd ed. (New York: Palgrave, 2002).

2. B. Jessop, *The Future of the Capitalist State* (Cambridge: Polity Press, 2002).

3. F. Fukuyama, *State-building: Governance and World Order in the 21st Century* (New York: Cornell University Press, 2004), ix.

4. T. Carothers, "The 'Sequencing' Fallacy," *Journal of Democracy* 18, no. 1(2007): 12–27.

5. G. Stoker, "Governance as a Theory: Five Propositions," *International Social Science Journal* 155 (1998): 17–28.

6. T. Carothers, "The End of the Transition Paradigm," *Journal of Democracy* 13, no. 1 (2002): 32.

7. C. Wolf, *Markets or Governments: Choosing between Imperfect Alternatives*, 2nd ed. (Cambridge: The MIT Press, 1996).

8. F. Scharpf, "Games Real Actors Could Play: Positive and Negative Co-ordination in Embedded Negotiations," *Journal of Theoretical Politics* 6, no. 1 (1994), 37.

9. B. Jessop, "The European Union and Recent Transformations in Statehood," *State and Society* (Taiwan), no. 1 (2006).

10. F. Fukuyama, *op cit.*

11. J. Kooiman, "Social-political Governance: Overview, Reflection and Design," *Public Management Review*, no. 1 (1999): 67–92.

12. Institute for Research and Debate on Governance, *Chronicle of Governance* (Beijing: New Star Press, 2007), 129.

13. B. Jessop, "The Rise of Governance and the Risks of Failure: the Case of Economic Development," *International Social Science Journal* 155 (1998): 29–45.

14. E. Sørensen and J. Torfing, "How to Achieve Effective and Democratic Network Governance?" Paper presented at the IRSPM-conference in Potsdam, April 2–3, 2007.

15. B. Jessop, *op cit.*, 242

16 F. Fukuyama, "Liberalism versus State-building," *Journal of Democracy* 18, no. 32 (2007): 11.

17. A. Giddens, *The Nation-state and Violence* (Berkeley, CA: University of California Press,1985).

18. Y. Zheng, *Globalization and State Transformation in China* (Cambridge and New York: Cambridge University Press, 2004).

19. Karl Marx, "The civil War in France (1871)," *Selected Works* (New York: International Publishers, 1968), 289.

20. T. Skocpol, *States and Social Revolutions* (London and New York: Cambridge University Press, 1979).

21. F. Fukuyama, 2007, *op cit.*, 11.

22. C. Anthony, "Africa's Refugee Crisis: State Building in Historical Perspective," *International Migration Review* 25, no. 3 (1991): 574–591.

23 M. Ravina, "State-building and Political Economy in Early-modern Japan," *The Journal of Asian Studies* 54, 4 (1995): 997–1022.

24. C. Boix, and S. Stokes, "Endogenous Democratization," *World Politics* 55, no. 4 (2003): 519.

25. L. S. Flint, "State-building in Central Southern Africa: Citizenship and Subjectivity in Barotseland and Caprivi," *The International Journal of African Historical Studies* 36, no. 2 (2003): 393–428.

26. J. Chalmers, *MITI and the Japanese Miracle: The Growth of Industrial Policy* (Stanford, CA: Stanford University Press, 1982).

27. R. Roett and R. Crandall, "The Global Economic Crisis, Contagion, and Institutions: New Realities in Latin America and Asia," *International Political Science Review* 20, no. 3 (1999): 271–283.

28. Z. Onis, "The Logic of the Developmental State," *Comparative Politics* 24, no. 1 (1991): 123.

29. T. Carothers, "The End of the Transition Paradigm," *Journal of Democracy* 13, no. 1 (2002): 5–21; J. Wong, "The Adaptive Developmental State in East Asia," *Journal of East Asian Studies* 4 (2004): 345– 362.

30. Fukuyama, 2004, *op cit.*, 15.

31. J. Linz and A. Stepan, *Problem of Democratic Transition and Consolidation in Southern Europe, South America and Post-communist Europe* (Baltimore: The John Hopkins University Press, 1996).

32. S. Wang, "The Cost of Power and the Path-dependence of Reforms (Quanli De Daijia Yu Gaige De Lujin Yilai)," *Strategy and Management* (Zhanlue Yu Guanli), no. 5 (2005): 114.

33. Skocpol, *op cit.*, 4.

34. E. Hobsbawm, *The Age of Revolution, 1789–1848* (New York: New American Library, 1977).

35. Jesso, *op cit.*, 1998

36. Fukuyama, 2004, *op cit.*, 42.

37. C.W. Barrow, "The return of the state: globalization, state theory, and the new imperialism," *New Political Science* 27, no. 2 (2005):123–45.

38. P. Aucoin, 1996, "Political science and democratic governance," *Canadian Journal of Political Science* 29, no. 4 (1990): 643–660.

39. H. Derlien, *German public administration: Weberian despite "Modernization,"* http://www.unibamberg.de/fileadmin/uni/fakultaeten/sowi_lehrstuehle/verwaltungswissenschaft/vw2/GermanAdmin.pdf (accessed June 20, 2011).

40. Z. Lan, "The Baseline of Decentralization and Boundaries for Innovation (Gei Fengquan Hua Dixian, Wei Chuangxin She Bianjie)," *Journal of Zhejiang University* (Humanities and Social Sciences), 6 (2007).

41. Y. Zheng, *Globalization and State Transformation in China* (Cambridge and New York: Cambridge University Press 2004), ch. 6.

42. K. Yu, *The Institutional Environment of China's Civil Society* (Beijing: Peking University Press, 2006), 63.

43. Y. Zheng, *op cit.*, 127.

44. D. L. Yang, *Remaking the Chinese Leviathan: Market transition and the politics of governance in China* (Stanford: Stanford University Press, 2004), 314.

45. Y. Zheng, "The Livelihood Economy is the Economic Foundation to China's Harmonious Society [Minsheng Jingji shi Zhongguo Hexie Shehui de Jingji Jichu]," *Singapore: Zaobao*, May 1, 2007.

46. D.L. Yang, *op cit.*

47. Compilation Committee of Chinese Financial Yearbook [Zhongguo Caizheng Nianjian Bianji Weiyuanhui], *Chinese Financial Yearbook 2002* (Beijing: Chinese Financial Magazine Press [Zhongguo Caizheng Zazhishe], 2002), 55.

48. The State Statistics Bureau, *China Statistical Yearbook 2006* [Zhongguo Tongji Nianjian 2006] (Beijing: Chinese Statistical Press [Zhongguo Tongji Chubanshe], 2006), 286.

49. J. Burns, "Downsizing the Chinese State: Government Retrenchment in the 1990s," *The China Quarterly*, 801 (2003).

50. Ministry of Civil Affairs of the People's Republic of China, *The Quarterly Reports of Civil Affairs Statistics* (the third season) (2009), http://files.mca.gov.cn/cws/200911/20091102104844314.htm (accessed June 27, 2011).

51. X. Ding, "Law and Order in Transition: Russian Phenomenon [Zhuanxing Shehui DeFa Yu Zhixu: E'Luoshi Xianxiang]," *Qinghua Sociological Review* [Qinghua shehuixue pinglun], 2 (2000).

Chapter 5
Local Governance Innovations and Their Sustainability

Xinjun Gao and Baogang Guo

Since the beginning of the 21st century, local governance in China has witnessed a period of active innovations and changes. A large number of experiments in areas of public services, public administration, political transparency, scientific decision-making, citizen participation, legislative work and poverty relief have been carried out at various localities, thanks to the institutional, theoretical, technological and cultural breakthroughs, Based on the level of innovations, degrees of local benefits, potentials for cost-saving and several other criteria, the China Center for Government Innovation Research (CCGIR) at Beijing University has selected many local innovations and issued the "China Local Innovation Awards" on a bi-annual basis since 2000. Five rounds of selections were made and over 1,300 projects were evaluated. Fifty finalists received the "Local Innovation Awards."

These innovations can generally be divided into three categories: political reform, administrative reform and public services reform. Projects involved in political reform include experiments in expanding inner-party democracy; cadre selection and assessment, supervision of the ruling Party and the government, civic participation, procedural designs for democratic decision-making, corruption prevention and detection systems; and legislative building and democratic consultation.

Projects involved in administrative reform include the development and management of neighborhood organizations; public budgeting reform; electronic government; electronic monitoring systems for administrative examination and approval processes; reform of village and township administrative management systems; forestry property right systems and reforms of new rural cooperatives medical services.

Projects involved in providing public services include the rural social security system; rural community development, representative agencies for public services, law enforcement information systems, harmonious community development; public financed home-care for the elderly; trade unions protecting workers' rights and reforms of the household registration system.

These innovations in local governance are of critical importance. Since large scale political reform at the national level carries greater risk to derail China's stability and economic development, the incremental changes at local level, which can minimize the risk and accumulate experiences overtime, offer an ideal, low-risk alternative to a top-down style of "shock therapy" used in the former Soviet Union. Thus, gradual political changes based on small scale of local governance innovations have been major contributors to the success of the so-called Chinese developmental model.

An Initial Assessment of the Development of the Local Governance Innovations

There are several reasons as to why local governance reform in China has progressed so rapidly in recent years. To begin with, the rapid economical development since 1978 has raised many challenges to local governance. One of the challenges is the need for a large number of well-qualified local cadres. The traditional cadre selection system is ill-equipped to meet the demands for promoting qualified young leaders into key government positions. The reform of the cadre selection system in Yi Zheng city in Jiangsu Province, for example, was the result of such a demand and was supported by the Central government's Personnel Minster and a member of Central Political Bureau of Communist Party of China (CPC), Li Yuanchao. Since its implementation in 2004, the results have been remarkable.

In addition, in the last few decades, China has developed a system of performance measurement and evaluation of governmental officials which tends to motivate local cadres to become more creative in order to have a fast-track promotion. In many cases, democratic decision-making is used not as an end in itself; rather it is used as a tool for official personal gains or reducing social tensions and criticism. In the Central and Western provinces of China, through making new institutional innovations, officials often find a shortcut through which their talents and achievements can be demonstrated, thus, opening up more opportunities for reorganization and promotion. The new process of selecting the Party committee secretaries through a new system of "public recommendation and direct election" at the township level in Pingchang County of Bazhong city in Sichuan province is a good example of how the promotional system has altered official behaviors.[1]

In recent years, the relationships between local government officials and local residents were not all that good. Tensions and contradictions have resulted in many mass incidents. Under such pressures, local officials can only survive if they attempt to make some changes to improve their relationships with the local residents and to acquire new sources of political legitimacy. This has produced local innovations such as the "Eight-Steps Method for Work" developed by Maliu township government of Kai County in Chongqing City. On June 14, 1999, angry farmers attacked the township government to protest their excessive tax burden. As a reaction to the escalating social tension, the township government developed and implemented the "Eight-Steps Method." Key to the new reform measures are the introduction of local township referendum on key policy and project decisions, financial transparency and democratic management.[2]

Not all innovations are results of official responses to the public demands at the grass-root level. Some of the pressures for change come directly from national authorities, and the innovation projects are merely a response the local officials made to demands or directives given by the high authorities. For instance, the system of "Automatic Approval for Over Timed Processing of the Licensing Applications" implemented in Nankai District in Tianjin City in 2002 was the result of the encouragement from leaders in the central government. The system was designed to cut bureaucratic red tape and improve government efficiency and transparency.[3]

In recent years, local innovations in China have manifested the following characteristics. First, the local government-initiated reforms and changes have been carried out across the nation and appeared in every province. Tibet's award-winning project on the management of and services to the Buddhist Monasteries, which was submitted to the fifth-round selection process organized by the Award Program of Innovations and Excellence in Chinese Local Governance (IECLG), was a good example of the extent to which local governance innovations have experimented.

Second, most of the local innovation projects are from the Eastern part of China rather than from China's Central and Western provinces. This is reflected in the fact that provinces in Eastern China received some two-thirds of the awards while the Central and Western provinces got only one-third of these awards. Although the impulse for innovation is much higher in the Central and Western part of Chins than in the East, it is the experiments in the Eastern province that have a better chance to survive and sustain. Experimental projects in the Eastern provinces have been concentrated in cadre selection, popular participation, development of non-governmental organizations (NGO), supervision of the Party committee and government and public budget transparency. In the Central and Western provinces, however, they are mostly centered in the development of inner-party democracy, grassroots-level democracy, the methods of cadre selection, etc.

Finally, the number of cases involving administrative reforms and public service innovations are higher than that for political reforms, which is a reflection of China's slow progress in this area.

Although the number of local governance innovation is impressive, our research indicates that the majority of these innovations are not sustainable and a considerable number of them are short-lived. According to data compiled by us, after several years, only one-third of these innovations are still in place. About one-third are semi-mordant and the remaining one-third ceases to exist completely. The rest of this chapter will analyze five recent cases of local innovation. The first case deals with commercialization of public utilities in Zhenzhen. The second case relates to the electoral change in county-level party committees in Changping County. The third case is about outsourcing essential public services in Xianing city. The fourth case involves opening up government decision-making process in Xuzhou city. The final case is about establishing deliberative democracy at grassroots level. Our goal is to determine the exact causes of variations in sustainability of these innovations.

Commercialization of Public Utilities in Shenzhen

Providing public utilities services such as water, gas, public transportation, energy are traditionally a function of local governments. But traditionally, the cost of providing these services have added tremendous burden on local governments' recourses. In order to improve service efficiency and save cost, Shenzhen City government in recent years attempted a reform to commercialize public utilities services with a goal to attract strategic investors and improve public utility supervisory and regulatory methods. This experiment is based the so-called French Model in which the government retains the control of the utility companies, but contract out the services to private companies on a franchised agreement.

The system contains two elements: the development of the public utilities services and public utilities service supervision and regulation. Starting from 2002, the city government invited biddings for providing public utility service. In 2004, five large companies won the bids. Among them, the New Hope Group and Hong Kong-based Towngas China acquired 40 percent shares of the Shengzhen Natural Gas Group and a long-term franchise for thirty years. Meanwhile, a French company, Veolia Environment, acquired 45 percent share of Shengzhen Water Group and a franchise for fifty years. The franchises created new private monopolies with a potential time trap to prevent the entrance of other competitors.[4] Shenzhen's seven-year experience with the system proved that as a result of this reform, the former function has become more vigorous and been completely marketized. The latter, however, has some serious problems. Apparently, the system design is ill-conceived and does not give the city government adequate supervisory and managerial power to regulate these semi-private utility providers. The third-party supervision and management is also lacking. This problem began to surface at the start of the system implementation and became more severe as the system continued to operate.

Privatization of public utilities services have been done in many countries before. Many researchers, including the authors, are concerned with two issues. First, how to determine utility prices once competitors have been removed? Second, how to ensure information transparency and supervision, and how to conduct necessary regulation of the service providers in a franchised setting? The answers to these two questions are so evident that after seven years of experience with the Shenzhen system that many people have questioned the merit of such a system and wanted other local governments to think twice before adopting the Shenzhen model of public utilities commercialization.

How to supervise and regulate the new market-based service providers who are literally in a monopolistic position is at the heart of these two issues. Although the government has the main responsibility for supervision after the contracting-out, the leasing agreement was poorly written. Instead of introducing market based competition, the system has allowed the service providers a total monopoly on public utilities. What has taken place is simple a role change for the government. The government transformed itself from a service provider to a share-holder of the new business entitlement. The related government agencies such as water-works department change their roles to regulators and enforcers of the rules and regulations. However, because information is asymmetrical under market conditions, the governmental supervision under market conditions tends to be very slow or inaccurate. It is for this very reason the transparency of the providers' production and maintenance cost and the third-party supervision has become critically important. Unfortunately, progress in these areas has been minimal. It was not a surprise when the government proposed a 30 percent price hike on water fees in early 2010; consumer representatives participating in the public hearing over the proposal were outraged over the lack of disclosure over the changes in production cost and profit margin. This in turn let people suspect that the regulatory agency has become a captive of the business companies, and yielded too much to business pressures.[5]

An official in the Reform Department of the Shenzhen government believed that the price hike after the public utilities being contracted-out was largely a result of the profit-seeking decisions of the strategic private investors in these areas who are concerned mostly with the returns of their investment.[6] But public utilities are by nature a low-profit business and can have a direct impact on the everyday lives of local residents. Therefore, it is always difficult to reach a consensus with local customers about the price increases. Every price increase causes a negative reaction from the Shenzhen residents. Consequently, tensions and disagreements between consumers and the private utility companies have developed. Because the government is still a stakeholder of the utility company, the city government appeared to side with the utility companies in the name of securing economic growth and social stability. When this happens, the public image of the city government will suffer.[7]

Thus, in the absence of competition and adequate "third-party supervision and regulation," the price adjustment mechanism for Shenzhen's public utilities such as public hearing has proven to be grossly inadequate. There is no incentive for private utility providers to cut the cost through internal improvement or efficiency-enhancement measures. Just like the situation before the reform, whenever there is an increase in operating costs, the utility companies will simply pass on the costs to customers without taking the effort to improve services and operating efficiency first.

The issue of lack of supervision is largely caused by the fragmentation and departmentalization of the bureaucratic structures. City government's supervisory functions have been traditionally dispersed among a number of departments, including the water authority, traffic department, etc. Supervisory methods used by these departments vary greatly, and their regulatory powers are far from being sufficient. In the end, they simply cannot do a good job. Although the relevant regulations on the "third-party supervision and management" have been made, no responsible organizations have been established and no technical and personnel support are provided.

Corruption is another factor that has compromised the regulatory effort. Many of these monopolistic companies hired the relatives of government officials who worked in the related governmental supervisory departments, and some of these positions are no more than "no-show" featherbedding. For instance: the Shenzhen Gas Company's archive office has basically become "the wives' room." The conflicts of interests also manifested in other areas as well. The president of the gas company is allowed to have four passenger vehicles; the entire family of pipeline company's executive manager was naturalized in Canada, while the manager himself frequently does not show up for work but allowed his relatives to finish his projects. Additionally, after a small gas leak, the Gas Company sought US$4.3 million from the municipal government for repairs and then the owner subcontracted the repair work to his own relatives.

The business operations have basically become a "black box," with no audits and third-party supervision and management. When the Shenzhen Water Group sought US$572 million in sewage treatment funds from the municipal government, it did not even consent to an inquiry conducted by the city's Finance Department or allow the Director of the Finance Bureau to enter the company's door. It nonetheless received the requested funds from the government. As a result of the total monopoly, staff salaries and wages in the Water Group are the highest in Shenzhen, and these payment systems have gone unaudited for a long period of time.[8]

Why can't a system of "third-party supervision and regulations" be slowly implemented in this reform project design? Why can't this type of mechanism, which is widely used in mature market economies, be realized in Shenzhen's public utilities enterprise marketability reform? Perhaps this cannot be blamed solely on the local governments. The structure restraints and lack of experience were partly responsible for the deficiencies in the reform. However, without necessary governmental and third-party supervision and regulation, the Shenzhen public utilities have acquired a monopolistic status, which can potentially heighten tensions between the providers and consumers and threaten social stability. Judged by this criterion, this particular case of local governance innovation is abused, flawed and not sustainable. Instead of focusing too much on role change and ownership transformation, the reformers should pay more attention to creating a market environment in which multiple public utility providers can compete with each other for improving and expanding services, customer satisfactory, and operating efficiency.

The Pingchan Experiments with Party Committee Elections

We believe that for a local innovation to be sustainable, it needs to solve two basic problems: one is the dynamics of the reform and innovation, and the other is its methods. Pingchang County's innovation in implementing inner-Party democracy, though celebrated by the media as a good example of local innovation in promoting inner-party democracy, has encountered institutional bottlenecks precisely on these two fundamental issues.

Pingchang County, located in Bazhong City in Western China's Sichuan province, has a population over a million people. It is one of the country's poor areas. In 2001 Pingchang County started the experiment with "public recommendation and direct election" (*gong tui zhi xuan*, 公推直选) for Party committee members in Lingshan Township. Its immediate cause of this new initiative was a serious legitimacy crisis resulting from the tensions and antagonism between the local cadres and the local people. Because at that time agricultural taxes and fees were still being levied, the farmers' burden was very heavy due to various fees collected by the township government. In a poor county like Pingchang, farmers have few opportunities to increase their income and benefit little from the national economic boom. Therefore, they are extremely sensitive when local authorities attempted to increase their tax burden and take away their resources.[9] Consequently, the township party committee, the main decision-making body of the township, enjoyed little public support or public confidence.

Traditionally, all key leadership positions in the township were either appointed or indirectly elected. The Party's Organization Department will typically prescreen and select candidates, and these candidates are always elected or confirmed by electors—usually deputies of the people or party members. These candidates were guaranteed to be elected since their nomination represented the party's will, not the individual candidate's will. Although the elections of county or township government leaders were experimented with in places like Buyun Township, they were challenged by some leaders in the National People's Congress (NPC) as unconstitutional since the practice was not endorsed by the existing provisions in the constitution. However, a direct election of local party leaders can avoid this constitutional controversy.[10]

The new electoral system, "public recommendation and direct election" shifted away from this controlled election exercise. Party members now can cast two votes in a three-round, direct election. The first vote is on the nomination of a candidate, and the second vote is on the actual election of the party leaders in a contested election. The first vote may look like a closed primary election in a typical American election, but on a much smaller scale. The rank-and-file party members will decide who will be nominated. Many members who are interested in running for positions can nominate themselves. When it comes to the actual election, the election of the party secretary will come first, and then followed by the elections of deputy party secretary and committee members. People who lost the first round of the contest are still eligible for being elected as deputy party secretary or committee members. This is truly an inner-party democracy at its best, and is no doubt a significant development in China's political reform.[11]

What has motivated Pingchang county party leaders to take this bold and risky step to reform the electoral system of the ruling party? Our research indicates that the need to demonstrate performance-based achievement was behind this earlier round of experiment in Pingchang. In recent years, the cadre system in China has undergone major changes. A large number of young and ambitious elites were promoted to serve official positions at the township and county level. When these cadres seek promotion, the primary criteria are achievements in promoting economic growth and maintaining social stability. Since Pingchang

County is an underdeveloped poor area and has very little opportunity for large-scale investments and impressive GDP growth rate. As a matter of fact, the county finance was heavily subsidized by the central and provincial government. For example, Pingchang County tax revenues were only US$11.5 million, but its annual expenditures exceeded US$157 million. Funds to fill in this huge gap came completely from central and provincial transfer payments.[12]

Political reform was considered the only chance to make difference in local cadres' performance, which, they hope, would in turn bring good chances for professional career advancement. Therefore, the introduction and the development of a semi-competitive election system in a county that is poverty stricken, makes sense in terms of rational personal interest calculation from the perspective of local political elite. Local party cadres understood the system of cadre selection and promotion very well. They knew clearly that there was no hope to obtain promotion through impressive GDP growth figures and foreign direct investment (FDI). For this reason, they are willing to implement a semi-competitive electoral system locally, even though this may mean that there will be temporary or partial loss of power. In the long run, their effort will pay off. And the political gains will outweigh the cost. When they get promoted, they will have more power and better opportunities for career advancement.[13]

The new political opening may also improve their public image and relationship with local residents. They want to create a populist image of being an advocate of local interests. Some of them even openly complained against some national leaders for their ill-conceived policies that allowed themselves a chance to move up without concerns of the interests of the other people.

This urge to reform at the local level often produced imprudent decisions that were not proper to the local conditions. Some of these decisions were too radical and too idealistic and doomed to fail. Furthermore, all of these decisions, including decisions to promote democracy, were made in the traditional autocratic manner without full-participation of the citizens involved. Thus a paradox appeared to be: the reformers must often use the highly centralized and undemocratic political power to carry out grassroots democratic reforms aimed at promoting a bottom-up democratic decision-making process, albeit in a top-down manner. The biggest flaw in using autocratic means to implement democracy is that it resulted in unconscious exclusion of the common people from making popular initiatives or participating fully in the decision-making process. These local innovations are often tied to a particular policy entrepreneur such as a county governor or the county party secretary. Very often, when the policy entrepreneurs left or transferred elsewhere, the innovations ceased to exist. The end result is that at least one-third of these innovations are not sustainable.

For example, in order to deal with the financial crisis, from 2002 to 2003 Pinching County government decided to merge sixty-one townships into twenty-seven. Although this drastic step of administrative consolidation saved the county a lot of administrative cost, it did create many unforeseen problems. Many people complained about the changes. As a result, after persisting in this way for several years, the county could not help but to restore the number of township from twenty to forty-three.[14]

Looking at the "popular recommendation and direct election" method for electing party committee leaders at the Township level in Pingchang County, the complications of reform began to surface at the outset. Since the driving force for the change was not from the grass-root demand, the initiative was taken entirely by the county's party chief (*yi ba shou,* 一把手) for the purpose of performance delivery. Its greatest propulsion comes from highly concentrated authority, from "the highest leader," and it has become one kind of "from the top down" reform. The tragedy soon took place. A theatrical contestation of power developed between the major leaders of Bazhong City and Pingchang County. This resulted in the departure of the Pingchang's county chief. This may have been the chance factor which led to a setback in Pingchang County's inner-Party democratic reform.

This tragedy in relations between top political elite reflects the problems in China's current political system. Because the Pingchang reform was implemented in a "top-down" fashion and was endorsed by a higher authority, that authority has no difficulty to reverse or stop the reform if mistakes were made by the reformers or complaints were registered with top government officials and departments. This is a good example of the classical case of "whatever explains a success also explains its failure."

The apparent setback of Pingchang County's reform in administrative and electoral changes may appear to be a result of the chance factors in personal relations among political leaders. However, fundamentally speaking, it reveals a bottleneck created by the existing system. This is precisely the paradox of reform that exists in China's political development. On the one hand, reform needs leaders who have the spirit of innovation and the power and authority to push reforms forward. On the other, a total dependency on the impulse from leaders with highly concentrated power can lead reform into a dead-end. That is, whenever the people in charge of the reform move out and the zeal for the reform cools down, which in turn leads to the eventual termination of the reform.

Based on this observation, the failure of Pingchang reform shows that grassroots reform and innovation have posted some serious challenges to the existing system. In order to sustain good reform measures, the system's bottleneck must be broken first. The blind race for performance-based achievement and the existing promotion criteria for cadre's career advancement lead to short-term political risk-taking. The inadequate incorporation of public input in the policy initiatives can only lead to a "political show" that will provide political leaders with personal gains.

The Reform of the Township Public Administration through Procurement of Services

After carrying out the reform of rural taxation and fee collection system in 2002, county and local governments all encountered serious financial difficulties. In order to cope with the large scale of reduction in township revenue, a reduction of the number of government employees becomes the only viable option.

Starting in 2002, the party committee and government of Xian'an District of the Xianning City in Hubei Province decided to target nine different service categories the county government used to support, including the animal husbandry and veterinary stations, farming technology assistance offices, the water conservation and irrigation offices, farm machinery offices, the suburban construction offices, the housing management offices, the cultural affairs offices, broadcasting offices, economic development offices, and birth control service stations. All together one hundred and twelve of these offices were closed down.

All former staffs in these service stations were encouraged to terminate their labor contract with their work units. Each of them received a one-time, lump-sum compensation. Among the 712 laid-off employees 194 met official retirement age or special rules pertaining to early retirement, and were placed on retirement. The remaining five hundred and eighteen employees displaced by the personnel reform received US$1.04 million in total compensation. In order to reduce their resistance, in September 2004, the District government established a township pension insurance system. All 712 former employees were enrolled and they paid a total US$735,000 for a one time, lump-sum insurance program premium payment for their coverage.

To continue to carry out these essential public services to farmers, District government outsourced most of the services to the former employees who worked at each of these stations or offices. The former government employees now became contract workers for the government. Instead of paying staff salaries, now the government simply contracts out services and pays for these services. The government does not simply downsize and reduce its service commitments to farmers and residents; instead, it provides financial safeguards, selects service contractors on the basis of bidders' qualifications, manages the contract, and compensates the services after satisfactory inspection. Locally, this new administrative innovation is known as: "service-based administrative system" (*yi qian yang shi*, 以钱养事), which is very different from the "staff-based administrative system" (*yi shi yang ten*, 以事养人). To support the reform, Hubei provincial government provided financial subsidies for the District government between 2005 and 2008. By 2008, the system was expanded to other service areas as well. The role and statuary change has not been easy for the former government staff as Chinese traditionally consider government employment to be more secure and prestigious. But majority of the laid-off staffs from their government posts continue to work in the service areas as private contractors. They were encouraged to form new service centers or companies. Many of these former employees now agree the reform has improved efficiency of government finance and services. [15]

The new service procurement system has been carried out for many years. The Xian'an District government has developed a "fine-tuned" set of management practices for supervision of the procurement contract. The District's main leaders are put in charge of the new system. All contracts are carefully managed. All service personals are required to keep daily log on services they provided.

Farmers are empowered to assess contract performance. They are issued service evaluation cards. When a service worker completes the service job, the farmers have to be happy with the service and sign the card. Assessment can be made on a single project assessment, a quarterly assessment or even a comprehensive year-end assessment.

Based on the successful experience with this reform, on November 4, 2003, the Hubei Provincial Party Committee and the provincial government issued a directive to encourage other parts of the provinces to carry out the similar reform. By 2004, seven counties carried out such experiments. In 2005, the practice was promoted throughout the entire province.

Xian'an experience has caught national attention. Some labeled the reform as "Xian'an Storm" and believed this "New Deal" will cause a major "earthquake" to the existing system of public administration.[16] The results of this process were uneven and many problems have surfaced. Consequently, considerable debate developed over this reform.

First, some argued that the reform was merely changing forms without changing substances. The bidding public services were essentially non-competitive; it was simply extended automatically to the existing individuals who once worked for the government. The way the procurement was conducted may have helped the former government employees to make a smooth transition, therefore, reducing potential for social instability. However, without a competitive environment, the cost and quality of these services cannot be properly assured. Furthermore, some of the towns which followed the Xian'an experiment did it without the termination of labor contract of these government employees, thus putting those employees in ambiguous status. Without substantial changes, there is no guarantee the same service providers will alter their behaviors.

Next, this reform has had a low level of popular participation in terms of contract assessment and evaluation. Although services recipients were given evaluation cards, effectiveness of these individual evolutions are not guaranteed. The lack of civic organizations in rural areas renders a third-party system of supervision to non-existent. The cost to print and process these evaluation cards can also add burden to the already strained township financial resources. Eventually, it all comes down to the chief town administrators. If he or she takes the individual evaluations seriously, it may make a difference. Otherwise, the reform is difficult to sustain and risks becoming an empty formality.

Moreover, the reform was not well coordinated. Under the current top-down vertical administrative structure, funds from ministries and commissions at the national and provincials must be transferred to the corresponding department or agencies. Since recent reforms at local levels have phased out many of these departments or agencies, the fund may never reach their destinations at local levels. As a result, many local governments developed a strong impulse to return to the original system and restore some of the government offices, even only with an empty name, in order to get the funding from the higher authorities. Some recent experiences with health pandemics such as the Bird Flu or SARS or natural disasters have made local governments think twice on the practice of contracting out public services. Many feel that government needs to return to these areas to provide services directly in order to ensure public safety.

Finally, this reform does not necessarily reduce local government's financial expenditures; it may enhance the efficient use of these funds to some extent.[17] For example, as the result of the personnel reform, Xian'an District's governmental expenditures were reduced by one-quarter. This was what the local reformers had hoped for since initial goal of the reform was to resolve the immediate financial crisis due to the elimination of agricultural tax. However, if one added all the direct and indirect subsidies from the government to the District and the substantial amount spent in dealing with several incidents of the health pandemics; the total government expenditures were not reduced.[18]

In fact, the services procurement reform in Xian'an District has been difficult to promote in other places for a number of reasons. When other places promoted this reform, they only emphasized government purchase of services, but did not actually transform the staff in the original township institution from government personnel to "people operating in the market." This reform may be difficult to duplicate because the resistance of government employees since no one is willing to leave the "Iron rice bowl" behind.

Government in the Sunshine: The Case of Jiawang District of Xuzhou City

In many Western democracies, government in the sunshine refers to the type of legislation which allows the widest possible public participation and supervision of the government. Its purpose is to make the government accessible, accountable and open. In recent years, the reform initiatives carries out by a district government of Xuzhou city captured people's attention.

Jiawang District, one of the five districts of Xuzhou city with a population of a half million, was once a major coal-producing area. On July 22, 2001, a huge gas and coal dust explosion in one of the small, unlicensed coal mines killed ninety-two miners, including twenty-three female miners who were not supposed to work in underground tunnels in the first place. This industrial incident revealed the dark side of the economic development in that region: unregulated coal mine exploration and development, official corruption, poor enforcement of government safety and labor regulation. The pubic was outraged by these uncovered stories and wanted to hold those responsible accountable for the tragedy. In order to reduce public pressure and regain public trust, the Jiawang District government felt it was necessary to set up a new set of mechanisms to enhance its ability to restrain and regulate the behavior of government departments and officials, bridge the gap between the government and the people, raise the government's credibility and control and prevent official corruptions. The new mechanisms were designed to "let the people have a place to speak and let people's voice be effective."[19]

After a period of thoughtful investigation and research, in May of 2004, the Jiawang District government began to implement a new system called "Public

Supervision of the Full Decision-making Process." The system has four major components: seeking public input, inviting public representatives to sit in official meetings, allowing public inquiries over government decisions, and evaluation of government officials by opinion polls.

Seeing public input is usually done in the form of public hearings before a government department or agency proposed new rules or new plans. Revisions will be made based on the feedback collected through these hearings. To open up government meetings, representatives will be selected from local People's Congress and the local residents. They will be allowed to participate in departmental meetings and hear the discussions but without the voting right. Having representatives from local People's Congress as listeners or observers is an unusual practice since it will be considered a distortion of the separation of powers and relations between the executive and the legislative. But it is considered acceptable anyway since the legislative members were never given as much prestige and power as legislative members in a Western democracy. The selection of the so-called representative is also controlled by the government. There were more 3,728 people designated as the representatives. Public inquiry is an important form of checks and balances in the Western democracy. It is usually carried by the legislative branch in the West. Jaiwang's practice is really another form of public hearing whenever a controversy arises over a project and or a decision. It allows affected residents to voice their concerns or register their complaints. The officials from related departments are supposed to answer their questions faithfully and solve as much problems as possible on the spot or on a fixed timetable. The evaluation poll is a poll conducted by a government-appointed, independent polling agency among groups or peoples whose interests are at the stake because of a government program or project. If 50 percent of the respondents find unsatisfactory the programs or the projects, the official in charge of the program or project will be held accountable.[20]

It is generally believed that for a local innovation to be sustainable and replicable there must be this type of institutionalization of the reform. In our opinion, this viewpoint contains some notion of "pan-institutionalization", especially in the present political and economic situation in China, in which this viewpoint has been institutionally sanctified.

Reliance on institutionalization is the normal and ideal approach through which all kinds of social groups can realize their interests and demands through structured arrangement instead of political manipulation or entrepreneurial role of political elite. In a transition period, most people believe that promoting continuous changes to the political system and decision-making process is the only viable choice to achieve long-lasting social transformation.

But regrettably, how things work in the field is actually very different from any scholarly design. Obviously, if we cannot find the flaw in the key link which causes the system to be truly ineffective, we will remain in a situation in which "one leg is long, one leg is short." This in turn not only hinders the transformation of local government functions, but also makes effectuating democratic governance, rule by law and scientific governance more difficult. Thus effectiveness of institutions will be closely linked to the balances of on relative strength of different social forces the political institutions are intended to restrain.

Based on our field observation, we would suggest that the marginal utility of supervision is the critical point for the effectiveness of the system. Here supervision refers to the reciprocal relations between the various social interest groups restrained by the system. Effective supervision can only be achieved if there is a balance of power among the various social interest groups. If the relations among social interest groups are imbalanced, and when one particular group's power is too strong while others are extremely weak, the institutions designed for normal conditions of bargaining and compromising will not work.

At the same time, in a multiplayer game involving various social interest groups, the marginal utility of mutual supervision and checks and balances is precisely the critical point where the system will function. In other words, if it goes beyond this critical point, the benefits of such a system will not only drop, but more significantly, decision rules established under the system of rules will no longer be observed and consequently, the entire system will cease to function.

Although institutionalization is a desirable outcome of any political change, the change, nevertheless, will not follow a linear direction. China's system transition will more likely follow a spiral path. The balance of power of various social groups will constantly evolve, shifting from being balanced to imbalanced, and to balanced again. At present, China is moving toward establishing a service-oriented government, creating public finance, promoting information transparency and democratic decision-making, and fostering sustainable development. These fundamental changes will stir the balance of power in a significant way. All the bottlenecks China is facing in carrying out these reforms are related to the defects in the way to ensure a proper balance and fairness in the multiplayer games of interest articulations and clashes.

Jiawang's system innovation was born out of a crisis situation. It was a retroactive response to the public pressure aimed at damage control. The system put in place did receive overwhelming public support. Official behaviors were modified to a great extent. The number of complaint letters and individual visits to register their grievances with government departments and agencies decreased and public approval rating of the district government went up. The new system provides some kind of safety valve to allow timely release of public pressure. However, the new system also put tremendous amount of pressure on local government officials.

The district government set up over thirty new procedures and requirements and hoped the new system will last regardless of a change in local level leadership. Nevertheless, once Wang Tianqi, the district chief administrator, was transferred to another county, many aspects of this new system started to crumble. For example, in Wang's last year as the district chief administrator, he held four public hearings meetings. District residents could raise questions about government performance. However, two years after his departure, there was not a single public hearing being held. It is startling to see how fast this new governance innovation died as the result of "when the leaders leave, their policies die with them."

This reflects the dilemmas for local innovations in China, namely, when the key policy innovators are present, the systems work, but when they leave the innovations cease to exist. Without the rule of law, changes made under the system of rule of men will certainly have the same fate as the experiments with government-in-the-sunshine undertaken by the Jiawang District. When the Jiawang District government implemented this reform, it indeed transformed the local political way of life, but without people to implement the system, it will not be sustainable.

There are many other defects in the new system. The people are still in a weak position and never had an effective way to monitor and control government officials. Therefore, for an innovation to be sustainable under China's current conditions institutionalization itself is far from enough. A number of prerequisites must be present: First, there must be many cadres who are seriously interested in reform and want to carry out the new innovations. Second, ordinary people must have adequate channels and means to be able to monitor and control cadres' behavior. Finally, people must be able to organize so that they can have a meaningful dialogues with the government based on equality and strength. Obviously, these requirements are beyond the power of scope of local government, and it may require higher-level changes in the political and administrative systems.

During this investigation it became apparent that the scarcest and the most precious resources for local governance reform in China are local cadres with a sense of creativity. They are the sponsors and primary advocates of local governmental innovation, and face huge political and the economic risks. Allocating such scarce resources in a rational manner is an important concern in making institutional transition and social transformation in China.

During this investigation, we contacted and interviewed many local officials, including Zhang Liyong, Chief Justice of the Superior Court in Henan province. Zhang was known for promoting mobile court system, publication of court case rulings on the Internet, and live coverage of trial proceeding in Henan. He had a history of initiating new governance innovations. When Zhang Liyong was the Party Committee Secretary in the Qindu District of Xianyang City in Shanxi Province thirteen years ago, he was famous for promoting local reform and innovation. Later he became the mayor of Xianyang City. He left behind many marks in establishing an open and transparent government.

Wang Tianqi, the former District Magistrate in Jiawang District in Xuzhou City and presently Party Secretary in Suining County of Xuzhou City is another good example. He not only established and pushed the "Public Supervision of the Full Decision-making Process" system we discussed earlier, he also carried out the "'New Deal' in Suining County" as the Party Secretary of Suining County to discipline county officials. For that reform, he was dubbed as "the Second Qiu He"[21] by the media. The "New Deal" started in February 2008 when he ordered an alcohol ban for county officials during working hours. Eighteen officials lost their job for violation of the ban. In August, he held county party committee meeting with live media coverage and 800 local representatives presented at the meeting. After revealing an opinion poll over the soft environment of the county, four officials who received lowest approval rating were removed from office on the spot. Wang also insists that county officials should work in a military style and make themselves available for work anytime that is needed. Their cell phone numbers were also made public so that people could contact them when they had an issue. He also paid great attention to the media and Internet. When he read a posted message from an Internet user entitled "who moved my pension," he took action to investigate the reported abuses in pensions. The county subsequently recovered US$16,714 from 1,188 households and 2,645 people who had lied about their qualification for the pensions. When investigating reported cases dealing with unlicensed building, he fired seven local government officials for corruption or incompetence.

Thus policy entrepreneurs continue to play an important role in the transitional phase of China's reform. To encourage more people like Zhang Liyong and Wang Tianqi to put their creativity into full use, China needs to create a more open political environment and to give full credit and greater recognition for their innovations. Additionally, the public should also be given the widest possible opportunities to participate in political decision-making process. Too much emphasis on institutionalization at this point may not be conducive to China's reform. Based on this analysis, we believe the Jiawang's innovation is not sustainable precisely because of the worship of institutional arrangements for local governance innovations.

"Democratic Dialogues:" the Case of Wenling City

So far, we have examined four cases of local governance innovation, and found them to be non-sustainable due to various reasons. However, there are also many local governance innovations surfaced in recent years have been sustained. In this section, we will take a look at the practice of "democratic dialogues" conducted between the government and local residents.

The "democratic dialogues" were first used in 1999 when a low ranking city official persuaded the officials in Songmen Town to hold a public discussion forum on promoting rural education. Over 200 farmers packed the meeting room and asked some tough questions to township leaders. Similar meetings were held elsewhere as well. However, the enthusiasm for promoting these kinds of dialogues was soon vanished since local officials became afraid to show up in these meetings and face tough questions. Starting from 2005, the city's People's Congress got involved in promoting democratic dialogues on budgeting and financing, the democratic reform was once again put back on track. Now democratic dialogues, public deliberation of key decisions, and public hearings are widely used at all levels. More than ten years has passed. This form of deliberative democracy has taken strong hold in Wenling and many other places in China.

The question now is why many of the local governance innovations have ceased to exist while the Wenling Model has survived. There are a number of reasons for this. First of all, strong support from keys leaders, such as Wang Jinsheng, the Party Secretary of Wenling City from 2001 to 2005, and his successor, Chen Weiyi, and Zhang Xueming, Chairman of Wenling City People's Congress, in the Municipal Party Committee and the Government was a critical factor. Successive directors of City Party Committee Propaganda Department, Dai Kangnian, Cao Hong and Lin Kang also supported the reform. Local cadres such as Chen Yimin and Jin Liangming also devoted their energy and time into the reforms with little concern about how the reform may affect them. Chen Yimin is an ordinary cadre in the Theory Division of the Party Committee Propaganda Department in Wenling. He was an active participant in the activities leading to the development of this reform since 1999. For more than ten years, he worked without interruption on this reform from his post. Later he became Director of the "Democratic Consultation Office" of the Theory Division of the Party Committee Propaganda Department. Jin Liangming was the Party Secretary of Xinhe Township and is presently the Director of the Water Conservancy Bureau of Wenling City. In 2005, he initiated the Public Budget Participation and Transparency pilot project (which was the precursor of the "Democratic Consultation" reform) in Xinhe. When a reporter asked why he was undertaking such a reform when it would limit his own authority and that of other cadres, he said that although his own power might be reduced significantly it would allow the Party Committee and the government to gain the people's trust.

Scholarly guidance from professors and researchers also contribute to the healthy development of the experiment. Many experts paid considerable amount of attention to this innovation. There were also a large number of media interviews and follow-up reports. Higher-level leaders also paid attention to it. All of which gave additional propulsion to make this reform sustainable.

In the recent past, nearly one hundred experts and professors, including some of the best known professors in China, went to Wenling city. They were fascinated by the democratic experiment because it touched upon some core issues in China local governance: participatory auditing and supervision of the city budget and public participation in financial management and operations. This innovation marks a breakthrough in the direction of China's local governments' administrative system reform and democratic political development. Scholars who went there were not only able to contribute their own opinions but also, as a result of Wenling's practice, to improve their knowledge and verify the theoretical hypotheses.

For any local cadres this new openness is a process of accepting and adapting to new things and ideas. Democratic decision-making as a mechanism for distributing social and political resources is new to many local-level cadres. What are the risks in giving up their decision-making power to the people? Could they lose control in face-to-face conversations with the populace? Government officials have long been used to making decisions for the people, but if suddenly they let the people make decision themselves, their own authority would shrink. Issues may become more complicated, and it may be time-consuming for issues to be resolved. A series of problems could influence the attitudes of local officials towards the reforms and their confidence in sustaining them. Precisely such concerns have become the conceptual barrier to the innovation and the sustainable development in China. If we want to solve this problem, preaching alone is no good, one must rely on practice.

Any innovation has risks. If at the beginning of reforms, people think the risks are too formidable, they could be too timid to act and back down. In such situations, we must choose appropriate methods to explain the risks of the reforms, such as doing it first and talking about it later and doing it first and reporting later so as to avoid risk and demonstrate that the new method has been tried with positive results. It is not a bad thing that local cadres have meritorious ideas, rather it at least shows local cadres want to handle matters and hope to make a difference. But, if people want to organically synthesize these kinds of successful ideas and with innovation and sustainability, they must introduce and use these ideas reasonably.

After "Democratic Dialogues" were developed in Wenling, they were promoted to numerous different domains. In the past ten years, some of these applications have not been successful while others have persisted with ever increasing vitality. In comparing the two, the key difference is whether or not the application of the reform has brought real benefits to the people. For example, the system for collective negotiation of wages in the wool sweater profession in Xinhe Township is an example of an application that has succeeded because it has brought real benefits to workers. The decade-long experiments with innovation in democratic decision making and deliberative democracy in Wenling has already broken, to some extent, some of the pre-existing superficial blockages to reform. We have reason to anticipate that reforms of local government structure in China will have a brilliant future.

Although the results of the democratic experiment are very encouraging, in the predictable future, they still have a long way to go to perfect the system. The reasons are very simple. At present, the environment in China for local innovation is still unsatisfactory. The transformation of the ideology of cadres at all levels is still far from being complete. The impulse for visible and major achievment is still very strong. Reformers who work quietly and wholeheartedly still are not used rationally and multi-layered barriers to local innovation remain very significant etc. This suggests that if people in Wenling really want to sustain these reforms, they still face many challenges.

Conclusions

Remembering the initial period of China's reform and opening policy, there were difficulties and debate when reforms appeared, leading some people to suspect that China could return to the planned economy. Thirty years have passed, and China is now is again encountering the similar difficulties and debates, but no one believes that China will return to the planned economy because China has already developed a degree of "path dependence" on the market economy and is locked into the market-economy track.

At present, local governance reform in China's social and politics domains is in its initial stage, much like initial period of the reform and opening policy, therefore, it is still quite far from being completed. In this stage, it is easiest for such reforms and innovations to wither away or fall back to the old system. At the same time, this will also be a period when reforms and innovations tend to emerge one after another. The accumulation of these incremental changes will eventually lead to a major breakthrough in China's political reform and a fundamental change in the framework of the political system.

Notes

1. Xinjun Gao, "The Failed Pingchang Reform," *Tongzhou Gongjin Magazine*, no. 7, 2009, http://www.tongzhougongjin.com/zazhi_detail.asp?id=533 (accessed Oct. 16, 2010).

2. "Speeches Made by Dang Guoying and Others at the Forum on "Village Governance Model in Qin County," http://www.chinaelections.org/ [in Chinese] (accessed Dec. 19, 2010).

3. China Center for Comparative Politics and Economics of the Central Compilation Bureau of the CPC, *Innovations and Excellence in Chinese Local Governance (2005–2006)*, 34–35.

4. Zhou Linjun, "The Trap of the Public Utility Privatization," Sina.com, March 3, 2006, http://finance.sina.com.cn/review/20060308/11342400825.shtml (accessed Dec. 20, 2010).

5. Zhang Ying, "Absurdity of the Proposed Shenzhen Water Fee Increase," http://bbs.oeeee.com/articles/2010-1/7/6832411_1.html (accessed Dec. 20, 2010).

6. An interview conducted by Xinjun Gao with the person in charge of the department in Shenzhen, on April 6, 2009.

7. An interview with Mr. Chen Guang, who is the division director of reform office in Shenzhen City government on April 6, 2009.

8. An interview with Ms. Li Hongguang, a senior professional staff in the Gas Company of Shenzhen City.

9. Wen Wu, "The Investigation and Thinking of the Debt of Village and Township in Tiexi District," *Bazhong Today* 12, (2001), 42; *The Summary of Re-election in Villages and Townships*, Party Committee of Bazhong City, Dec. 20, 2001.

10. Wang Yongbin, "A Study of the 'Public Recommendation and Direct Election' in Pingchang County and Village Party Committee Elections in Sichuan Province," *Gaige* (Reform Magazine), January, 2010, http://www.cser.org.cn/index.php/2010-01-11-05-37-14/2009-12-21-10-40-01/447-2010-01-10-09-41-50 (accessed Dec. 20, 2010).

11. Wang Changjiang, Zhou Hongyun and Wang Yongbing, eds., *The Innovation of Party Inner Democratic Institution: One Case Study of Grassroots Party Committee Leadership Group "Public Recommendation and Direct Election"* (Beijing: Central Translation Press, July 2007).

12. Interview with Mr. Liu Qianxiang, who was Party Secretary of Pingchang County. He is currently the division director of the Attractive Traders Bureau of Sichuan province.

13. Lai Hairong, *The Comparative Study on Financial Situation, Governance Capability, Democracy and Rule of Law in Grassroots in Chinese Towns and Counties*," September 2008.

14. An interview with Mr. He Xiude, who was Deputy Director of Personnel Department of Pingchang Party Committee. He is now Director of Legal Office in Pingchang County Government.

15. Xinjun Gao, "The 'Service-based Administrative System' as a Way to Reform the Township Administration in Xian'an District of Xianning City of Hubei Province," http://www.chinaelections.org/NewsInfo.asp?NewsID=140560 (accessed Dec. 23, 2010).

16. Liu Xiaoping, "The 'Service-Based Administrative System:' a Case Study of the Xin'an District," http://www.cdrf.org.cn/a/yusuan2/6yangxuedong8.pdf (accessed Dec. 23, 2010).

17. An interview with Zhou Qingsong, who was vice secretary of Xianning City Government in 2008.

18. An interview with Mr. Li Changping, who was Director of Rural Comprehensive Reform Office in Xian'an District in October 2008. Also see records of the interviews with Mr. He Qing, who was Deputy Party Secretary of Shuangxiqiao Township, and with Mr. Fan Tiansong, who was Director of Center for Rural Public Service in Shuangxiqiao Township in 2008. Also see records of the interviews with Mr. Wu Guoqing, who was the Deputy Director of Dingsiqiao Township, with Zhou Dayong, who was Deputy Party Secretary, with Yang Bing, who was Deputy Director of Dingsiqiao Township, and with Zhang Wenbing, who was the director of Center for Rural Public Services in Dingsiqiao Township in 2008.

19. See "All around Public Supervision Government Affairs" issued by the Jiawang District Government of Xuzhou City in Jiangsu Province; report of the investigation team to Jiawang District from in The Third Local Innovation Award Program in 2008.

20. China Center for Comparative Politics and Economics, *Innovations and Excellence in Chinese Local Governance (2005–2006)*, 62–63.

21. Mr. Qiu He was Party Secretary in Shuqian City of Jiangsu Province; he led the reform of economy and health insurance in rural China, and was successful in the past few years. Lately, he has become a lieutenant governor in Jiangsu province and right now he is Party Secretary in Kunming City of Yunnan province. He is a very well-known reformer in China.

Chapter 6
The (D)evolution of Human Rights in China

Michael Kilburn and Vitaly Kozyrev

The selection of Chinese dissident and democracy activist Liu Xiaobo as the recipient of the 2010 Nobel Peace Prize, and China's furious overreaction to it, has once again drawn international attention to the state of human rights in China. Liu is currently serving an eleven-year sentence for his role in authoring and publishing Charter 08, a manifesto based on the anti-Soviet Czechoslovak Charter 77 calling for political reform, democratization, and respect for human rights in China. While the official charges are "inciting subversion of state power,"[1] the document chiefly consists of entreaties to the Chinese authorities to abide by their own Constitution and treaty obligations, and engage in constructive dialogue with their own citizenry. Indeed, Liu's defense was that he had "merely exercised a citizen's right to free speech as conferred by the Constitution."[2]

After diplomatic pressure failed to dissuade the Nobel committee from its choice, the Chinese Foreign Ministry dismissed supporters of the prize as "clowns" and accused them of orchestrating an "anti-China farce."[3] Flexing its growing economic and political influence, the Chinese government organized a boycott of the ceremony, convincing nineteen of the sixty-five countries with embassies in Oslo not to send representatives to the ceremony. Even the United Nations High Commissioner for Human Rights, Navi Pillay declined to attend, though she had earlier issued a statement of concern that the sentencing of Liu Xiaobo represented "a serious setback for the protection and promotion of human rights in China."[4] The Chinese authorities also detained Liu's supporters, signatories of the Charter, and other leading opposition figures, preventing them from leaving the country. Liu's wife, Liu Xia, was placed under house arrest to prevent her from accepting the award on her husband's behalf and it was presented, for the second time in Nobel history, to an empty chair. As a final petulant gesture, the Chinese government announced a rival "Confucius Peace Prize" awarding it to a mystified Lien Chan, honorary chairman of the Kuomintang, who didn't even bother to pick it up.

To international observers, China's virulent reaction to the award is only the latest illustration of the government's general restrictive policies on freedom of speech and the press and a symptom of a broader systemic cultural and religious repression. According to this view, the arrest of Liu Xiaobo is in the same category as the conflict with Google over internet neutrality and cyber-surveillance, the ongoing suppression of practitioners of *Falun Gong*, and the heavy handed response to the protests in Tibet and Xinjiang in 2009: all manifestations of a reflexive intransigence toward unauthorized expressions of democratic values and rights.

Despite Hillary Clinton's obsequious deference to real-ekonomik in her first visit to China as Secretary of State in February 2009,[5] the official position of the United States regarding human rights in China has been and remained at least formally critical. In the "2009 Country Reports on Human Rights Practices" released by the U.S. Department of State, for example, China is qualified as a country where "human rights record remained poor and worsened in some areas." According to the data provided by the U.S. Department of State's Bureau of Democracy, Human Rights, and Labor, nothing changed in the sphere of the basic civil and political liberties, "the party and state exercised strict political control," "citizens did not have the right to change their government."[6]

Such criticism is practically de rigueur protocol in U.S.-China diplomatic relations and Beijing has been increasingly willing to engage in the diplomatic charade,[7] especially since such formal protestations have been more or less decoupled from any substantive policy effects. But the uncharacteristic tactlessness of the response to the Nobel Prize affair suggests a deeper nerve was touched, demonstrating both the Chinese government's extraordinary sensitivity to dissident or critical views of its human rights record and its growing hegemonic influence on the terms of symbolism and discourse in the field of human rights. The case of Liu Xiaobo does not demonstrate so much the "power of the powerless"—as Vaclav Havel once famously characterized the function of dissent in authoritarian societies[8]—as the "powerlessness of the powerful,"[9] an unforgiveable loss of face.

The embarrassment of the Nobel Prize award and perfunctory critical assessments by the State Department, the United Nations Human Right Commission (UNHRC) and various NGOs, however, cannot overshadow the cumulative impression that, at least in formal terms, China's advancement in the human rights sphere over the last decade has been unprecedented. Historically, for the Chinese leaders, the struggle for human rights was unalienable from the "self-determination" process, embedded in the conception of "collective human rights" which became popular among the third world countries.[10] It was in the era of economic reforms since the late 1970s, when the ideas of "universal" human rights and freedoms were gradually included in China's political agenda. The Tiananmen events of 1989 were a critical turning point for the Chinese leaders' strategy of political reforms. Since the political turmoil of the late 1980s, Beijing authorities have continuously proclaimed China's turn to the era of political reforms, including an integrative approach to rights both civil and human in the broader context of social reform and modernization. In one of his speeches China's former president Jiang Zemin, who represented the "third generation" of the Chinese leaders, stated that, for the success of reform and reconstruction, it was necessary for the Chinese people to "broadly implement freedom, democracy, and human rights."[11]

Jiang's statement was indeed significant, even if the exact significance is yet unclear. Students of Chinese politics have noted Beijing's incorporation of human rights law from the outset of Jiang Zemin's sole leadership in the Communist Party after Deng Xiaoping, the patriarch of Chinese reforms, passed away in 1997. By that year, China had recognized the *Geneva Convention Relative to the Protection of Civilian Persons in Times of War* (in 1952), and, in 1980s, it signed the subsequent additional protocols to this document, as well as signed and ratified the *Convention Relating to the Status of Refugees* (in 1982) and *Convention on Prevention and Punishment of the Crime of Genocide* (in 1983). In the 1990s China's international legal activity in the sphere of human rights broadened: Beijing became a signatory party of ILO (the International Labor Organization) conventions. Most importantly, in 1997-98 China became a party of the *International Covenant on Civil and Political Rights* (ICCPR) and signed *International Covenant on Economic, Social and Cultural Rights* (ICESCR). Major treaties regulating the Rights of the Child have been recently signed and ratified by the Chinese legislature. By late 2009 China joined twenty-five international treaties in the human rights sphere, and it became a party to six and signatory to two of the thirteen core international human rights treaties.[12] Indeed, in de jure terms at least, China compares favorably or even surpasses the United States, the self-proclaimed bastion and defender of human rights, in the number of international human rights treaties signed and ratified.

China's attention to human rights frameworks in the sphere of domestic lawmaking has sparked interest in the West toward Chinese accommodative practices within the international legal system. Many observers noticed the shift from China's resistance to the western pressure toward more cooperative approach in the sphere of human rights legalization. By revising the 1982 Constitution in 2004, the Chinese government opened "a new era" of human rights development in this country, where the state is obliged to "respect" and "protect" human rights.[13] The statistical data publicized in April 2004 by the central newspapers, illustrating enormous activity of the Chinese authorities aimed at institutionalization and internalization of international human rights norms, has been broadly cited in the western literature.[14] Since 2006 China as a member of the UN Human Rights Council has been actively coordinating its human rights policy with the respective UN activities. Finally, in April 2009 the National Human Rights Action Plan of China (2009–2010) was approved by the government, which expressed its determination to promote and protect human rights.[15]

Thus, the Chinese case is broadly considered as an example of the so-called "socialization" of authoritarian regimes resulted from the diffusion of universal international norms, standards, and ideas. Driven by the "constructivist turn" in international studies theory in the late 1990s, some analysts assessed the normative processes through which China came to comply with the human rights norms as crucial for China's "discursive enmeshment" into the global human rights regime. Rosemary Foot referenced the role of human rights norms, rhetoric, and language in the formation of a "shaming discourse" that affected China's international behavior and identity-formation. She found the "spiral" model of internalization of human rights norms (proposed by Risse et al. in 1999) applicable to China's advancement to the "rule-consistent behavior."[16]

Does this process of China's "socialization" truly represent a substantive movement to reframe and incorporate human rights in the Chinese context? Or, alternatively, is this rhetorical strategy—as the critics claim—merely prevarication: a cynical attempt to distract the international community from serious rights violations from Tibet to Darfur; from the death penalty to freedom of expression to environmental degradation? Does a reanimation of the "Asian values" debate signify bluntly—as the Chinese delegate to the 1993 Vienna World Conference on Human Rights put it—that "individuals must put the state's rights before their own"? Or might the broader project to promote sustainable development and social harmony function as a counterweight to the first generation bias of western Enlightenment notions of rights and finally provide the basis for the integration and full exercise of human rights, including the civil and political?

This chapter suggests that these developments in Beijing's human rights policy should not be considered as a mere progress in the domestic "human rights lawmaking" in accordance with the existing international norms, i.e. not simply assessing to western cum "universal" standards, but rather must be seen as part of a larger and longer view toward reforming and reframing the normative reference itself. Rather than finally "talking the talk" of human rights as conventionally understood, China's current human rights discourse reflects its ambition to become a "normative power" capable of creating a new set of values, norms and regulations for the international community. The policy and politics of human rights have become an operative legitimizing factor for the ruling Communist party. By developing its own autochthonous human rights strategy, one that deprioritizes so-called first generation rights in favor of social and economic rights, the Chinese leaders seek to utilize the human rights issue as a powerful instrument of "class struggle" in the international arena, and a key element of Beijing's far-reaching efforts to reshape the international order under the banner of a "harmonious world" concept, while simultaneously trying to "soften" class struggle rhetoric domestically to secure social and political consolidation under the banner of Confucian "harmony." It is a subtle distinction: domestically, the Chinese leaders tend to downplay the significance of human rights discourse, especially as it pertains to "coordination goods" of civil and political rights, advocating a kind of *perestroika* without *glasnost*. Yet it is not necessarily disingenuous. We conclude that the development of human rights discourse in China should be taken seriously and examined in the context of a complex interaction of domestic and external factors conceptualized in China in the respective programs of building a harmonious *society* and striving for a harmonious *world*. The historical discourse of "people's rights," as part of a broader narrative of restoration of China's core historical heritage, plays an instrumental role reinterpreting human rights norms and values to counter the alleged moral universalism of western values. Hence we argue that Beijing's human rights policy is an important component of China's overall "normative, value-driven" external interaction strategy, aimed at the accomplishment of a specific mission to reshape the political and moral global order. The incorporation of human rights discourse into the larger project for sustainable development, social harmony and soft power thus has transformative potential both for China and for the meaning of human rights itself.

China's Theory of Political Development: the Dual Use of Human Rights Discourse

Recent progress in the adoption of international human rights norms in China, and the gradual institutionalization of its human rights regime may be considered as part of Beijing's comprehensive strategy of "global constructivism," which sets important political guidelines on the way to modernization. This strategy helps the Chinese authorities to develop at the nation-state level an adequate political response to the dynamic domestic transformation of Chinese society in a complex global environment. To maintain domestic stability in the era of reforms and opening-up to the outside world, the Chinese leaders have carefully separated the political and economic aspects of modernization, prioritizing the latter as a prerequisite for domestic political reforms and prospective social change in China.

The "economization" of the CCP's domestic political agenda since the beginning of the reforms in the late 1970s was a strategic decision to secure fast economic modernization and to underpin the CCP's legitimacy by broadening the social base of the party rule. Over more than thirty years of reforms, the Chinese leaders—Deng Xiaoping, Jiang Zemin and Hu Jintao—were guided by the assumption that any reform effort would become legitimate only when it was approved by mainstream society and accepted by the public. To win popular support, the reform needed to produce quick results, and priority was given to generating wealth and increasing production, rather than securing equal distribution or social justice. The role of the state remained crucial: much effort was paid to mitigate the inevitable contradictions and tensions during the reform, and to prevent collapse of the constitutive order in the country.

However, these reforms inevitably led to broadened income disparities, and the resultant social tensions forced the party to make improvements in the sphere of income distribution and ownership relationships. The "rural-urban" divide worsened in China at the turn of new millennium, when rural incomes averaged for about one-third of those of the coastal areas. Apparently, the imbalanced distribution of economic resources exacerbated political and cultural tensions, and the government had to work out effective measures to mitigate regional, ethnic, religious, and social conflicts, as well as to prevent even deeper polarization of the rich and poor. In other words, by the late 1990s the Chinese leadership realized that the developmental model originally proposed by Deng Xiaoping was no longer sustainable. Firstly, the CCP leaders had to revise the policies that prioritized market efficiency over parity and social justice. Secondly, the market-induced fragmentation of society and elitist authoritarianism could be suicidal for the party which had continued to proclaim the ideas of socialism as its official ideology.

Jiang Zemin's theory of "Three Represents" appeared to be the first attempt to resolve the "legitimacy crisis" by political means. In the late 1990s, the "Shanghai group" of the party leadership, led by CCP General Secretary Jiang

Zemin, tried to reconcile the party's program, the interests of new influential groups, and the preferences of the broader public. During his inspection tour of south China's Guangdong province in February 2000, Jiang formulated the tenets of his new theory, trying to reinterpret the role of the Communist Party, to broaden its social platform, and to blur the borders between multiple social and economic groups. To downplay the role of class division in China's sociopolitical life, Jiang referred to Deng's proposal of the early 1980s to build a new "social spiritual civilization" that would be supported by the majority of population and guided by a reinvigorated party.[17]

Jiang's efforts signaled to the world that China would no longer be able to separate economic reform from political change. Besides, external aspects of political development became critical as China integrated itself more deeply into the global economic system. Jiang's initiative spurred heated debate among the Chinese political elite about the outcome of economic reforms and the role of the party: in the eyes of leftist "neo-socialists," for example, the theory of "Three Represents" could simply transform the CCP into an amorphous organization similar to Euro-communists or, even worse, into a replica of the Communist Party of the Soviet Union (CPSU) in the period of the "all-people" political regime of the early 1980s. What China needed was a conceptual reinterpretation of its strategy and political objectives both at home and abroad. The new concept ought to secure political change in China, fueled predominantly by this country's domestic needs, rather than external factors. Stability in China required a proactive international policy, rather than simply continuation of Deng's "observe calmly" approach and "keeping a low profile" strategy of the late 1980s.[18] China's development within the existing global capitalist system, or its "intra-systemic" rise,[19] therefore, required from the rising "dragon" that it would adequately "express itself" (□□) in the world arena and to "have a say" (□□□) in world affairs, in order to secure its role in shaping a new international order, as well as to protect its economic interest, pursue moderate political change, and act carefully on the level of institutional decision-making.

Hence, reconciliation of economic development and political reconstruction, and the coordination of domestic change and global competition, appeared to be the most challenging task for the fourth generation of the Chinese leaders (since 2002). In his comments on China's "peaceful development" strategy one of the leading CCP ideologists Zheng Bijian stated in 2001 that China made its strategic choice by accepting economic globalization and accommodating itself to its influence.[20] By simultaneously integrating with the world economically and accommodating itself to international law in the 1990s and early 2000s (including internalization of human rights norms), China successfully secured its "entrance into the system." The new era of transition from "entering the system" toward "assuming higher international responsibility" prescribed that Beijing would restrain the expansion of global capitalist forces by peaceful means, quietly contesting America's "hegemonic behavior," limiting the spread of its political values, and competing with the world's sole superpower at the systemic level.[21] As Aaron Friedberg noted, "instead of attempting a premature, frontal assault on

America's strategic position, Beijing has taken a low-key, indirect approach, using newly acquired instruments to chip away at its foundations."[22]

Moreover, the adoption of useful American experiences is considered in China as a necessary condition of its intra-systemic rise.[23] The CCP leaders believe that it is only the economic expansion of a rising nation that will ultimately secure China's preeminent standing internationally. To operate within the capitalist system, it is therefore important to protect China's national interest by strengthening its own national capital which thus becomes the agent of the "national idea," turning global class struggle in a global era into the cross-border struggle between the capitals of different national origins.

Capitalist competition in the global market should not necessarily lead to conflict. The key objective of China's global strategy is to harmonize the world by soft power means, demonstrating the harmonious character of its own society and thus becoming a "hegemon by example." Trying to synchronize the needs of China and the global community, Beijing is ready to deliver systemic "impulses" to the world; a peacemaker as pacemaker. This new formula for peaceful development implies a dynamic relationship between economic and cultural norms, postulating that the rise of China as a great power will contribute to maintaining global peace, order, and sustainability. From the outset of the reform era, China's economic success was dependent on a stable domestic and international environment. At present, a peaceful global environment is increasingly dependent on China's rise. Building a harmonious world, therefore, becomes a natural extension of China's effort to harmonize its own society. This Sinocentric orientation is consistent with traditional Chinese self-conception and global positioning as a gravitational center of civilization and order.

China's "exceptional" role in the world may be maintained only if Beijing successfully makes a compelling case for rapid economic growth and finds a balance between market and social justice. Furthermore, China may become an integrative force in the world if its "national characteristics" do not contradict with the universally adopted legal and political practices, such as the rule of law, the separation of powers, democracy and people's participation. The reinterpretation of the discourse of human rights is thus central to Beijing's global agenda. It is no longer sufficient to claim exceptionalism. While acknowledging each country's right to choose its own national road to modernization, the Chinese leaders insisted that excessive stress on specificity of the national model may leave the country on the sideline of global progress. The "fourth generation" of the Chinese leaders, Hu Jintao in particular, developed their new perception of a successful reform strategy which would integrate reforms with development and stability, and coordinate economic development with "social justice" and "political democracy." To mitigate internal contradictions, the party leaders have proposed a "human-centered" approach to modernization, embedded in the key theoretical concepts, namely, "realizing scientific development," "building a harmonious socialist society," "building a new socialist countryside," "building an innovative state," "fostering a socialist outlook on honor and disgrace," "promoting the building of a harmonious world," and "strengthening the building of the Party's advanced nature." Hu Jintao has clearly picked up the neo-socialist argument against China's "national characteristics" concept that may eventually make the Chinese example inapplicable for the rest of the world and would not help China to effectively confront western ideologies and values under the banner of restoration of "real" human values, rather than institutions of corporate democracy.

This "scientific" approach to development is a strategy to amalgamate some traditional Chinese "human-centered" concepts with the imperatives of modernization. Her growing economic influence would help Beijing to fulfill another systemic obligation, namely, its participation in the formation of new international norms and rules. To harmonize the world, Beijing utilizes the idea of *organic mutual complimentarily* of western and eastern cultures and civilizations, seeking the balance between morals, justice, and power. As a potential promoter of a new developmental model and a prospective pacifier of the world conflict-prone system, China might obtain a tremendous cultural influence worldwide. The Chinese leaders hold that China, by linking its struggle for a harmonious society with the building of a harmonious world would help the international system develop from the socially degenerate practices of the free market—exemplified by the greed, corruption, and social chaos of the early post-Soviet "wild east" liberalization in Russia—toward more civilized (and centralized) socio-economic practices under the guidance of a Chinese Leviathan. Responding to the expansion of American liberal universalism, the Chinese strategists have tried to demonstrate a new type of power growth which would not lead to ideological or civilizational conflict. China is apparently striving for the establishment of its own "cultural diocese" where it will play the role of an integrative force.[24]

It is noteworthy that the growing international influence of China is not regarded there as a development of its model of "cultural nationalism," much less cultural imperialism. As Beijing University Professor Yuan Xingpei stated in 2006, China's goal is simply "to secure that the human beings with different cultures can but mutually tolerate with an attitude of enlightenment and open-mindedness, and can but co-exist in peace and harmony, before the goal of mutual development and prosperity is attained."[25] China does not want to isolate itself from universal values—on the contrary, Beijing seeks to promote these values, though with its own spin. Effectively, China is turning the tables on the demands of uniformity and standardization of western globalization by appealing to the universality of Chinese traditional values. The operationalization of this approach, however, entails an incorporation of means that may have unintended consequences.

In the concept of "socialist harmonious society" introduced by the 4th Plenum of the 16th Central Committee (September 2004), for example, a special emphasis was placed on the use of legal means in the settlement of social conflicts. The Party's objective was to build democratic, law-based, just, and orderly society, based on a harmonious relationship among the people and between men and nature. Along with Hu Jintao's "eight standards of honor and disgrace" (2006), these principles laid the foundation for developing a civic ethics of a "socialist harmonious society." In Hu Jintao's plans, "socialist democracy" and "a human-centered model" play a decisive role in the building of a "social spiritual civilization."

The new cultural epoch of human-centrism is considered in China as a revolutionary development from the age of imperialism to the new system based on justice and righteousness. The CCP leadership argues that in the capitalist world, the primacy of capital is secured at the expense of "workers' rights" and causes the exhaustion of national resources and limitation of national sovereignty. To secure "real rights" of a human, the state should put an end on the use of humans as just the instruments for capital growth. Focus on the "growth environment," rather than a physical growth of the GDP, in Beijing's view, would contribute to the adequate quality of growth, the improvement of human capital and social welfare. To develop an effective "growth environment," a balance between the state/party and corporations should be achieved. China's criticism of western models of democracy is based on the assumption that the role of private capitalist corporations in western societies is unreasonably decisive in the formation of the sets of values and securing social guarantees for workers. To build a harmonious society, the corporation should be responsible for economic efficiency, and the party should help "liberate workers" from the corporate rule, by impartially regulating social relations, promoting "right" social values, and securing timely feedback from the broader public.

Ming Wan rightfully notes that that the reason for China's dramatic move to human rights law lies in the domestic politics of reform and shifting national identity on the one hand, and, on the other, in the changing strategic interaction on the international level, where human rights law remains weak[26] and susceptible to manipulation. China's new self-proclaimed role as a defender of international human rights norms is a chance to use its growing power capabilities to actively develop the international human rights regime, based on the "real rights of the people liberated from the oppression of capitalist corporations."[27] The human rights issue is becoming a powerful instrument of "class struggle" in the international arena for the establishment of a "harmonious world." Domestically, the issue of human rights has become a part of the comprehensive concept of "a socialist harmonious society," reducing social tension and solidifying the regime's legitimacy. Now that the human rights genie is out of the bottle, however, it remains to be seen whether it will only serve one master.

The Chinese Model of Human Rights Protection: Taming the "Three Dragons"

Beijing's far-reaching strategy of internalization and concurrent "purification" of international human rights norms requires a new model of human rights protection that would block the dissemination of the allegedly "universalist" liberal interpretation of human rights and inspire sympathy of the world community for China's specific modifications of those norms and values. The Chinese project to revise the western engineered system of basic rules and institutions of international justice and governance seems too ambitious. As John Ikenberry aptly noted, this system is "hard to overturn and easy to join."[28] This mission might be successful if China's revisionist claim is grounded in deep political foundations which will gain broad support within the country and be shared by the other members of the evolving world system as an alternative to the existing liberal legal norms. The Chinese mission, therefore, is an attempt to tame the "three dragons"—the western liberal legacy of human rights protection, Chinese traditional "human-centrism," and the Marxist narrative of the class nature of social change. The complexity of the matter, as well as the need to operate both domestically and internationally explains Beijing's emphasis on publicity and the demonstrative effect of its norms-adaptation process. High priority is given to the development of a relevant institutional infrastructure and the systemic elements of human rights protection: the new institutes are instrumental for the CCP's theoretical guidance and practical control of the sphere of human rights in China.

Three elements of the CCP strategy are essential for "smart" governance: a "scientific" approach, "democratic" development, and a "law-abiding" behavior. The scientific approach to the human rights issue should secure China's smooth and risk-free "discursive enmeshment" into the international human rights regime. This approach helps the government to set priorities in the system of human rights protection and determine relationships between the human rights institutionalization process, the role of the state, social change, identity formation, and the realization of the political reform. The party leadership attributes a "scientific" role to human rights cause by making the latter a part of Beijing's grand strategy of development. Wang Chen, director of the State Council Information Office, considers the human rights theme as a key agenda issue in China's economic construction and social progress.[29] To promote the Chinese model of human rights protection, the CCP government has elevated the human rights issue from the slogan of "full realization of human rights" announced in the first white paper on China's human rights conditions in 1991 toward codifying of the concept of human rights in the PRC Constitution revised in 2004, and punctuated by the inclusion of the principle of "respect for and protection of human rights" into China's Eleventh Five-Year Plan adopted the 10th National People's Congress in March 2006.

The new political doctrine, formulated by the 17th National Congress of the CCP in 2007, set the parameters of socio-political transformation in China which prioritized the rule of law and people's political rights to "be informed, to participate, to be heard and to oversee." At the opening of the Party Congress, President Hu Jintao recalled the 2004 constitutional provision stating that the state "must respect and safeguard human rights, and ensure the equal right to participation and development for all members of society in accordance with the law." It is noteworthy, however, that the CCP today acknowledges the role of "individual morality" inalienable from collective ethics, family virtues and responsibilities, patriotism, and the "socialist ideology." In China's democratic development the political role of the state is critical: the state is a guarantor of human rights, and the party-led government is obliged to establish "role models" for society, to guide people in carrying out their obligations, and enhance "people's awareness of integrity." Initiatives outside this framework, therefore, are by definition subversive of the state interest in securing human rights according to its own definition and priorities.

Institutionally, the development of China's human rights cause requires the optimal distribution of responsibilities and duties among state agencies and non-governmental (people's) associations.[30] The CCP's Central Committee and the State Council coordinate the activities of numerous divisions at state agencies, as well as public and non-governmental organizations in the sphere of human rights protection and information. A number of special committees, commissions and working groups in the legislative and executive branches of the government at each level have been involved into the process of development of the country's human rights cause. To publicize China's position on a variety of human rights issues in China and abroad and promote China's perception of human rights the above-mentioned governmental organizations coordinate their activities with the State Council Information Office and China's Foreign Ministry. Established in March 1993 as a "non-governmental" think tank organization, the China Society for Human Rights Studies works in collaboration with dozens of China's universities and research institutions and develops theoretical foundation for China's model of human rights protection.[31]

The "democratic" character of the process of human rights development is secured, as Beijing believes, by the involvement of numerous "people's organizations" that embrace more than 200 thousand "social" and 174 thousand "non-enterprise" associations and clubs.[32] In addition to the China Society For Human Rights Studies, the following organizations—the China Society of Law, All-China Lawyers Association, China Legal Assistance Fund, China Society of Education, All-China Federation of Trade Unions, All-China Women's Federation, China's Disabled Persons' Federation, All-China Youth Federation, China's Women's Development Fund, China Disabled Persons' Welfare Fund—play a key role in the realization of human rights-related programs in China. More than twenty specified networks with web-based platforms provide up-to-date information about human rights development in China. The CCP actively "promotes and guides" non-governmental organizations as "a buffer zone between the civil rights claimants and the government," though the legal documents regulating registration and administration of social organization remain confusing and incomplete.[33]

The approval of "National Human Rights Action Plan of China (2009-2010)" is considered in Beijing as the manifestation of state-society collaboration and one of the signal achievements of China's democratization process. To facilitate the work, the government established the "joint meeting mechanism" for elaborating the Action Plan. The Information Office of the State Council coordinated the activities of fifty-three organizations which included the related committees and divisions of the key governmental agencies representing the three branches of government. Among the contributors to the plan were China's leading universities, research institutions, non-governmental organizations and private think tanks (the China Law Society, All-China Lawyers' Association, China Legal Aid Foundation, China Foundation for Human Rights, and the others). Labeling this Action Plan as "an important event" in the history of China's human rights development, the CCP ideologists maintain that the Action Plan is a step forward in the party's effort to combine the universal principles of human rights and the concrete realities of China.[34]

The plan, in fact, introduces the major premises of Beijing's reconceptualization of human rights. Firstly, the CCP leaders believe that China has a long road ahead in its efforts to improve its human rights situation, and, given the challenges that China faces, the government "gives priority to the protection of the people's rights to subsistence and development, and lawfully guarantees the rights of all members of society to equal participation and development on the basis of facilitating sound and rapid economic and social development."[35] It should be noted that this single conceptual reframing not only includes, but *reintegrates* the three generations of rights disaggregated by the Cold War and post-colonialism. Subordinating the rights claims of both liberalism and socialism—often construed as irreconcilable—to the so-called third generation rights of self-determination, development, and environmental integrity and re-ordering the traditionally antagonistic or servile relationship of the individual and the state obviate many of the tensions and contradictions that have dogged the implementation of an effective global rights regime. By focusing on the realization of a social and international order requisite to the enjoyment of *all* rights and freedoms (Article 28 of the UDHR) rather than prioritizing either civil–political or social-economic rights, the Action Plan, however self-serving, is a potentially radical and liberating conceptual advance.

The right to subsistence is guaranteed by society and secures individual freedom, self-respect, and creating conditions for satisfying material and spiritual needs of each citizen. The right to development implies citizen's participation in development and some benefits this individual gains from it. The Action Plan creatively embodies the principle of "putting people first," formulating the goal: "Development is for the people, by the people, and with the people sharing its fruits."[36] Unlike the western liberal tradition, in China the rights to subsistence and development do not separate the individual from society and state. The interconnectedness between state and society brings about cooperation and mutual dependence, or even creates a merger between them.[37] The Chinese state is the main guarantor of these basic rights, and therefore, state sovereignty becomes a prerequisite for the implementation of the latter.

This second premise—the importance of state sovereignty for human rights protections—rooted in the specific historical experiences of "one hundred years of national humiliation," when China's sovereignty was violated by western powers and therefore the struggle for human rights was a function of China's fight for national independence. Similar to the current Russian concept of "sovereign democracy," the notion of sovereignty as part of human rights creates a direct challenge to the western perception of human rights as a matter of higher priority than state's sovereignty. Luo Haocai, President of the China Society for Human Rights Studies, characterizes the essence of human rights protection in China as a balance between "respect for national sovereignty and protection of human rights, protection of individual and collective human rights, and protection of civil and political rights and economic, social, and cultural rights."[38]

Thus "conditionality" of political rights in China, vis-à-vis economic and cultural rights, becomes the third conceptual component of human rights discourse in today's China. The dialectical relationship between political/civil rights and economic/cultural rights is seen in China as a reincarnation of the Marxist principles that explain the role of state power (the proletarian dictatorship) as an instrument to secure economic rights of the masses, and the importance of "economic reconstruction" for helping the "people" to hold the power and exercise it by the means of political participation. Giving the priority to protecting the people's right to subsistence and development, the Chinese government tries to balance development of the first two generations of human rights. The Action Plan laid out the arrangement for protecting twenty-two human rights in three categories.[39] Focusing on social guarantees, education, environmental rights of the public, the CCP authorities demonstrated their adherence to the idea of people-oriented scientific development in times of crisis. Governmental effort to improve politically sensitive spheres of employment, social security, education, and health is portrayed as a positive development along the way of human rights protection in China.

According to the authors of the Action Plan, the government persists in ensuring the people's position as "masters of the country." The government guarantees people's rights "to be informed, to participate, to be heard, and to oversee." To secure the right to be informed, the State Council on April 5, 2007 adopted "Regulations of the People's Republic of China on Open Government Information,"[40] aimed at the improvement of public affairs management and securing higher transparency of the work of the government. A matter of special concern is "village affairs,"[41] which lack publicity and the tradition of good governance: local bureaucracy remains one of the most corrupt in the world.[42] To protect the right to participate, the CCP is trying to improve the mechanism of political representation, and consolidate the interest of diverse social and political groups, beyond the reach of the ruling party. Broad political consultations is seen as an essential part of human rights protection, since the dialogue between the public, interest groups, experts, and the party will improve, as the CCP believes, the decision-making process. At the local level, the system of self-governance is seen in Beijing as a means for strengthening democratic control and limiting the outreach of bureaucracy. Despite some pitfalls in the development of village institutions of public representation,[43] the government seeks to boost the role of the Villagers Committees, and further expand the system of "democratic management" over urban neighborhoods. To stimulate "scientific" decision-making, a variety of elements of civil society is planned to be developed, including mass organizations, minority groups, industry associations, trade unions, and non-governmental entities.[44] Those mushrooming groups are considered critical for the further implementation of the rights to participate and "to be heard." To guarantee the latter, more channels and sources of information are promised to be unblocked, though "in the orderly way," and the people's rights of self-expression may be interpreted as keeping the window open for dealing with some new claims and requests of the people.

In the development of human rights protection, two "basic relationships" are important: the ones between rights and obligations (relationship between individuals), and the ones between rights and power (relationship between individuals and government). These relationships are secured by legal means. However, the principle of harmony is supposed to turn these relationships into a non-confrontational practice, tailoring contradictions between individuals and between the people and government into the model of a "mutual positive influence between rights and power."[45]

Regarding civil and political rights, the Chinese government prioritizes the rule of law as a necessary prerequisite for implementing democracy. The fundamental principles of the plan are: to uphold human rights in China in accordance with the law, to encourage the coordinated development of economic, social and cultural rights as well as civil and political rights, and the balanced development of individual and collective rights. Special emphasis is placed on the expanding of the "channels of democracy" and strengthening of China's legal system in general. To protect the "rights of the person," the state prohibits the extortion of confessions by torture, illegal detention by law enforcement agencies, and inappropriate application and procedural abuses of death sentences. The state pledged to secure an impartial trial for litigants and improve the rights of detainees and law enforcement in prisons. China is willing to further the freedom of religious belief, ensuring the positive role of "religious circles" in the promotion of social harmony and socio-economic development.

As human rights development is seen in Beijing as inalienable from the rule of law, the fourth conceptual element of the strategy includes the establishment of a functional judicial administration. As early as 1994 the system of "legal assistance" was introduced to help local governmental agencies to respect law in their administrative practices. The CCP leaders called for the development of the law-based state at the 15th CCP Party Congress in September 1997, which opened the gates for a judicial reform in the country. In March 1999 the constitutional principle of "running the country in accordance with the law" was approved by the Second Session of the Ninth National People's Congress. The principle of "equality before the law" played an important role for resolving a traditional "state-society" tension in China: constraining the power of government officials which was essential for the process of human rights internalization. Some important measured were adopted to prevent arbitrary judicial decisions on the cases involving the death penalty, as well as to investigate cases of extended custody and illegal violence by law enforcement agencies. The Civil Procedure Law was revised in 2007 and the government has made efforts educate the juries, diversify penalties, and pursue different anti-corruption procedures.[46]

The fifth element of China's concept of human rights protection is the policy of coordination of government's "sovereign" efforts to protect human rights in a specific socio-cultural setting and China's norm-creating policies in the international arena. To tackle globalization-generated challenges to human rights of the Chinese people, Beijing has become an active member of the global human rights regime, developing dialogue and cooperation with international institutions to forward the cause of human rights in China. The Action Plan is considered as China's response to the United Nations' call for pursuing a national human rights action plan. Being a signatory to twenty-five international covenants on human rights (January 2010), and a signatory party to six of the eight core UN covenants on human rights, China is close to ratifying the International Covenant on Civil and Political Rights.[47]

In the course of human rights development, the Chinese government has had to regulate delicate relations between state and social groups, individual and collective, economic and political. Special emphasis on "obligations vs. rights" and the legal aspects of human rights protection in China sets some limits to the full realization of political and civic rights and signals about the complexity of balancing between post-Marxist "global constructivism" and the spread of western liberal norms supported by growing influential middle class groups with their preference of open, integrated, and rule-based western norms. There are heated debates in the literature on the role of the Chinese middle class which looks different from normative roles played by these groups in the west.[48] However, the prevailing leftist discourse among the CCP ideologists drives Beijing away from a risk-prone "universalist" interpretation of western norms, values and institutions toward the Chinese tradition. The party leadership, to further modernize the country, has to paradoxically appeal to China's classical heritage.

Wen Jiabao appraised many luminous ideas brought by the Chinese tradition: the philosophical precept of "harmony without uniformity," the political belief that "people are the foundation of the nation," the educational guideline of "respecting teachers and valuing education," and the moral ethic of "do not do to others what you would not have them do to you."[49] Yuan Xingpei argues that the "primacy of the people", "harmoniousness", "tolerance", enlightenment, collectivism, the role of law, strive for reforms, openness, and public debate create the invaluable asset that may secure the boom of civilization.[50] Stephen Angle holds that China's simultaneous commitment to human rights and to harmony is both coherent and desirable.[51]

One may find the three traditional sources of the present human rights discourse in China: Confucianism, the "democratic" discourse of Republican China ("Three Principles of the People'"), and the lessons of public (direct) democracy, learned in the Mao period and applied to the current reality of China in the information age. While acknowledging the solidity and the significance of the many traditional Chinese virtues in Beijing's soft power projection, some important historical legacies may become either an impediment or a great asset on the way to real democratization of China.

The notion of enmeshed economic and political rights, without clear parameters of full realization of both, recalls some imperial practices of building social semi-administrative units or self-government experiments in Republican China which were oriented on the creation of a new citizen but ended up instead as a policy of preservation of a semi-traditional social organization. The tradition of "self-government" and local elections has always been just the other side of the process of power centralization in China. Guided local "participation" of the masses in social activities or public campaigns was merely a manifestation of the indispensable role of the government, the party-state, which had long cherished the ideal of the minimized "bureaucratic rule" (*guanzhi*) and the expanded people's power (*minzhi*). In Republican China, the need for the guidance of uneducated masses was a justification of the supreme role of the party as "a guarantor", educator, and mobilizer for a political action. The tutelage of the Kuomintang between 1928 and 1937 never left room for dissidents. The enlightening role of the CCP seems too important for China's global competition and strategic consistency, but to some extent it revitalizes Sun Yat-sen's principle of a managed and controlled "involvement of the public in political affairs" measured by the standard of common benefit, pre-set by the leaders of the party-state.

In today's China, human rights are often indistinguishable from "people's rights," where the notion of "people" may have a different connotation, certainly than the traditional individualistic preference of liberalism. For some it is comprised of a variety of social groups irrespective of their status and economic condition. Such a broad interpretation of the "people" bears resemblance with the "three people's principles" promoted by Sun Yat-sen who saw a distinction between "people" as an integrated entity, the "bureaucracy" (*guan*), and the individual. By some Chinese politicians, this might be helpful to interpret human rights as the rights of the people in the spirit of Jiang Zemin's "classless" "Three Represents Theory." For other (neo-socialist) politicians, the use of the "people" reminds of the "cultural revolution" practices, when "the people" was seen as an instrument to "mold" intellectuals and check the loyalty of state officials, in the interest of the majority and the party leadership.

Apparently, the appeal to "immortal values" might help the party to secure "cognitive infallibility" in the country that has always been invoked as a pillar of legitimization.[52] On the other hand, the restoration of state paternalism, public conformism, moral absolutism, and the edifying role of the party-state may reverse China from its current strategically important universalist claim to purify western values to one of excessive cultural relativism, which would impede its mission of "global constructivism." Direct appeal to public opinion on democratic grounds, widely promoted by the left wing in the party, may, if poorly managed, lead to people's protests against either capitalism or Party rule and cause instability, possibly leading to another authoritarian reaction. But if Beijing manages to tame the dragons and maintain the balance between global class struggle, harmonization, and western liberal humanism, it has the potential to become real norm-generating power.

Toward a New Universalism

With the rise of China as an increasingly normative voice in the discourse of human rights, the universalist/cultural relativism debate is shifting into one of relative universalisms. The resolution of this debate might finally reintegrate the fragmentation and incompetence of the current human rights regime.

In the 20th century, the original universal intent and aspiration of the Declaration of Human Rights propounded by the UN in 1948 was undermined by a Cold War bipolarity that divided humanity into first and second worlds with corresponding first and second generations of rights. So-called "first generation" civil and political rights were embraced and propounded by liberal capitalist democracies who drew on 18th century Enlightenment theories of Locke and Adam Smith, and put into practice by the American and French revolutions—which highlighted a rational, integral and self-interested individual as the basic unit of society. According to this theory, governments were then instituted solely to protect the self-evident and inalienable rights (life, liberty, and property, excuse me, "the pursuit of happiness") of these individuals from the depredations of others whose self-interest did not correspond to their own and especially of the government itself.

So-called "second generation" social economic and cultural rights emerged as a response to the inadequacies of the Enlightenment conception of humanity as atomized selfish self-propagators and the widespread social injustice wrought by its marriage with the productive capacity of the industrial revolution and abetted by corporate interests (constitutionally construed as bearing the same rights as individuals). According to this model, the narrow philosophical and institutional focus on the individual as the bearer of rights counter intuitively undermined the realization of rights for the majority of humanity. By contrast, proponents of the second generation model—especially Marx and his followers—claimed that human rights and dignity could only be realized in a social collective.

These ideological differences were institutionalized in the conceptual and framework of the of the International Bill of Rights. Though the General Assembly had declared in 1950 that "the enjoyment of civic and political freedoms and of economic, social and cultural rights are interconnected and interdependent," the integrity of the nascent rights regime was to be compromised by the political exigencies of an emerging postwar bipolarity. Within a year, despite the "Unity Resolution" put forward by the Soviet bloc, the mandate of the Human Rights Commission was redirected toward the creation of two distinct covenants. While differences of implementation and justiciability were factors in the decision, ideology and superpower politics also played a key role. The twin covenants, which should have been conjoined, were instead separated at birth and transformed into political currency.

Following the successful Communist revolution in 1949, China was often lumped in with the Soviet bloc in its predilection for social and economic rights over civic and political and continues to be criticized by the HRC and Western opinion on these grounds. Its unique culture and path of development, however, particularly the dramatic Sino-Soviet in the early 1960s and embrace of aspects of capitalism in the late 1970s, problematizes this facile characterization. China's later advocacy of the so-called Asian values debate threatened to undermine entirely the ideal of universalism and enshrine cultural sovereignty as a hedge against the effective implementation of a global rights regime.

The events of 1989 threw this distinction into sharper relief. The harsh crackdown on pro-democracy protesters at the Tiananmen Square only months before the successful democratic revolutions in Eastern Europe appeared to validate the West's negative preconceptions of the state of human rights in China. Unfortunately, it also obscured the larger story of the evolution of rights discourse in China and the potential role it might play in the reintegration of the generational divide. The end of the Cold war provided an historic opportunity to reconcile the cold war divisions that had crippled and distorted the human rights regime in both theory and practice since its inception. Unfortunately, any serious attempt to harmonize civil and political with economic, social and cultural rights; to reunite/conjoin the twins separated at birth and thus re-consecrate the original intent of the UDHR was confounded by the self-congratulatory rhetoric of the western liberal cohort, the triumphal march of global capital, and the two generations long institutionalization of the bipolar system.

Even the assertion of the Vienna Declaration at the 1993 World Conference on Human Rights that, "the universal nature of these rights and freedoms is beyond question" didn't manage to undo the fundamental bipolarity writ into the basic structures of international human rights law and administration, not to mention the fatal flaw of statist sovereignty and governance. Nor did it entirely put to bed the relativist "Asian values debate." The ambivalence of the concluding statement by the Chinese representative to the Vienna conference has been well parsed by Randall Peerenboom in his analytical review of Stephen Angle's book *Human Rights and Chinese Thought*. Min Wang summarizes it as: "On the one hand, there are some basic and universal elements in human rights. Assuming that the economic-social rights assertion, the cultural relativism, and the state sovereignty doctrine are all justified, the universal nature of core human rights elements still cannot be refuted."[53]

The universalist finesse is subtle, but China's official position that countries may have different concepts of human rights depending on their national characteristics does not necessarily imply a return to "Asian values" style relativism. On the contrary, it may well demonstrate an evolution in thinking that bodes well for the state of human rights globally.

China's current policies aimed at harmonization apparently coincide with the emergence of a discourse on so-called 3rd generation human rights. This is no coincidence, as China considered itself until recently—and not only for strategic reasons—as a developing country. As Min Wang outlined, from the perspective of the third world, modernism, while increasing the capacity of the realization of rights in the 1st and 2nd worlds, was a disaster, signifying slavery, colonialism, and a systemic pattern of exploitation and discrimination that continues to this day.[54] The articulation of claims to self-determination, environmental integrity and sustainable development, articulated at the Rio summit in 1992 and reiterated most recently at Copenhagen, is rooted in Article 28 of the UDHR, which asserts the right to "a social and international order in which the rights and freedoms set forth this Declaration can be fully realized."

Far from the subversive tone of the Asian values debate of the 1990s (subversive of universalist claims, that is) China's apparent current strategy, which we describe above as "organic mutual complimentary," seeks to redefine the meaning of universalism itself. Whereas the former debate sought a kind of Chinese exceptionalism to prevailing and ostensibly universal norms, the current strategy seeks to recenter universal human rights in Chinese terms. In many ways, China is the ideal actor and catalyst for such a project. It has a long history of absorbing and "sinicizing" foreign values, structures, institutions, and peoples and then successfully re-exporting them via a specifically Chinese form of social imperialism based on the overwhelming strength of culture and values, underwritten by the strategic use of economic co-dependency. Given the dismal failures and hypocrisies of the current rights regime, which never satisfactorily addressed the cold war schism, and continues to fail in its mission to alleviate human suffering and the global epidemic of war, torture, genocide—not to mention the systemic denial of basic healthcare, education and development—this might not be such a bad thing. Compared to the Western practice of ideological arrogance and gunboat diplomacy, the emerging Chinese model would seem a more appropriate vector for human rights. The equivocal failure of the human rights regime, sixty years after the bold assertion of its principles, to achieve much more than rhetorical or normative results, demands a reexamination and honest reappraisal of its premises and practice. The current Chinese experiment at the convergence of limited liberal economic values with collective rights and responsibilities and duties has promise, despite its many contradictions, fragilities and unintended consequences; to redefine Universal Human Rights, hopefully in a more substantive way than has been managed so far.

China has been and may be fairly accused of instrumentalizing this redefinition of universal human rights for reasons of the consolidation of political power and international legitimation. Jack Donnelly, for example, says that China has adopted the language of internationally recognized human rights "as an inescapable precondition to its full recognition as a great power."[55] But the adoption of the language of human rights also functions to legitimize state authority in the eyes of the world and its own citizens as well, building trust and community by speaking the established language of international law, even while shaping the and reframing its signification. China would not be the first state to strategically and selectively adopt human rights norms for instrumental reasons. Intervention in humanitarian missions, for example, is usually tied to the national interest, whether on a realist or cultural basis (US intervention in the Balkans, for example, but not Rwanda). From the Chinese perspective, the current human rights claims against it on behalf of Liu Xiaobo or others may legitimately be seen as part of a self-serving liberal offensive from the West, regardless of their legitimacy.

But even if the base motivation for adopting human rights norms is purely rhetorical or even cynical, their formal recognition can sometimes have a substantive effect despite the worst intentions of the framers. This was the result of the 1975 Helsinki Accords, for example, when the Soviet Union and its East Bloc client states cynically agreed to respect human rights in exchange for a recognition of Soviet sovereignty over Eastern Europe. While this was seen by dissidents and human rights activists at the time as another sell-out by the west of its ideals for real political gains, the ratification of basket three of the Helsinki Accords provided the legal opening and basis for Charter 77 and other dissident non-governmental human rights organizations that ultimately undermined the monopolistic control of the state in that region.

This process of socialization—that principled ideas become norms in the sense of collective understandings about appropriate behavior which can lead to changes in identities, interests and behavior[56]—applies both to states and individuals. Adherence to customary international norms of human rights is the clearest way states can demonstrate their legitimacy and become members of an international society. In the Chinese case, particularly given its self-conception as a great power and foundational civilization, policies in this area do not aim to simply satisfy western demands, but to effectively reshape the discourse. Human rights norms-making is part of China's global "charm offensive" aimed at the change of international norms, values, and rules favorable to national stability and economic prosperity. Thus, the norms, and the consideration of international prestige may be crucial for some behavioral patterns of the leaders. They want the others think well of them, and they want to feel well of themselves.

But socialization to human rights norms also functions at an individual level, which may present a threat to the legitimacy of the regime and to political order, as demonstrated in the case of Eastern Europe in 1989. Following the example of the dissident Charter 77 in Czechoslovakia, the Chinese Charter 08 has made its demands for democracy and freedom based on the state's endorsement of human rights claims, specifically the signing of the International Covenant on Civil and Political Rights in 1998. Whether or not Liu Xiaobo will one day emerge from prison to become president of China, as Vaclav Havel did in 1989 in Czechoslovakia, remains to be seen. Such an outcome depends on a convergence of several factors apparently missing in the Chinese case, but it does demonstrate the fine line that the Chinese authorities have to walk in taming the dragon of human rights discourse. Of course, the Czech Chartists suffered repression and reprisal for more than a decade before their claims bore fruit, so perhaps it is too soon to tell. Perhaps in the case of Liu Xiaobo, given the extraordinary efforts put into human rights initiatives and institutionalization in China, his crime was not so much the substance of his claims, but his usurpation of the state's role in making them. In this sense, perhaps the charge of "subversion of state power" is technically accurate.

Conclusions

The current Chinese orientation regarding human rights suggests two interpretations. A cynical take is that the regime is paying lip service to human rights to calm its western and domestic critics in order to defuse any threat to its political and economic legitimacy and nascent cultural hegemony. A more comprehensive reading is that the rhetorical and institutional gestures of the past few years toward greater awareness, respect, and institutionalization of human rights are integral to the Chinese vision of a harmonious global society.

Moreover, if this strategy is effective, it could signal a substantive improvement in the integrity of the global human rights regime, which has been compromised since its inception by the ideological divide of the Cold War and the vested interest of state sovereignty.

The evolution of Beijing's policy orientation toward human rights has signified a tectonic change in China's political life, both domestically and internationally. Throughout the reform years, China has emerged as a prospective "normative power" capable of generating a new set of values, norms and regulations for the international community. While adapting certain measures of international human rights norms, Beijing seeks to justify its own interpretation of the principles of human rights through the creation of a new set of norms which does not simply mirror or reiterate broadly adopted human rights standards, but reinterprets, "purifies," and sinicizes these standards by construing a "human-centered" approach based on a specific understanding of individual human rights as part of the collective human rights of each nation. Rather than haggling over interpretations and implementations of specific *rights*, in other words, it has recast the entire debate by reinterpreting the meaning of *human*.

The incorporation of human rights discourse into the larger project for sustainable development, social harmony and soft power has transformative potential both for China and for the meaning of human rights itself. The endgame of China's engagement is unclear, but it has clearly assembled the conceptual, legal, and infrastructural mechanisms for a fundamental recalculation of the global human rights regime. While many may legitimately fear that China's growing hegemony in the field of human rights could bode ill for individual victims of the Chinese regime—be they religious or ethnic minorities that trouble the ideal *organic mutual complimentarity*, or too rash and ambitious rights avant-gardists like Liu Xiaobo, the larger project has the potential at least to reboot the tragic mesalliance of the rhetoric and reality (or theory and practice) of human rights and truly create a harmonious world. It may seem contradictory that one of the worst offenders of fundamental human rights (currently construed) might also be its salvation, but the Chinese experience consistently illustrates the dialectical nature of change and progress. The incontrovertible success of the Chinese model of authoritarian capitalism, for example, has also produced contradictions and social pressure on the very system that inculcated it: a rising middle class whose prosperity inevitably breeds a desire for political sovereignty, and an increasing income and opportunity gap and emerging class tension. Given these stresses and threats, the current evolution of human rights discourse and institutionalization in China may be cynically read as an attempt to downplay the more liberal (civil political) aspects of universal rights in favor of a return—both ideological and historical-to the social and cultural aspects. But it could also be that they are right—the western dominated rights regime certainly has precious little to show for its 60 year reign—and that they will manage to reintegrate the seemingly contradictory, but essentially integral aspects of social, economic, civil, political, cultural and environmental rights into a coherent and justiciable regime. Maybe someday there will even be a resurgent "western values" debate reiterating western values and contesting the universalist claims of a human rights discourse framed by Chinese values of sustainable development, social harmony, and soft power.

Notes

1."Verdict against Liu Xiaobo," Beijing Municipality First Intermediate People's Court, Verdicts in Criminal Cases (2009), First Intermediate Court, No. 3901, http://www.hrichina.org/public/contents/press?revision%5fid=173860&item%5fid=172713 (accessed December 19, 2010).

2. Ibid.

3. Associated Press, "China denounces Nobel prize supporters as clowns," December 7, 2010, http://abcnews.go.com/International/wireStory?id=12330143 (accessed December 20, 2010).

4. United Nations, "UN Human Rights Chief Deeply Concerned by Extremely Harsh Sentencing of Liu Xiaobo," press release, December 25, 2009, http://www.unhchr.ch/huricane/huricane.nsf/view01/51E11DED60ED6C7EC125769A00384ED3?opendocument (accessed December 20, 2010).

5. Richard Spencer, "Hillary Clinton: Chinese Human Rights Secondary to Economic Survival," *The Telegraph*, February 20, 2009, http://www.telegraph.co.uk/ (accessed December 20, 2010).

6. State Department, U.S., 2009 *Country Reports on Human Rights Practices*, March 11, 2010, http://www.state.gov/g/drl/rls/hrrpt/2009/eap/135989.htm (accessed December 20, 2010).

7. Yang Jiechi, "Although Differences Exist, China Is Willing to Conduct the Dialogues with the U.S. to Push Forward the Human Rights Situation on the Premise of Mutual Respect and Noninterference in Each Other's Internal Affairs," Chinese Foreign Minister Yang Jiechi cited in "Clinton: Chinese Ruman Rights Can't Interfere with Other Crises," *CNN*, February 21, 2009, http://articles.cnn.com/ (accessed December 20, 2010).

8.Vaclav Havel, "The Power of the Powerless," http://www.vaclavhavel.cz/ (accessed December 20, 2010).

9. To paraphrase Kerry Brown, "China and Liu Xiaobo: the Weakness of Strength," *Open Democracy*, October 11, 2010, http://www.opendemocracy.net/kerry-brown/china-and-liu-xiaobo-weakness-of-strength (accessed December 20, 2010).

10. Yu Shilin, "On the Legal Relationship between 'State's Respect' and 'State's Protection' of Human Rights" (Guojia zunzhung he baozhang renquan'zhi falüguanxijiedu), *Faxue zazhi (Journal of Legal Studies)* 6 (2007), 30; Wang Shoulin and Zhang Meiping, "On the CCP's Perception of Human Rights" (Lun zhongguo gongchandang de renquanguan) *Dangdai Makesizhuyi yanjiu* (*Contemporary Marxist Studies*) 5 (2007): 12–14.

11. *Jiang zemin wenxuan* (Selected Works of Jiang Zemin) (Beijing: Renmin chubanshe, 2006), vol. 2, 56.

12. Luo Haocai, "The Chinese Model of Human Rights Protection," Lecture at Vrije University Brussels, Belgium, September 21, 2009. *Human Rights*, Beijing, no. 1 (January 2010), 6; Ming Wan, "Human Rights Lawmaking in China: Domestic Politics, International Law, and International Politics," *Human Rights Quarterly* 29 (2007), 729; 730–32. Based on the official data from the Office of the High Commissioner for Human Rights (http://ohchr.org/english.law) and the Chinese Foreign Ministry, Ming Wan pro-

vides a comprehensive list illustrating the process of China's engagement in the system of international human rights regulations.

13. See Yu Shilin, *op. cit.*, 28–29.

14. The *People's Daily*, for example, reported that, by April 2004, there were 451 laws adopted by the NPC, and the State Council issued 966 regulations, and local authorities made over 8,000 regulations on the human rights issues. *People's Daily* (Chinese edition), April 1, 2004.

15. Information Office of the State Council, P.R.C., "National Human Rights Action Plan of China (2009–2010)," http://news.xinhuanet.com/ (accessed December 20, 2010).

16. Rosemary Foot, *Rights beyond Borders: the Global Community and the Struggle over Human Rights in China* (Oxford: Oxford University Press: 2000), 256; see also: Thomas Risse, Stephen C. Ropp, and Kathryn Sikkink, *The Power of Human Rights: International Norms and Domestic Change* (Cambridge: Cambridge University Press, 1999): 11–17; 20. On the normative function of human rights legal frameworks, see also Daniel Thomas, *The Helsinki Effect* (Princeton: Princeton University Press, 2001).

17. The idea of "civilizational change" was originally proposed by Deng Xiaoping who in 1980 envisaged many cultural and political challenges that China would face as the country develops its market economy. Jiang Zemin's "Three Represents" referred to the party's representation of the development trend of advanced productive forces, the orientation of advanced culture and the fundamental interests of the overwhelming majority of the people in China. See, for example, "The Three Represents Theory," June 25, 2001, http://news.xinhuanet.com/english/20010625/422678.htm (accessed December 20, 2010).

18. The strategy "Observe calmly; secure our position; cope with affairs calmly; hide our capacities and bide our time; be good at maintaining a low profile; and never claim leadership" was aimed at securing favorable environment for Chinese reforms. See a detailed survey: *Taoguang yangmei, yousuo zuowei—Deng Xiaopingwaijiao sixiang jian yi* (Observe calmly, secure our position, have something to do—the general meaning of Deng Xiaoping's foreign policy thought), *Guangmin Daily*, August, 9, 2004, http://news.xinhuanet.com/world/2004-08/09/content_1741467_2.htm (accessed December 20, 2010).

19. See Tang Shiping, "Zailun zhongguo de dazhanlue [Re-examining China's Grand Strategy]," *Strategy and Management*, no. 4 (2001): 31–32; "On China's Strategic Perception and the New Global Order" in *Guojianzhongguo da zhanlue de kuangjia: guojia shili zhanlue guannian yu guoji zhidu* [The Framework for Shaping China's Grand Strategy: Strategic Perception of State Power and International Order] (Beijing: Beijing University Publishing House: 2005).

20. Zheng Bijian, "China's 'Peaceful Rise' to Great-Power Status," *Foreign Affairs* 84, no. 5 (Sep/Oct 2005), 18.

21. "China's Rise Will Be Peaceful," Interview with Zheng Bijian, *New Perspectives Quarterly* (Winter 2006): 50–51.

22. Aaron L. Friedberg, "Are We Ready for China?" *Commentary* 124, no. 3 (Oct. 2007), 39.

23. Tang Shiping, ibid.

24. Peng Peng, ed. *Heping Jueqilun: shongguo congsu daguo zhilu* [The Theory of "Peaceful Rise:" China Re-formulates its Great Power Program], (Guangzhou People's Publishing House, 2005).

25. Yuan Xingpei, "The Historical Revelations from the Chinese Civilization," *Beijing Forum Newsletter* 2, no. 2 (October 2006), 32.

26. Ming Wan, *op. cit.*, 728.

27. Randall Peerenboom maintains that China presents a normative challenge to the human rights regime. China is likely to take advantage of its growing economic and geopolitical influence to defend and advocate rights policies and normative vision of the world at odds with current rights policies based on secular liberalism even in the face of Western opposition. See: Randall Peerenboom, "Assessing Human Rights in China: Why the Double Standard?"*Cornell International Law Journal* 38 (2005): 71–172.

28. John G. Ikenberry, "The Rise of China and the Future of the West. Can the Liberal System Survive?" *Foreign Affairs* (January/February 2008).

29. "Action Plan to Promote All-Round Progress in China's Human Rights Cause. An Interview with Wang Chen, Director of the State Council Information Office," *Human Rights* (Beijing), no. 4 (July 2009), 2.

30. In the Chinese context, GONGO (government organized non-governmental organizations) is perhaps a more appropriate term.

31. On the role and functions of China Society for Human Rights Studies, see more details at its official web-site http://www.humanrights.cn/cn/zt/qita/zgrqyjh/index.htm. The partners of this Society include, for example, such prestigious organizations as the Institute of Human Rights and Humanitarian Law of China Politics and Law University, Research Center for Human Rights and Humanitarian Law at Beijing University Law School, Human Rights Study Center at Guangzhou University, and the like.

32. Wang Qiyan and Jiang Zhiqiang, "China's Human Rights Cause and Non-Governmental Organizations," *Human Rights* (Beijing), no. 6 (November 2009), 15.

33. Ibid, 18.

34. "National Human Rights Action Plan of China (2009–2010)," The Information Office of the State Council, April 13, 2009, *Human Rights*, no. 3 (May 2009): 5–20.

35. Ibid, 5.

36. Ibid, 5. Wang Shoulin and Zhang Meiping, *op. cit.*, 12.

37. Dorothy Solinger, "Urban Entrepreneurs and the State: The Merger of State and Society", in *State and Society in China: The Consequences of Reform*, ed. by Arthur Lewis Rosenbaum (Boulder: Westview Press, 1992). David Yang Da-hua contends that with very few exceptions, "Chinese civic organizations remain closely linked to the state" and "their general lack of autonomy apparently renders them ineffective as counterweights to state power." David Yang Da-hua, "Civil Society as an Analytic Lens for Contemporary China," *China: an International Journal* 2, no. 1 (March 2004), 3.

38. Luo Haocai, *op. cit.*, 6. To define the contours of state's interference into the sphere of human rights, the idea of "positive" and "negative" aspects of freedom in the concept of human rights has been developed by many Chinese experts into the concept of the indispensable role of the state in safeguarding human rights in the era of the "welfare state." (See in details Yu Shilin, "On the Legal Relationship between "state's respect of human rights" and "state's protection of human rights," *Legal Studies*, Beijing 6 (2007), 31.

39. Luo Haocai, *op. cit.*, 7.

40. State Council, P.R.C., "Regulations of the People's Republic of China on Open Government Information," effective May 1, 2008, Order of the State Council No. 492, http://www.greenlaw.org.cn/files/laws/State%20Council%20Information%20Disclosure %20Regs.pdf (accessed December 20, 2010).

41. "National Human Rights Action Plan of China," 14.

42. See, for example, "The red and the black," *The Economist* 392, 8651 (October 3, 2009): 28-30; Ting Gong, "Corruption and Local Governance: the Double Identity of Chinese Local Governments in Market Reform," *The Pacific Review* 19, no. 1 (March 2006), 85-102; on anti-corruption work and the operational secrecy in the Discipline

Inspection Commission see: Jeffrey Becker, "Tackling Corruption at its Source: The National Corruption Prevention Bureau," *Journal of Chinese Political Science* 13, no. 3 (2008): 287–303.

43. Sylvia Chan demonstrated that Villagers' Representative Assemblies failed to check and balance the role of local executive agencies and appeared to be "undemocratically constituted" and subservient to village branches of the CCP and Villagers' Committees. See Sylvia Chan, "Villagers' Representative Assemblies: Towards Democracy or Centralism?" *China: An International Journal* 1, no. 2 (September 2003):179–199.

44. "National Human Rights Action Plan of China," 14.

45. Luo Haocai, *op. cit.*, 8.

46. Substantial changes occurred in the legal sphere to secure the functioning of the judicial branch of government and a more open and independent court procedure. Xiong Qiuhong describes the process in his article: "Running China in Accordance with the Law" Ensures Development of Human Rights," *Human Rights* (Beijing), no. 1 (January 2010): 26–28.

47. Luo Haocai, *op. cit.*, 9.

48. For example, Luigi Tomba contends that the Chinese middle class appears as the most desirable type of subject for an authoritarian state: politically docile, but willing to participate in an ethical and moral community in the name of social stability, consumer rights, and virtuesLuigi Tomba, "Of Quality, Harmony, and Community: Civilization and the Middle Class in Urban China," *Positions* 17, no. 3 (Winter 2009), 591.

49. Wen Jiabao, "Our Historical Tasks at the Primary Stage of Socialism and Several Issues Concerning China's Foreign Policy" *China Daily*, March 4, 2007.

50. Yuan Xingpei, *op. cit.*, 23–32.

51. Stephen C. Angle, "Human Rights and Harmony," *Human Rights Quarterly* 30 (2008): 76–94.

52. David Yang Da-hua, *op. cit.*, 25–26.

53. Min Wang, *op. cit.*, 148.

54. Ibid.

55. Randall Peerenboom, "Human Rights, China and Cross-Cultural Inquiry: Philosophy, History and Power Politics," UCLA School of Law Research Paper No. 04–4: 289. *Philosophy East & West* 55 (2005); see also the Social Science Research Network Electronic Paper Collection: http://ssrn.com/abstract=506382 (accessed December 20, 2010).

56. James F. Barnes, Marshall Carter and Max J. Skidmore, *The World of Politics: A Concise Introduction* (New York: Palgrave Macmillan: 1980), 35.

Chapter 7
China's Religious Policies in the Post-Mao Period: Co-existence of Atheists and Theists

Yiran Zhou

Chinese religions have witnessed a momentous revival in the last three decades since China's reform and opening in 1978. The number of clerics, faith believers, and religious sites has increased astonishingly. Buddhist temples and Taoist monasteries teem with worshippers and pilgrims, Buddhist academies are being restored, and popular religions in rural areas are coming alive.[1] Tibetan Buddhism and Islam have been flourishing in the western part of China. Christianity has been expanding in a way that is "more vigorous than at the height of Jesuit influence in the seventeenth century, or during the Protestant evangelization in the 1920s."[2] China's official figure put the number of religious followers at 100 million while scholars inferred through surveys that China has at least 300 million religious followers.[3] The faith plurality and the flourishing religious activities in contemporary China demonstrate the people's inner desire for spiritual fulfillment in a modernized society.

Despite the reality of religious renaissance in China, the relations between the state and religion are still a controversial topic discussed heatedly in scholarly studies. Scholars in the West largely remain suspicious of China's religious policies, arguing that the Chinese Communist Party (CCP) never changed its policy in the "fight to maintain control over the rapidly expanding religious activities."[4] Anthony Yu concluded in his *State and Religion in China*, "The People's Republic . . . is using [political] religion to police religion."[5] H. H. Lai wrote, "The state has indeed developed relatively effective strategies and tools for differentiated management control of mushrooming social groups . . . . Religious groups and their agents are co-opted, deterred, restricted, or suppressed, depending on their potential political threat as measured by their ideological assertiveness and, especially, their organizational strength, independence and readiness to challenge the state."[6] By means of textual analysis of law documents on religion, Sister Beatrice Leung observed that laws and regulations have turned into the tools of the CCP to maintain its governance and control over religious matters. Most Western scholars share a theoretical presupposition regarding religious idealism and communist materialism—that is, they are in an irreconcilable and life-or-death conflict and cannot co-exist on good terms with each other.

However, religious studies within China—flourishing along with religious revival and becoming less ideological and more academic-oriented[7]—hold different views from western mainstream thoughts. Scholars maintain that religions are developing in the process of mutual interaction and adaptation with the state; therefore, mutual accommodative religion-state relations corresponding to China's actual situation are taking shape. Mr. Zhuo Xinping, a leading scholar on Chinese religious science, contends that contemporary Chinese religion has entered an era of pluralistic development and that mutual interaction represents the relations of religion and state, which are intricately interwoven with each other.[8] Another noted scholar, Zhu Xiping, wrote, "Because of the profound changes in the social system and in religion itself, it is now possible for religion, influenced by patriotism and socialist ideology, to be in harmony with socialist society and to contribute to society."[9] Still, a Chinese researcher observed that "mutuality between religion and socialist society is affirmed as long as religion is not an expression of class conflicts or of anti-Party."[10] Chinese scholars' viewpoints are based on the proposition that Chinese socialism is changing internally with an input of capitalist market economic behaviors; and that a pragmatic party-state would acknowledge religions as part of its United Front policy for uniting theists and atheists together to achieve its supreme goal of building a modern socialist state. At the same time, religions would accommodate the updated state regime to ensure their existence and development while this opportunity exists.

This controversy in the evaluation of Chinese religions is by far most intensive between the political arenas of China and western nations, the U.S. in particular. In the two yearly reports released by the U.S. government—*The Country Reports on Human Rights Practices* and *International Religious Freedom Report*—Chinese religious issues were always a topic tensely scrutinized and heavily criticized.[11] An illustration of this was found in the 2008 country report: "The government tried to control and regulate religious groups, particularly unregistered groups, and repression and harassment of unregistered religious groups intensified in the run-up to the Olympics," and "The government's repression of religious freedom intensified in Tibetan areas and in the XUAR [Xinjiang Uyghur Autonomous Region]." As a counteraction against U.S. criticism, China has issued its own yearly report for ten straight years on American problems in human rights. The wording in the reports were no less stern and severe than the U.S. used in its reports, as shown in the *Human Rights Record of United States in 2008*: "The U.S. practice of throwing stones at others while living in a glass house is a testimony to the double standards and hypocrisy of the U.S. in dealing with human rights issues and has undermined its international image."[12] In the last two decades, China has also published a number of white papers regarding China's freedom of religious belief and human rights, promoting their achievements in religious freedom in order to offset negative influences of opinionated Western reports. This cycle of verbal exchanges and counteractions has not shown any sign of abating.

In addition, the assertiveness of both the Chinese camp and Western camp in defending their claims regarding Chinese religions seems to make their controversy irreconcilable while putting one at a loss over how to view contemporary Chinese religions. To gain an insight into the relations of Chinese state and religion, several questions need to be addressed: What are the root causes that divided the two camps and shaped their opposing views? What is really happening in China regarding religions and religious affairs? Moreover, how did Chinese regime of managing religions evolve in recent decades, and how would it possibly continue to evolve in the future? To accomplish these tasks, this chapter starts with an analysis of the core reasons behind the divergence of Chinese and western understandings of Chinese religions. It then explores how the state and religion interact in contemporary China by discussing the evolution of China's religious policies in post-Mao period—phased in three eras of the Party leadership with Deng Xiaoping, Jiang Zemin, and Hu Jintao successively at its core. Finally, this chapter forecasts the specific policies that the state would likely adopt, through an examination of the characters of five government sanctioned religions and their levels of adaptability to the state (Buddhism, Taoism, Islam, Protestantism and Catholicism). My conclusion is that the mainstream trend of the state-and-religion relations would be mutual adaptation and accommodation, in a setting where the Party being more pragmatic, people's beliefs being plural, and China's integration with the world community growing closer. In the meanwhile, conflicts between the state and religion would emerge sporadically due to an enduring existence of incompatibilities between communist ideology and religious faiths.

Root Causes of Different Understandings of Religions by Westerners and Chinese

While referring to contemporary Chinese religions, people often focus on the clash of religious ideologies and Marxist doctrines propagated nationwide by the CCP. However, in a country with a 5,000-year history of civilization and rich cultural diversity, an exploration of the truth regarding Chinese religions—short of historical and cultural inputs—would be incomplete and unreasonable. When it comes to the comparison of Chinese and western religions, a common error with western scholars is that they impose their understandings and judgments of religions, based on western cultural values, on Chinese religiosities in a cultural setting different from theirs. As a noted scholar on Chinese religions Jordan Paper observed, "Until recently, the tendency in Western studies has been to force Western assumptions and categories on non-Western traditions and artificially create religions that do not exist in actuality . . . ." It is encouraging that there are intellectuals who have begun to take on a comparative approach which explores Chinese and western religions and their relations with states by putting them in a web woven with history, culture, and politics.[13] Without resorting to a comparative approach to the distinctive contexts in which Western and Chinese religions have been evolving, the tightly-knotted controversy in this area between both sides could not be disentangled. The subsequent part of this section serves as a summary of the results of this approach, which is also a revelation of the deep-rooted causes for different understandings of religions by westerners and Chinese.

Etymological Connotation of Religion

The word religion in English, originated from Latin *religio*, is defined in Merriam-Webster's Online Dictionary as "the service and worship of God or the supernatural," and "commitment or devotion to religious faith or observance." In a sense, the definition reveals that religions in the western concept involve believers in the worship of supernatural, and always monotheistic, divinity. For an exhaustive explanation of "religion", the definition given by Clifford Geertz is popularly recognized as comprehensive: "a *religion* is a system of symbols which acts to establish powerful, pervasive, and long-lasting moods and motivations in men by formulating conceptions of a general order of existence and clothing these conceptions with such an aura of factuality that the moods and motivations seem uniquely realistic."[14] Another aspect of the western understanding of religions manifested itself as "a structured system of beliefs and practices, separate from society."[15]

In the Chinese concept, religions were thought to be exported from abroad; and there is no religion in a western sense that gave birth.[16] Even in traditional Chinese, there is no "linguistic equivalent to the word religion." *Zongjiao*, the modern Chinese term for religion, contains a broader and more complicated connotation than the western concept of religions. Nominally, the graph *zong* means "ancestor, ancestral lineage, and ancestral temple itself,"[17] while "the semantic field of the singular *jiao* itself in classical Chinese texts seems to combine the transmission of knowledge with authoritative instruction, in such a way that both content and action of the process are expected to modify affective orientation and behavior."[18] Therefore, Chinese religiosity is characterized by diversification that displays itself in such religious behavior as "the state, clan, and family sacrificial complex, of well over four millennia in age."[19] And the core of this religiosity is reflected in the reverence and worship of ancestors and saints, as in the cases of Confucianism in honor of Confucius and Taoism in honor of Lao Zi. These "gods" being worshipped are real human beings rather than supernatural deities living in people's mind, as with western religions.

Relations of State and Religions in History

The relations between state and religion in Western world and China evolved on different tracks. In early European history religions and political rulers went through incessant conflicts and tensions in struggling for political ascendency, finally forged the balance in the form of mutual reliance and mutual support for a common development. As Jordan Paper generalized, "Christianity, in its embryonic development, was conscious of its opposition to the state, but after Constantine it became increasingly identical with the state . . . a separation of Church and state became normative to many but not all Western European and North American countries."[20] Throughout history, religions have been playing an influential role in Western states in terms of both political and social lives. It was often so that religious power accorded state power of supreme governance while state power offered protection for religious power. An illustration of this was in Medieval Europe where emperors were coroneted by the Pope for their enthronization while elections of the Pope were ratified by emperors (sometimes, religious clergy took official state positions, directly engaging in politics). And religious influence in contemporary western politics and society was prevalent, as was shown by American elected presidents' swearing on a Bible and taking oaths in front of their pastors. So it could be said that the history of the interaction of state and religion constitutes a major part of the Western history; and the essence of their finally formulated relations is one of mutual-support (even in some historical periods, religious forces controlled secular governments and acted as real monarchs).

In ancient China, with more than 2,000 years of feudal system (beginning in 221 B.C. when Qing dynasty was founded, till 1911 when the last emperor of Qing dynasty was dismissed from the throne), such orthodox religious traditions—ancestor worship, state sacrifices to heavenly God (and a variety of Gods of natural phenomena), and Confucianism—were all tools utilized by imperial states to maintain their unchallenged governance, either in the way of enhancing the mindset of revering ancestors and patriarchs or deifying descending royal power. With regard to the implication that ancestor worship represented a patriarchal system, Anthony Yu observed, "By his own submission to his designated ancestors, in principle regarded as all inclusive, the emperor would at the same time acquire absolute power over all his subjects."[21] Furthering the analysis of the nuanced interaction between the imperial state and religions, a Chinese scholar maintained:

> The successive rulers in China all regarded their power as having been authorized by the gods, held that they had orders from Heaven and were sons of Heaven, and claimed their powers were superior to the power of the gods. Thus, they took advantage of the role of religion and, at the same time, kept a certain distance from religion, adopting the policy of inclusion and tolerance towards all religions.[22]

This explanation hinted at the root cause for Chinese rulers to borrow religious elements to strengthen the "divine rights of king (*junquan shenshou*)," while preventing religious extension from threatening their royal powers. This relationship between state and religion was affirmed by Confucius in the *Analects* (recording Confucius' lectures and conversations), "respect the gods and immortals, but keep one's distance from them (*jingguishen eryuanzi*)." Subjected to the harnessing by the state, religions in China were put in a disadvantaged place, often times perceived heterodox phenomena, especially reminiscent of the movement of suppressing Buddhism in the mid-eighth century and the status of Islam and Christianity traditionally perceived seditious heterodox outside of Chinese normal life.

Christianity vs. Confucianism

Christianity and Confucianism, two mainstream religious cultures prevalent respectively in Western and Chinese societies, differ in the social and cultural contexts in which they came into being. Christianity spread rapidly in the Roman Empire at a time when its primitive religions and heterodox philosophies (either decadent Epicureanism or rigorous Stoicism) has been unable to offer exalted moral principles and spiritual forces strong enough to bring together various ethnic groups in the large territory of the Empire. And Christianity—owing to its preaching of such virtues as equality, philanthropy, and abstention—emerged among Romans. Roman rulers, in the fourth century, assigned Christianity the status of state religion as an effective tool to strengthen its power; and in later centuries, with the support of European secular governments, Christianity gradually developed into a popular religious faith followed by the majority of westerners. In this process, Western governments and Christianity formed into their mutual-supportive relationship. Rather than the governments taking control of Christianity, they sometimes held an attitude of awe and respect in view of its popularity in society.

Different from Christianity's status in western society, no Chinese religion was ever mainstreamed by feudal rulers into an ideological tool, let alone elevated to the position of state religion. Traditionally, Confucianism as an ideology had been holding a predominant place in Chinese political and social cultures, since the 2nd century BC when a Han dynasty emperor adopted the policy of putting Confucianism in shrine while removing all other ideologies. The core ideas of "five relations" and "five cardinal values"[23]—supported by all subsequent imperial rulers as a useful spiritual tool in maintaining their ruling—constituted as Chinese essential life values and basic framework of social relations. Confucian values contained elements that constrained religious development, as McInnis analyzed: "Because of the contradiction between the patriarchal social system and the Confucius emphasis on ethics and moral principles and the religious idea of worshipping supernatural powers, the orthodox Confucian had to suppress the social functions of religion."[24] While attacking religions, Confucianism also absorbed Buddhist and Taoist elements and evolved into an identity with a combination of religion and ideology. And Confucianism's powerful influence among Chinese was a major factor in leaving religions in a disadvantaged place. The majority of Chinese people were non-religious laymen, who viewed religions as something out of normal life and only occasionally used them when they needed spiritual consolation.

The above comparative analysis of religions in the West and China proved that they evolved in different manners: Christianity held an important role in terms of its leverage on western politics and society and culture; while in China, religions were historically held in a limited space with Confucianism as a dominant ideology in the country. This detailed analysis will help in understanding contemporary China's religious policy that will be discussed below, from historical and cultural perspectives. It should be no surprise that, looking at the religious policy in the Post-Mao period, religious status under the communist regime shared similarities with its past experiences in imperial history. As a recent book, *Making Religion, Making the State*, remarked, "The congruence between Communist and Confucian hostilities to the religion and their capacity to influence state policy is not haphazard coincidence, of course."[25]

An Analysis of Religious Policies in Post-Mao Eras

Before exploring Post-Mao religious policies, there is a need to briefly review Mao's policy regarding religions, which left an ideological impact on today's religious regime in China. In the early years of the PRC (1949–1958), Chairman Mao and his comrades—with the realistic purpose of uniting various sectors of people to rejuvenate a country having gone through years of warfare (anti-Japanese and civil wars)—formed their religious policy. A corporatist United Front was established with various official sanctioned religious leaders at its core. Recognizing the reality of religion's existence, they created the theory of "five characteristics of religions," which recognizes that religions are "mass-based, complex, long-lasting in character, ethnic and international."[26] This theory constituted a cornerstone with which the Party state made their religious policies over the course of various periods. Other evidence showing Mao's accommodation of religions was Article Five of the "Common Program"—a temporary constitution of the PRC from 1949 to 1954—which clearly stated the people's right to freely practice their religious beliefs.

Religious activities during the first decade of the PRC were mainstreamed with self-independence, patriotism, anti-imperialism and anti-feudalism. Guided by the government, various religions carried out their patriotic and democratic reforms: the Protestant Church launched Three-self (self-government, self-support, and self-propagation) program, aiming to replace the control of foreign missions over Chinese religious affairs; the Catholic Church took on anti-imperialist patriotic movement, cutting ties with the Vatican. Various Buddhist and Taoist and Islamic groups in China waged a democratic campaign to get rid of feudal elements and the system of oppression and exploitation in these religions.[27] In this period, the state's policy of cooperation and reform of religions won the full support of the so-called patriotic religious groups. And the concerted interaction between the religious circle and the government facilitated the continuance of religious activities within the new-born communist regime.

Since 1958, when the country became immersed in waves of leftist movements that culminated in the Cultural Revolution (1966–1976), religions sunk to its lowest valley, in a suffering situation. As a Hong Kong scholar Beatrice Leung described,

> Religious life in China was dismantled in the 1960s. Religious discipline was ridiculed, church/temple property was confiscated, church education and service institutes (orphanage, school and medical service) were nationalized, foreign missionaries were expelled, places of worship (churches, mosques and temples) were closed, religious houses (monasteries, convents, and seminaries) were disbanded.[28]

Deng Xiaoping's Era (1979–1989) and the No. 19 Document

With the end of the Cultural Revolution in 1976, China ushered in an era of reform and open-door—the new policy initiated by Deng Xiaoping, successor to Chairman Mao. Deng focused on developing economy and pushed aggressively on China's development and modernization. He gradually replaced Mao's revolutionary ideologies with pragmatism. In a Deng-led movement called "Setting Wrong Things to Right"—so named because the new leader was correcting Mao's leftist policies and actions—Chinese society was brought back to its normalcy. Against this backdrop, the religious policy in the early period of the PRC was restored, religious sites reopened to the public, and official religious associations resumed their work.[29]

Deng's religious policy was written into the "The Basic Viewpoint and Policy on the Religious Affairs during the Socialist Period of Our Country," referred to as the No. 19 Document, issued by the CCP Central Committee and the State Council in 1982. This important document laid the groundwork for subsequent improvement in the new religious policy. The core idea regarding the freedom of religious belief under the regulation and management of the Party government has since remained unchanged. The Document, which reviewed the CCP's lessons and experiences in dealing with religions from the 1950s to 1960s—stressed that "the basic policy the Party has adopted toward the religious question is that of respect for and protection of the freedom of religious belief," and "this is a long-term policy, one which must be continually carried out until that future time when religion will itself disappear."[30] The Document explicitly stated that "under socialism, the only correct fundamental way to solve the religious question lies precisely in safeguarding the freedom of religious belief."[31] This in fact was a reaffirmation of an earlier policy adopted in the 1950s wherein there was a total denial of Mao's persecution of religions, broadly interpreted as feudal superstition and spiritual opium. The purpose of this policy was to reestablish a United Front that would incorporate religious believers in the cause of socialist construction. Their manifesto insisted that it was crucial "to unite the mass of believers and non-believers and enable them to center all their will and strength on the common goal of building a modernized, powerful socialist state."[32]

The Document detailed how to understand religious freedom. The Document's connotation was defined as follows: "every citizen has the freedom to believe in religion and also the freedom not to believe in religion," and ". . . the freedom to believe in this religion or that religion," ". . . the freedom to believe in this sect or that sect." One central point of the policy is "to make the question of religious belief a private matter, one of individual free choice for citizens," a point that could never be imagined to exist under Mao's leadership.

Regarding the relations between religions and the state, the Document clearly pointed out that political power could not "be used to promote any one religion, nor can it be used to forbid any one religion," and that "religion will not be permitted to meddle in the administrative or juridical affairs of state, nor to intervene in the schools or public education which have been abolished or to return to an exploitative and oppressive religious system. The Document underscored that religions would not "be permitted to make use in any way of religious pretexts to oppose the Party's leadership or the socialist system, or to destroy national or ethnic unity."[33] The policy provided that no CCP members are allowed to believe in any religion. The Document further cited that religions cannot force people to convert, nor "propagate or preach religion outside places designated for religious services."[34] Per the text, all religious activities were subject to the administration of the Bureau of Religious Affairs (BRA) at various governmental levels, in order to guarantee that religions did not operate across the political line set up by the Party, thereby preventing the infiltration of "hostile religious forces from abroad" and "destructive espionage" in the process of religious exchanges with foreign countries.[35]

While stressing the Party's leadership in managing religious affairs, the Document actively called upon Party cadres and officials to redress the injustices against religious personnel during the Cultural Revolution. The Document stated that it was necessary to "win over, unite and educate religious professionals," to help religious organizations restore their religious sites and train young religious personnel who "fervently love their homeland and support the Party's leadership and the socialist system and who possess sufficient religious knowledge.[36] Religious organizations were encouraged to build and develop friendly relations with foreign religious groups while putting efforts in training talented religious personnel adept in foreign exchanges.[37]

Seen from the No. 19 Document—which was in line with Deng's pragmatic thoughts—it affirmed the imperative of communists and religious believers cooperating with each other to build the country. This thought was evident in the narration of the Document wherein it was written that ". . . in terms of political action, Marxists and patriotic believers can, indeed must, form a united front in the common effort for socialist modernization."[38]

The Document contained a few ambiguous points, such as how to differentiate normal versus criminal religious activities, and the issue of religions versus superstitions. These ambiguities resulted in local officials confusing legal religious activities with crimes or feudal superstitions, causing them to infringe upon legal religious rights and leading them to commit religious persecution in extreme cases.

With the propagation across the nation of Deng's new policy of religious tolerance, China witnessed a period of religious revival. Although there were no official statistical records depicting Chinese religious status in the 1980s, bits of information sourced from academic literature offered a glimpse of the religious momentum during that period. Catholics, estimated at three million in 1949, reached ten million by late 1980s. A conservative estimate put the number of Protestants at six million compared to around one million in 1949.[39] In the late 1940s, there were roughly 4.6 million minority Buddhists (worshipping Tibetan and Pali branches of Buddhism); by 1991, that number increased to 9.1 million according to a National Minority Census.[40]

The revival of religions, thanks to the relaxation of the religious policy, paralleled Chinese "faith crisis" under during this period. The rapid development of the market economy whipped up economic consumerism and money worship, while the communist rhetoric peaking in Mao's period gradually lost its ideological appeal to the common people, even some CCP members. Along with the abating influence of Communism throughout the country, China was left in a spiritual vacuum where religions emerged to fill in.[41] Cognizant of the risks the Communist "faith crisis" and moral degradation posed for the Party, the government inaugurated what came to be called the "Socialist Spiritual Civilization and Anti-Spiritual Pollution" campaigns, aiming to reestablish the Communism-cored national spirit. This campaign did not produce the intended result; instead, it was submerged by the overwhelming tide of consumerism and commercialism sweeping the country. This paved the way for religions to revive and expand across the country, as people sought for spiritual solace and peace in the social milieu of money worshipping and harsh competition.

In the late 1980s, however, the momentum of religious revival slowed down, as Chinese authorities turned to a policy with "tightening controls over religious practice," in the wake of collapses of East European communist regimes. The role of the Churches played in the social upheavals sent an alarm signal to the CCP leaders.[42] With Deng's successor Jiang Zeming taking helm of the Party in 1989, he faced a tough test in how to reconcile the intra-party pressure against religious expansion and reestablish the predominance of the communist ideology with the reality of people's pursuit for diverse religious faiths. The following section will specifically discuss Jiang's religious policy and its impact on Chinese religious movement.

Jiang Zemin's Era (1989–2003) and "Three Sentences"

In the first two years since President Jiang Zemin was sworn in to office, the pressure from leftist groups to crack down on illegal religious activities (e.g., underground Catholic churches, restlessness in Muslims and Tibetan Buddhists in Western China) intensified. These groups linked non-approved religious organizations and activities with foreign hostile forces plotting to infiltrate into and sabotage the socialist state by means of religions. However, the CCP leadership with Jiang at the core did not turn a blind eye on the reality of the expansion of religious idealism which emerged to fill in the moral void with waning socialist virtues. They recognized that the virtues preached by these religions—such as sincerity, benevolence, and love—could be exploited to offset the evil trend of moral decadence and relieve social stress in an increasingly mercantile society. Thus, how to deal with religions in this new situation became a major topic of the Party.

In December 1990 Jiang's new approach to religious affairs came to the surface. In the then-held State Council's National Work Conference on Religion, Jiang called for the tolerant treatment of religions, asserting that this would help maintain social stability and state unification. Following this speech, Jiang received leaders of five national religious organizations in *Zhongnanhai*, the headquarters of the central government, reiterating the policy of protecting normal religious activities while repressing heterodox, and further emphasizing that the people who believe in religions and those who do not can unite and cooperate politically while respecting each other's faiths.[43] Jiang's religious platform was later written into four major points in Document No. 6 (Circular Issued by the Central Committee of the Chinese Communist Party and the State Council on Some Problems Concerning Further Improving Work on Religion, published on February 5, 1991). Specifically, these points include: (1) protecting rights of believers and non-believers, (2) regulating religious affairs according to the law, (3) giving support for patriotic religious organizations to serve as a bridge between the government and religious personage, and (4) resolutely curbing those who use religion to engage in criminal activities.[44] In 1993, at a National United Front work conference, Jiang further summarized his religious approach into "three sentences or tenets (*san ju hua*)"—a condensed representation of Jiang's thoughts regarding how to manage religions. These three tenets included the correct implementation of Party policy of freedom of religious belief, strengthening management of religious affairs according to law, and actively leading religions to accommodate to socialism.[45]

The first sentence illustrated that the policy of religious belief freedom laid down in the Document No. 19 would remain unchanged. Jiang's new thoughts were reflected upon the latter two sentences. The second sentence, to regulate religious affairs with laws, has two meanings: the government, recognizing the legal status of religions, would protect the legitimate religious rights by incorporating religious activities into the framework of laws; while employing laws as a weapon to prevent illegal religions from stirring up social turmoil, particularly the kind of anti-government and anti-society. And following this mandate, two central government-issued regulations were promulgated and entered into force in 1994—one Document No. 144 (Regulation on the Management of Sites for Religious Activities) and the other Document No. 145 (Regulation on the Management of Religious Activities of Foreigners Within Chinese Borders)—setting down specific requirements on religious affairs ranging from registration, management, personnel and operational activities of religious sites, to foreigners' missionary work, proselytizing, religious materials distribution, and religious exchanges with Chinese counterparts. With these two documents serving as a guideline, provincial and municipal governments also made their own regulations governing local religious affairs. These official regulations assigned religions a legal status in the society and brought them into the framework of the civil management—a breakthrough from the past when religions were regarded as alien in the society. Certainly, they also facilitated the government supervising religions to ensure that their activities follow state rules and laws.

Jiang's other new thinking, entailed in his third sentence, was on the adaptation of religions to socialist society. Jiang positioned religions at a place where they should adjust themselves to the socialist regime in order to develop a symbiotic relationship between religions and the atheist state. The specific connotation of this new thought was related in a white paper on the freedom of religious belief, published by Chinese government in 1997:

> Religion should be adapted to the society in which it is prevalent. This is a universal law for the existence and development of religion. Now the Chinese people are building China into a modern socialist country with Chinese characteristics. The Chinese government advocates that religion should adapt to this reality. However, such adaptation does not require citizens to give up religious belief, nor does it require any religion to change its basic doctrines. Instead, it requires religions to conduct their activities within the sphere prescribed by law and adapt to social and cultural progress. This conforms to the fundamental interests of religious believers as well as to those of the various religions themselves.[46]

Seen from this official explanation, the government required religions to adapt to the socialist system, a one-way adaptation; and not vice versa. While in the religious circles, there were proposals that the "adaptation" be endowed with a meaning of a two-way, mutual interaction of religion and state. That is, religions should actively play their part in serving the society; while at the same time the state should accommodate the reality of religious development that satisfies people's spiritual needs increasingly intensified with a weakening influence of communism across the country, engaging religions further as a reliable social force in assisting the government to build a civil society. The proposition of the "two-way adaption" has never been echoed by the government; however, for all practical purposes, the policy shift towards accommodating further about religions has been ongoing since the mid-1990s, particularly in the aftermath of the incident of *Falun Gong*.

Falun Gong, a newly emerging spiritual faith in the 1990s that mixed Buddhist and Taoist beliefs with *qigong* exercises, was banned by the government as a heretical cult posing a threat to society in 1999 (when *Falun Gong* practitioners staged protests in Beijing and some other cities in defiance of criticisms that they thought distorted the truth about their faith). It is beyond the scope of this study to analyze why *Falun Gong* had been growing fast across the country and why it was outlawed by the government eventually. Alarmed by the growing influence of *Falun Gong*, the Party begun to reconsider how to reconstruct spiritual civilization (*jingshen wenming*) in the face of the reality of the withering communist ideologies without hope of resurrection, and how to prevent evil cults such as *Falun Gong* from seizing the opportunity of filling the spiritual vacuum. Recognizant of the role of official religions in restraining heterodox cults, the Party leadership came to sense that to give due support for official religions may help attract adherents who would otherwise turn to unofficial or illegal spiritual activities.[47]

Against this background, Jiang Zemin—in his speech at a national religious work meeting held in December 2001—called for Party/state cadres to apprehend and promote positive aspects of religions as a stabilizing force in society, commanding them to actively seek consultations from religious personnel on how to better manage with religious affairs based on the current status of religions. He emphatically reiterated three characteristics of religion including its long-time survival, important influence on social stability and national development, and strong relevance to international political dynamics. This speech appeared containing a soft tone on the management of religious affairs, disclosing the inclination of the Party leadership to adopt a more tolerant approach to religions for tapping into their role in meeting people's hunger for faiths while resisting an invasion of unorthodox spiritual faiths.[48]

In sum, in the Jiang administration, the policy incrementally shifted towards soft-handed treatment of religions, intended for employing religious virtues (honesty, love, uprightness, compassion and trust—these virtues that had been held high in the Mao's era were fading away in a mercenary social environment) to save the society from spiritual degradation, relieve social distress and conflicts arising from the social transformation, and maintain social stability. Also, an establishment of mutual accommodation of state and religion would help in silencing the criticisms from the West regarding China's religious status, thus creating a favorable international environment for domestic economic development. Whatever political considerations existed for the Jiang administration to actively engage religions in social construction, the trend of mutual interaction and accommodation between state and religion did well to religious development as well as the state. Going further along this line, Hu Jintao, the successor to Jiang Zeming, launched his new policy of developing a religious role in promoting social harmony, which will be discussed in the following section.

Hu Jintao Era and Decree No. 42 (2003–Present)

Hu Jintao, who succeeded Jiang as the core of the fourth generation of CCP leadership, advanced Jiang's tolerant religious policy with a platform that emphasized the role of religions in serving social harmony. Hu formally put forward his new thinking at the 17th Party Congress held in October 2007, stating that a promotion of religious harmony "plays an irreplaceable role in enhancing unity and pooling strengths," and demanding that all CCP members "fully implement the Party's basic principle for its work related to religious affairs and bring into play the positive role of religious personages and believers in promoting economic and social development."[49] Hu's religious policy built upon the CCP's

United Front Policy, endowing it with new meanings of uniting with religious communities in order to develop the economy and maintain social harmony. Most noteworthy, though, the Party Congress passed an amendment to the Party constitution that incorporated religious principles formulated in recent years—an unprecedented move that signified the Party's formal accommodation of religion in a socialist system.[50] One month later, Hu stressed the need for a full implementation of free religious policy while speaking at a meeting of the Politburo of the CPC Central Committee that was exclusively convened for the study of religious issues at home and abroad. Promising a full implementation of free religious policy, Hu stated, "We shall fully carry out the Party's policy of free religious belief and manage the relevant affairs in line with law."[51] Hu called on all levels of local governments to support the self-governance of religious groups by helping them to address the concerns of religious believers, train religious professionals, and improve legal consciousness. Throughout Hu's administration, a number of state-sponsored training programs were established at academic institutions to teach religious leaders on subjects including religious history and ethics as well as management sciences, law, and psychology, with the intent of improving their knowledge and skills (*zong jiao su yang*) in communicating with worshippers and managing religious sites.[52]

Furthermore, the legalization of the management of religious affairs advanced one step further in Hu's era. In March 2005, Regulations on Religious Affairs (RRA)—the first comprehensive administrative regulation on religions—was officially published by the State Council. There were scholars who believed the RRA still served as a tool for the state to control religions, without a hint of a positive development in the Party's religious policy line.[53] However, in order to gain insight into the document, there are two main points that need to be highlighted. First, the law—detailing various aspects of religious affairs (religious bodies, sites, properties, personnel, etc.)—offered transparent, systematic explanations on how to manage religions and religious activities.[54] Second, the new law did not mention any particular religion by name, only referred to religions in general. This could be construed as the government intentionally having left the vagueness in place to impart a flexibility in considering future accommodations of existing religions that have not been officially recognized (such as the Orthodox Church, concentrated in Northeast China). Of course, the function of the law still remained as a tool for the state to regulate and supervise religions, as reflected by certain ironclad principles: for example, unswervingly sticking with the Party's leadership and socialist system and the self-independence of Chinese religions against foreign domination and infiltration. Nonetheless, for all practical purposes, this new law played its role in promoting close interaction and cooperation between the state and religion, in a standardized, legally regulated framework, for the common task of building social harmony.

Compared to the policies of his predecessors, Hu's religious policy advocated a more active engagement with religions. It sent a signal that "the state is no longer content merely to monitor and control the grassroots upsurge of religiosity but is assuming an active, leading role in managing, guiding and rebuilding the various bodies of religious clergy, theological doctrines, and institutional religious structures."[55] This strategy of engaging further with religions was the best solution the Party state could find in the face of religious expansion amid the setting of an unstoppable social transformation.

Interesting questions arise when we attempt to forecast the future of Chinese religious policy. In what possible directions could that policy evolve? Will the current trajectory of benign interaction between the state and religion continue, or do some uncertainties lie ahead? The following section will predict the future of the state-religion relationship and analyze what differentiated policies the state may adopt toward specific religions.

Prognosis of the Future of Chinese Religious Policy

As seen from the above analysis, there is a telling trend that Post-Mao religious policy was tilting toward a more accommodating and tolerant approach in dealing with religious affairs. Suffice it to say that the Party has been adapting to the momentum of religious development, during the previous three decades in an increasingly open and progressive society. The emergence of faith pluralism, the bestowing of legal status upon religions, the positive force in society acknowledged by the Party, as well as religious principles written into the Party constitution—all these new phenomena that could never have taken place in the Maoist era illustrate that the Party was trying to build a mutual-accommodative relationship with all religions to engage them in the participation of the establishment of a stable and harmonious society.

The current religious status bodes well for the relations and future of state and religion in China, regardless of the underlying Party motives that state harbored in accommodating religions, either employing them to strengthen its governance or elevating national moral standards. If anything, the state-led institutionalization of religions is in the making through processes that are mutually constructive.[56]

Given the current reality of a post-totalitarian China—where various social forces including religions play their part in society while the state still maintains its authoritarian power over social affairs—the state-religion relations are evolving further toward mutual interaction and adaptation. In the meantime, mutual restraints and conflicts are sporadically occurring over the issue regarding whether religions remained within the scope the government allows, that is, within the requirement that religion cannot oppose government or society. The state-religion tensions sometimes emerge as competition between Communism and religion for mass believers (that is, for a larger influential power among people). The government adopts differentiated strategies for different religious groups depending on the extent and potentialities of their compliance and support with the regime. The following will explore what strategies the government may employ toward five established religions in the future and why it would likely adopt these strategies.

Tacit Support: Buddhism and Taoism

Buddhism and Taoism are more easily accepted by Chinese, compared with other religions, due to their absorption in the development of traditional Chinese cultural values. Both these religions have experienced an astounding revival in the last three decades along with China's economic reform and social transformation. Official statistics in 1997 showed that there were more than 13,000 Buddhist temples and 200,000 monks and nuns, and 1,500 Taoist temples and 25,000 masters.[57] About forty Buddhist academies across the country offer Buddhist training and an education of general knowledge, and Buddhist and Taoist religious ceremonies and relevant cultural activities (such as music, *kung fu*, and body cultivation) have been restored and developed.[58]

In recent years it has seemed that the government has been intentionally giving support to the promotion of those virtues of the two religions that it deems are beneficial to social stability, harmony and national unity. One indication of this was the First World Buddhist Forum, held in 2006, titled "A harmonious world begins from the mind/heart." This was the first time in history that China took initiatives to hold such a large-scale international religious assembly, covered by media at home and abroad, which convened about one thousand Buddhist monks and scholars from thirty-seven countries.[59] Following that, the Second World Buddhism Forum, titled "the harmony of the world," took place in 2009, with its attendees coming from about fifty countries and areas. This forum was co-hosted by Buddhist communities on both sides of the Taiwan Straits. Also, the promotion of Taoism was gaining strength, as illustrated by several international Taoism symposiums and cultural festivals held successively in Southwest China in the last few years.

Why was the government tilted towards a favorable support for these two religions? First, the values that the two religions preach—harmony, compassion, righteousness, tolerance, etc.—are what the state needs in current times for elevating people's minds above worshipping money in an increasingly commercialized society as well as for achieving the national goal of harmony. Also, these two faiths are identified as less threatening, among religions, to the state power, as they promote the ideas of detachment from worldly affairs and laissez faire. Second, they serve as a tool to strengthen the sense of affinity of Taiwan people and overseas Chinese to China. Originated from same cultural sources, Buddhist and Taoist circles across the Taiwan Straits have been keeping close communications and interchanges in recent years. Their intimate interaction contributed to the unity between two peoples in the mainland and Taiwan. In addition, there were a number of overseas Chinese believing in Buddhism or Taoism; they often return to pay respect for their religions' holy sites in China while making contributions to their motherland by way of business investment or charitable donations. Hence, the emergence of Buddhism and Taoism, as part of Chinese civilization, is conducive to improving national cohesion among all Chinese, both at home and abroad. Lastly, Buddhist temples and Taoist monasteries, mostly historical relics with ancient cultural heritage, attracted tourists to pay a visit, thus promoting the development of local tourism. In those areas with well-known religious sites, the earnings from religious tourism even constitute as a major source of fiscal revenues of local governments. In a period, there appeared a widespread wave of building temples and monasteries in local areas, as governments rapaciously wished for promoting tourisms as well as attracting business investments from Taiwanese and overseas Chinese. This phenomenon, jestingly called "build the religious stage to sing the economic opera (*zongjiao datai, jingji changxi*)," was halted by the central government as an abnormal model of economic development by making use of religions.[60]

As seen from the above analysis, it is being acknowledged by the government that Buddhism and Taoism played positive roles in serving the country for its political stability, economic development, cultural protection, and spiritual purification. Given this truth, the state would continue to adopt a favorable policy towards Buddhism and Taoism in the way of active interaction and support for them, which would naturally usher in a thriving period of development for the two religions.

Differentiated Management: Islam

According to official sources, there are ten minorities who believe in Islam.[61] Based on the year 2000 national census of China, the total Muslim population of that country was close to 20.3 million. Most of these minorities are accommodative to the state's ethnic and religious policy.[62] The only Muslim minority in open defiance of the governance of the PRC is the Uyghur, a minority Turkic-speaking group. These almost nine million people live in the Xinjiang Uyghur Autonomous Region (XUAR), a northwest frontier province bordering South Asian Islamic countries such as Pakistan and Afghanistan as well as Central Asian states.

In recent years, riots between the Uyghur and the Han Chinese (the majority ethnic group of China) occurred sporadically, and brought much attention to the restive Xinjiang region. External and internal factors interacted behind the ethnic conflicts in Xinjiang: First, China's open-door policy facilitated Uyghur building close connections with the Islamic World through cross-border trading or pilgrimage to Mecca. In this process, various thoughts of religious extremism and ethnic separatism, such as Islamism, Fundamentalism, and Pan-Turkistanism (calling for all Turkic groups to establish a Pan-Turkistan country), flooded into Xinjiang, stirring up Uyghurs' anti-government and anti-Chinese moods. Second, the economic development in the region, while raising the overall living standards of all ethnic groups, also expanded the wealth disparity in favor of the Han Chinese and against Uyghur; this deepened the disharmony and antagonism between them.[63] Third, geographically, Xinjiang's location—about 3,000 miles away from the eastern part of China where the Han majority is concentrated—historically restrained Uyghur-Han cultural and social exchanges, leading to the Uyghur group lagging behind in integrating with the Chinese-culture-dominated society.

In face of rising religious and ethnic conflicts in the region, the government in 1998 launched three-year Strike Hard campaign, aiming to crack down on "three forces" (that is, ethnic separatists, violent terrorists, and religious extremists). Soon after this campaign, the worldwide anti-terrorism movement in the aftermath of 9/11 incident also helped put a check on the Uyghur separatist activities with some of their groups (such as the East Turkistan Islamic Movement) designated as terrorist organizations by the UN and Chinese government. In this context, the region since entered a period of relative peace. However, this did not mean the tense relations of Uyghur Muslims and the Han Chinese had been truly harmonized. Just days before the opening of the Beijing Olympics Games in August 8, 2008, a terrorist attack in a border town of Xinjiang killed sixteen-police officers; and about one year later, in July 2009 there arose a new wave of Uyghur-Han violent conflict that crippled Urumqi, the capital of Xinjiang, for several weeks, leaving 197 people dead and about 1600 injured.[64] To look ahead, the strained relations between the Uyghur Muslims and the Han Chinese would not be ameliorated in a short period of time, given the complexity of various factors (religious, ethnic, political, economic and cultural) interwoven together. And how to resolve the Uyghur issue would pose a challenge for China's Islamic policy as well as its ethnic regional autonomous system.

However, Xinjiang's case alone cannot demonstrate that China's Islamic policy failed itself. After all, the root cause for the conflicts in the region lies mainly in ethnic disharmony, as seen from above analysis; religions are often utilized by ethnic nationalists and religious extremists as a tool to serve their discourse of independence. In fact, the Islamic policy itself did not gain much controversy in Xinjiang, and in most cases normal religious activities can be carried out, as illustrated from the fact that there are more than 20,000 mosques in the region according to official figures.[65] Furthermore, if looking at other Muslim minorities, they are basically well-suited to the institutionalized religious and ethnic policy, keeping traditionally harmonious relations with the Han group, without a desire to challenge the current system. Suffice it to say that Chinese Islamic policy since the early 1980s has been faring well, with religious teaching and rituals and traditions resorted gradually and smoothly, such as Koran study, sermon, pilgrimage to Mecca, and foreign exchanges with Islamic countries. Also, Chinese Muslims, as minorities, enjoyed preferential policies in education and employment. They are basically satisfied with the current status where their religion has established a mutual respectful and accommodative relationship with the state; and that is why Muslim activism (such as fundamentalism and extremism) had little, if any, appeal amongst the majority of Muslim groups in China.

On the way ahead, it is forecasted that China would continue its preferential policy towards Muslim-concentrated areas, taking Muslims as dual identities of religion and ethnic minority. The Party state assures themselves of this policy's properness by recognizing the fact that most Muslim areas are stable and peaceful compared with Muslim turbulence occurring often times in other countries. Xinjiang, as a special case in China's Muslim communities in terms of its ethno-religious complexity and political sensitivity, would be given differentiated treatment. It would be little wonder that Chinese government continues to apply restrictive measures to Islamic activities as a precaution against separatist infiltration and destruction. A series of harsh measures the Chinese government has adopted against the Uyghur riots in recent years are sending out a strong signal that its attitudes are resolute in, more than anything, maintaining the stability and sovereignty in the region. At the same time, the government would continue to tap into the potentials of developing ethnic economies in easing Uyghur Muslim tensions. A recent evidence of this is that the Party boss in charge of Xinjiang for more than a decade, who was unpopular for its heavy-handed policy against ethnic minorities, was replaced with a new bureaucrat who is familiar with economic affairs.

Management and Reconciliation: Christianity

Christianity, which the Chinese call "foreign religion (*yang jiao*)," has been consistently mainstream in every administration of the PRC, with the enhancements of patriotism and resistance against foreign intervention. In the 1950s, under the direction of the Party, Chinese Christian communities launched the Three Self Patriotic Movement (TSPM) across the nation, calling for self-governance (*zizhi*), self-support (*ziyang*), and self-propagation (*zichuan*), with the purpose of cutting off religious ties to foreign imperialist powers. In the post-Mao period, two slogans were repeatedly promoted among Christian communities: "love one's country, love one's religions/church" (*aiguo aijiao*), and "independence and self-administration" (*duli zizhu ziban*). Christians were instructed to be "good citizens", a term which means loving the homeland, setting moral examples for others, doing charitable work, and keeping the principle of independence in mind in the exchanges with foreign counterparts. And government leaders in their speeches have often emphasized taking precautions against religious infiltration, which kept Christians always on high alert regarding subversive activities of anti-China forces dressed in the cloak of religions.[66]

Another indication of the importance to the government of a role for patriotic education in Christianity is its dual-track management system, which differs from other religions. For Catholics, there is a pair of organizations, the Chinese Patriotic Catholic Association (CPCA) and the Chinese Catholic Bishop College (CCBC); and for Protestants, there is another pair, the TSPM and the CCC. The first organization in each pair oversees church-state relations, including supervision of church registration; the second organization focuses on pastoral matters (sermons, missions, etc.) as well as church exchanges with international communities. This dual-track system guarantees that the Party's religious policy will be digested and implemented by Christians while churches manage their own affairs with relative independence. In recent years a momentous theological reconstruction movement—engaging Chinese ministers, theologians, and scholars—unfolded among Christian churches. Its tenet was to explore, through broad discussions and research, how churches adapt themselves to socialism—a task mandated by the state and embraced readily by Chinese ecclesiastical leaders.[67] It is therefore true to say that Christianity, seen traditionally as an alien faith outside of Chinese culture, experienced a kind of baptism in the waters of accentuated sinonization and patriotism. The purpose of this process, politically, was to prevent this *yang jiao* from becoming a tool of Western nations for their cultural intrusion into China as had occurred in the nineteenth century.

An abundance of data reveals that Christianity was expanding rapidly in China since the 1980s, and that this growth was remarkable and astounding. With regard to Protestant Christianity, the number of officially sanctioned churches and meeting points increased from 1,600 in 1984 to more than 12,000 churches and 25,000 meeting points, with 18,000 clerics in 1997. The number of Protestants was approximately three million in 1986, and in the order of seventeen million by 2003, while in 1949 only one million Protestants lived in China.[68] As of 2006, there were about 50,000 churches open to the public, 70 percent of them newly established.[69] For Catholics, official data in 1997 estimated that there were over 4,000 churches, 4,000 clergy, and four million believers. And information from official sources revealed that every year some 50,000 laymen converted into Catholicism.[70]

With the expansion of Christian religiosity, some clerics and Christian believers emerged to challenge the state's religious management system with its intervention and co-option through intermediary patriotic organizations. They called for restoring a system of self-management by churches without the state's intervention and building close links with foreign Christian communities. In Chinese Catholicism, two camps divided themselves along the lines of pro-Vatican and pro-government. The former, often called the underground church, maintained a secret contact with the Holy See, and carried out activities such as consecrating bishops, ordaining priests, and organizing Episcopal conferences, with the Vatican's directive without regard to the state's regulations and laws.[71] It has been estimated that as of the year 2000, about seven million people were involved with the underground church.[72] For Protestant denominations, unauthorized house churches were growing as rapidly as official ones. And western sources reported that there existed about the same number of unregistered Protestant believers as those participating in the official churches.[73] The seemingly unstoppable growth of these unofficial churches stemmed from their winning Christian converts at an increasing pace outrunning the official churches. This growth also shows the undercurrent of the Christian autonomy movement gaining momentum in challenging the state-supported mainstream churches and theology. How to reconcile the interests of the authoritarian state with those of an expanding Christianity in the process of Chinese modernization poses a tough test for the state-regulated religious regime.

Facing the reality of increasing numbers of unofficial churches—accompanied with international pressures—the government is softening its attitude and attempting to adopt a flexible and pragmatic policy that ameliorates tense relations in return for a peaceful and stable society. It is holding out an olive branch to signal its willingness to reconcile with unregistered churches, while taking the position that the legitimacy of worshipping places necessitates their registration with state-sanctioned patriotic organizations. For instance, in November 2008, a seminar—hosted jointly by governmental and non-governmental research institutes, and attended by house church leaders and religious experts and scholars—concluded with the announcement that house churches would be willing to start a dialogue with the government; following this seminar, the Three-self Patriotic Movement (TCPM) and China Christian Council (CCC) leaders also expressed supportive attitudes, recognizing and cooperating with house churches if they did not preach heretical doctrines.[74] The Chinese government also is seeking to resolve the issue of Catholic underground churches through a normal dialogue with the Vatican. One sign of detente is that recently consecrated bishops received the approval of both the Vatican and the government-sanctioned church. Those Bishops included an auxiliary Bishop in Shanghai diocese and a coadjutor bishop in Guizhou province and Beijing's bishop.[75] The development brought hope of a possible solution to the problem of clandestine churches, although Beijing and the Vatican remain at an impasse. China steadfastly maintains its self-autonomy in Catholic affairs while the Vatican demands incorporating Catholic churches into its hierarchical church system. Once can predict that the state's evolving policy towards Christianity will continue to oscillate between principled control to flexible tolerance, depending on the extent to which churches run their activities within the parameters set by the state.

Conclusions

In addition to the five officially recognized religions we have discussed, popular religion is gaining a momentous revival in China. Having been dismissed and prohibited as the equivalent of superstitions in the early years of the PRC, popular religion began to grow from the early 1980s onward as the state turned a blind eye to it, focusing instead on the five official religions. In some areas, popular religion was regarded as a folk custom and received legal protection and promotion by local governments, such as the restoration of the worship of Mazu (Goddess) in the south-eastern coastal areas of China. The state's lax control over popular religion has something to do with its dispersed distribution, which limited the supervisory ability of the government. More importantly, popular religion, which is less structured and short of established canons and doctrines, poses little threat to the regime. Rather, it helps maintain social stability by offering spiritual asylum to people who are suffering. It is forecasted that popular religion would continue to spread in a space outside of state intervention, because the government lacked resources and the desire to restrain this less provocative worship.

Looking back at the evolution of the post-Maoist religious policies, there has been a clear shifting from tight control and regulation, through accommodation and adaptation, to an active promotion of religion's positive role in constructing social harmony. The change in religious policy mirrored the overall picture of the current Party/state regime as it adjusted to profound social transformation. A progressive, increasingly open Chinese society calls for a state that can accommodate social plurality and attend to civil needs; and the state incrementally improves its methods of governance for maintaining its legitimacy. In this socio-political context, contemporary Chinese religious policy evolved in a positive, progressive manner. It could be said, in a sense, that how the state treats religions reflects how the regime adjusts itself to the changing social reality—just as the title of a new book suggested, "*Making Religion, Making the State*."

Looking ahead, it cannot be denied that the discord between the Party/state and religions will persist due to the incompatibility of their ideologies. Tensions will sporadically erupt in the way of mutual restraints and completion, between communism and religiosity, for a scope of spiritual influence. However, the mainstream trend of the state-religion relationship would be predicted to go toward the mutual adaption and accommodation, based on the above analysis of the post-Mao religious policy; and this trend is irreversible in the milieu of social modernity and internationalization. We must presume, of course, a stable political environment without intra-Party factious fighting. This judgment is evident in a remark by the former head of China Religious Affairs Bureau, Mr. Ye Xiaowen, on the thoughts on the formulation of China's future religious policy:

> We today must make and implement the religious policy in consideration of two-sided factors, domestic and international: that is, doing our religious work on both arenas while thinking inward and outward. It is necessary not only to maintain domestic stability but create a sound international environment, not only pay attention to domestic issues but observe the world with a globalized perspective. While keeping up consistently our principles and policies, it is an imperative for us to study how to adjust our strategy and tactics to the shifting circumstances; and the purpose is to maintain national unity, social stability, and an international environment favorable to domestic construction.[76]

Notes

1. Mayfair Mei-Hui Yang, ed., *Chinese Religiosities: Afflictions of Modernity and State Formation* (Berkeley, CA: University of California Press, 2008), 27–28.

2. Arthur Waldron, "Religious Revivals in Communist China," *FPRI Wire* 7, no. 3 (1999), http://www.fpri.org/fpriwire/ (accessed January 15, 2010).

3. Zhongjian Mu, "How to View Chinese Religious Issues," *Friends of Leaders*, no. 1 (2009), 36.

4. Yoshiko Ashiwa and David Wank, eds., *Making Religion, Making the State: The Politics of Religion in Modern China* (Stanford, CA: Stanford University Press, 2009), 2.

5. Anthony Yu, *State and Religion in China: Historical and Textual Perspectives* (Peru, IL: Carus Publishing Company, 2005), 145.

6. H.H. Lai, "Religious Policies in Post-totalitarian China: Maintaining Political Monopoly over a Reviving Society," *Journal of Chinese Political Science* 11, no. 1 (2006), 71.

7. For the detail regarding the status of Chinese academic research on religion, see Zhufeng Luo, ed., *Religion under Socialism in China*, translated by Donald MacInnis and Xi'an Zheng (Armonk, NY: M.E. Sharpe, Inc., 1991), Foreword; David Yu, ed., *Religion in Postwar China: A Critical Analysis and Annotated Bibliography* (Westport, CT: Greenwood Press, 2009), Foreword, IX, 1.

8. Xinping Zhuo, "Zhongguo zongjiao de dangdai zouxiang [Contemporary Trends of Chinese Religions]," *Academic Monthly*, Issue 10 (2008).

9. Zhufeng Luo, *Religions under Socialism in China*, 154.

10. David Yu, ed., *Religion in Postwar* China, Annotation 0028, 40. And the annotated essay is tilted "Guan-yu wo-guo zongjiao ton she-hui-zhu-yi she-hui xiang xue-taio wen-ti di qian-jien " [My View on the Problem of Mutuality between Religion and Socialist Society in China], written by Zhenyu Jin, published on ZJXYJ, no. 13 (1988), 47–51.

11 . Department of State, USA, http://www.state.gov/g/drl/rls/hrrpt/, and http://www.state.gov/g/drl/rls/irf/2009/index.htm (accessed January 20, 2010).

12. Anonymous, "China Hits Back with Report on U.S. Human Rights Record," *People's Daily Online*, February 26, 2009, http://english.peopledaily.com.cn/90001/90776/90883/6602049.html (accessed January 21, 2010).

13. Jordan Paper, *The Spirits Are Drunk: Comparative Approaches to Chinese Religion* (Albany, NY: State University of New York Press, 1995); Yoshiko Ashiwa and David Wank, *The Politics of Religion in Modern*; Anthony Yu, *State and Religion in China*; Jordan Paper, "Foreign Religions and Chinese Culture: Comparative Paradigms," in Kangsheng Dai, Xinying Zhang, and Michael Pye, *Religions and Modernization in China*, proceedings of the Regional Conference of the International Association for the History of Religions held in Beijing, China (Cambridge, UK: Roots and Branches, 1992).

14. Clifford Geertz, *The Interpretation of Cultures: Selected Essays* (New York: Basic Books, 1973), 90.

15. Vincent Goossaert, "The Concept of Religion in China and the West," *Diogenes* 52, no. 1 (2005), 14.

16. Anthony Yu, *State and Religion in China*, 5.

17. Anthony Yu, *State and Religion in China* , 9.

18. Anthony Yu, *State and Religion in China*, 15.

19. Jordan Paper, *The Spirits are Drunk*, 2-4.

20. Jordan Paper, "Foreign Religions and Chinese Culture," 167.

21. Anthony Yu, *State and Religion in China*, 146.

22. Xinchuan Huang, "China's Religions and China's Traditional Culture," in Kangsheng Dai, Xinying Zhang, and Michael Pye, eds., *Religion and Modernization in China*, Proceedings of the Regional Conference of the International Association for the History

of Religions held in Beijing, China, April 1992 (Roots and Branches, Cambridge, 1995), 16.

23. Five Relations means the relations—between ruler and subject, husband and wife, father and son, elder and younger brothers, and older and younger friends—should be obedience and respect of the latter in return for benevolence and support of the formers. Five Cardinal Values include *ren* (benevolence), *yi* (righteousness), *li* (rites), *zhi* (wisdom), *xin* (trust). For the detail about Confucianism, go to the website: http://www.religionfacts.com/a-z-religion-index/confucianism.htm (accessed April 10, 2010).

24. Donald E. MacInnis, *Religion in China Today: Policy and Practice* (Maryknoll, NY: Orbis Books, 1989), 14–15.

25. Ashiwa and Wank, *Making Religion, Making the State*, 40.

26. Karin Aalderink, "Totally Expunge Evil, Pursue It to the End," graduation paper in the Department of Chinese Studies of Leiden University of The Netherlands, Sept. 2001. http://website.leidenuniv.nl (accessed December 6, 2009).

27. Zhufeng Luo, ed., *Religion under Socialism in China*, 55–71.

28. Beatrice Leung, "China's Religious Freedom Policy: The Art of Managing Religious Activity," *The China Quarterly*, no. 184 (2005), 910.

29. Fenggang Yang, "Tripe Religious Markets in China," *The Sociological Quarterly*, 2006, 93–122. Chinese official religious associations include the following: the Chinese Buddhist Association; the Chinese Daoist Association; the Chinese Islamic Association; the Chinese Catholic Patriotic Association (CCPA); the China Catholic Administrative Committee (CCAC); the Bishop's Conference of the Catholic Church in China (BCCCC); the National Committee of Three-self Patriotic Movement of the Protestant Churches in China (NCTPMPCC); and the Chinese Christian Council (CCC).

30. See "Section IV, The Party's Present Policy toward Religion," in Document No. 19, included in Donald E. MacInnis, *Religion in China Today: Policy and Practice* (Maryknoll, NY: Orbis Books, 1989), 14–15.

31. No. 19, "Section XII, The Role of the Party and State Organs in Handling the Religious Questions," 25.

32. Document No. 19, 25.

33. Document No. 19, 16.

34. Ibid.

35. Document No. 19, 14-19.

36. Document No. 19, 13-23.

37. Document No. 19, 24.

38. Document No. 19, Section V, 17.

39. Alan Hunter and Kim-Kwong Chan, *Protestantism in Contemporary China* (New York: Cambridge University Press, 1993), 67.

40 . See "Summarization of the Development of China's Buddhism," http://www.tese.me/html/guojiatese/include/zongjiaogaikuang/2009/1022/37770.html (accessed February 23, 2010). Han Buddhism, the largest of the three Buddhist branches, had uncounted numbers of unregistered Buddhist laypersons; so it is difficult to calculate the Buddhist population with a reliable number.

41. Arthur Waldron, "Religious Revivals in Communist China," *Orbis* 42, no. 2 (1998), 325.

42. Human Rights Watch, "Freedom of Religion in China," no. 28 (1992).

43. Pitman Potter, "Belief in Control: Regulation of Religion in China," *The China Quarterly*, no. 174 (2003), 321.

44. See Mickey Spiegel, *Freedom of Religion in China* (Human Rights Watch: New York, 1992), Appendix I.

45. Beatrice Leung, "China's Religious Freedom Policy," 908.

46. See Section II, "Legal Protection of the Freedom of Religious Belief," in *The White Paper: Freedom of Religious Belief in China*, Information Office of the State Council of the PRC, October 1997.

47. Leung, " China's Religious Freedom Policy," 911.

48. Leung, "China's Religious Freedom Policy," 910.

49. Hu Jintao, "Hold High the Great Banner of Socialism with Chinese Characteristics and Strive for New Victories in Building a Moderately Prosperous Society in all," Report to the Seventeenth National Congress of the Communist Party of China, October 15, 2007. http://www.china.org.cn/english/congress/229611.htm (accessed March 10, 2010).

50. Geroge Thomas, "China's Communists Get Religion," *Christian World News*, May 8, 2009. http://www.cbn.com/cbnnews/ (accessed March 9, 2010).

51. Embassy of PRC in the U.S., "Hu Stresses Full Implementation of Free Religious Policy," December 19, 2007. http://big5.fmprc.gov.cn/gate/big5/us.china-embassy.org/ (accessed March 8, 2010).

52. Embassy of PRC in the U.S., "Hu Stresses Full Implementation of Free Religious Policy."

53. Fuk-Tsang Ying, "New Wine in Old Wineskins: An Appraisal of Religious Legislation in China and the Regulations on Religious Affairs of 2005," *Religions, State & Society* 34, no. 4 (2006), 9, 12; Caolee Harmin, *China's New Regulations On Religious Affairs: A Paradigm Shift*, The Congressional-Executive Commission on China, 109th Congress House Hearings (US Government Printing Office: Washington, 2005).

54. State Council, PRC, "Regulations on Religious Affairs," Amity News Service, http://www.amitynewsservice.org/page.php?page=1289 (accessed March 10, 2010).

55. Yang, *Chinese Religiosities*, 28.

56. Ashiwa and Wank, *Making Religion, Making the State*, 6.

57. Ashiwa and Wank, *Making Religion, Making the State*, 1.

58. Yang, *Chinese Religiosities*, 27.

59. Yang, *Chinese Religiosities*, 29.

60. Yang. "Triple Religious Markets in China," 17–18.

61. Dru Gladney, "Islam in China: State Policing and Identity Politics" in Yoshiko Ashiwa and David Wank, eds., *Making Religion, Making the State*, 152-153; Hui (9,816,805); Uyghur (8,399,393); Kazakh (1,250,458); Dongxiang (513, 805); Kyrgyz (160,823); Salar (104,503); Tajik (41,028); Uzbek (14,502); Bonan (16,505); Tatar (4,890). The actual number of Muslims may be more than this census that count population figures by nationality, not religious identity (at least nonminority converts to Islam are not counted).

62. Gladney, *Islam in China*, 153.

63. See Yiran Zhou, "The Road to Ethnic Harmony: An Analysis of Internal Causes to the Ethnic Issues in Xinjiang," in Baogang Guo and Dennis Hickey, eds., *Toward Better Governance in China* (Lanham, MD: Lexington Books: 2010), 191–193.

64. See "Official: Real Purpose of Urumqi Riot 'Xinjiang's Independence'," Xinhuanet.com, July 21, 2009, http://news.xinhuanet.com/ (accessed April 20, 2010).

65. Colin Mackerras, "Why Terrorism Bypasses China's Far West," April 23, 2004. http://www.atimes.com/atimes/China/FD23Ad03.html (accessed March 20, 2010).

66. Ryan Dunch, "Christianity and Adaptation to Socialism," in Yang, ed., *Chinese Religiosities*, 164,

67. Dunch, "Christianity and "Adaptation to Socialism," 173.

68. Dunch, "Christianity and "Adaptation to Socialism," 169.

69. See China related Facts and Data. http://www.china.com.cn/ (accessed March 26, 2010).

70. Alan Hunter and Kim-Kwong Chan, *Protestantism in Contemporary China* (New York, NY: Cambridge University Press, 1993), 243.

71. Lai, *Religious Policies in Post-Totalitarian China*, 68.

72. Beatrice Leung, "Communist Party-Vatican Interplay Over Training of Church Leaders in China," *Journal for the Scientific Study of Religion* 40, no. 4 (2001), 658.

73. John Pomfret, "Evangelicals on the Rise in Land of Mao," December 26, 2002. http://www.christianpost.com/article/20011226 (accessed February 23, 2010).

74. See "China Reaches Out to House Churches; Raids, Arrests Continue," *One-newsnow.com*, December 11, 2008. http://www.onenewsnow.com/ (accessed March 27, 2010).

75. See "China, Vatican Agree on New Bishop," *USA Today*, September 21, 2007, http://www.usatoday.com/news/religion/2007-09-21-china-vatican-bishop_N.htm (accessed March 27, 2010); "Beijing and Rome Agree on Bishop's Appointment," *CatholicCulture.org*, June 28, 2005, http://www.catholicculture.org/ (accessed March 27, 2010); "Chinese Government, Vatican Agree on Bishop's Ordination," *CatholicCulture.org*, September 7, 2007, http://www.catholicculture.org/ (accessed March 27, 2010).

76. Xiaowen Ye, *Religious Question: How to See and How to Do* [Zongjiao wenti zenmekang zenmeban] (Beijing: Religious Culture Publishing House, 2008), 418–419.

Chapter 8
China's Petition System and Its Effects on Social Stability and Regime Legitimacy

Lacey Bradley-Storey

Due to restrictions on activism and political opposition, non-democratic states frequently lack reliable communication channels between the leadership and the populace.[1] Although expressions of dissatisfaction are often met with repression, authoritarian states sometimes solicit input from their citizens in a process known as "contacting."[2] While these dual approaches appear paradoxical, they often work in conjunction with one another so that the central leadership can gauge grassroots conditions and advance regime legitimacy. In China, the centuries old petition system (*xinfang*, translated as "letters and visits") serves this function by enabling individuals to report on government officials' malfeasance and appeal to higher authorities for redress.[3] Despite this, there remains some measure of uncertainty regarding the effects of *xinfang*. Specifically, how does this particular contacting institution actually impact state-society relations? Does *xinfang*, by offering a channel for citizens to articulate their concerns and suggestions, enhance social stability and help the regime maintain legitimacy?

Given the increase in incidents of disruptive action, from 8,700 in 1993 to 87,000 in 2005, it would seem that citizens are lacking in both political and legal recourse and that they have few other channels through which to voice their grievances.[4] In other words, popular protest movements bring to mind the appearance of a dissatisfied and increasingly marginalized segment of the population and the failure of government institutions to meet that population's needs.[5] The forms of resistance vary markedly, from the more powerful images of strikes and violent demonstrations to subtle, everyday forms of protest that slowly undermine normative and institutional structures.[6] In any case, each form of resistance represents a potential challenge to the legitimacy of the governing institutions that have—for a variety of reasons—failed to restore justice to the marginalized.

Challenges to legitimacy do not always occur outside of legally sanctioned avenues of dispute resolution, however. In China, the petition system, *xinfang*, presents citizens with the opportunity to seek redress from authorities for a perceived wrong committed against them and/or to report on any wrongdoing on the part of government officials. Although a legally sanctioned mode of dispute resolution, *xinfang* exists outside of the Chinese legal system and as such, petitions carry no legal weight.[7] Nonetheless, petitioners base their claims on law.[8]

In spite of this, however, the majority of petitioners never receive redress, prompting them to engage in disruptive behavior—such as protests, kneeling in front of government buildings and even rioting—in order to both draw public attention to their case and pressure authorities into a resolution. Indeed, petitions now represent "the basic mode of social disruption in China."[9] Aside from social disruption, however, the failures in the petition system have also led many petitioners to lose trust in the central leadership.[10] For its part, the center has recognized this. At the Fourth National Complaint Bureau Conference, the national leadership expressly stated that complaint bureau work is critical to the survival of the Party.[11] Given the acknowledged importance of *xinfang*, its failures seem puzzling. Why is a system meant to resolve disputes and preserve stability actually generating it? Why is it undermining petitioners' confidence in the regime?

This chapter will attempt to answer these questions by arguing, first, that the petition system not only embodies a complex and often conflicting mandate, but it is also a legitimating institution, meaning that it functions in a way so as to bolster (or undermine) the legitimacy of the regime. Second, this chapter will argue that as a result of its conflicting mandate, the actors who participate in *xinfang*, specifically the central and local governments and petitioners themselves, have competing perceptions of the purpose and function of the system. For the central government, *xinfang* is inherently political—a tool of governance. For the local governments, *xinfang* is often considered a potential threat to the positions of local officials and to the legitimacy of local government institutions. Finally, petitioners view the purpose of *xinfang* as inherently legalistic, meaning that their participation in *xinfang* stems from a legally based claim to justice. Because *xinfang* is used for different, often-competing purposes, its ability to function in a legitimating role is necessarily hampered.

Defining *Xinfang*

Although petitioning exists outside of the Chinese court system, it is legally recognized with roots in both traditional Chinese political thought and historical practice. Historically, the notion that the central government—as embodied in the emperor and his officials—would correct the transgressions of lower-level officials and thereby, restore justice to the people, originated in Chinese Confucianism.[12] According to Confucian thought, the emperor and his officials had a moral obligation to maintain social order and stability. By doing so, they could both achieve and maintain harmony in the world.[13] Under the Qing Dynasty (1644–1911), for example, petitioners, who had been unable to find satisfactory justice at the provincial-level, could travel to Beijing and bang the "grievance drum" located near the offices of the censorate and capital police. These officials would then decide whether or not the petitioner's case merited imperial attention. For some petitioners, the censorate and capital police proved to be yet another hindrance in their quest for justice and as a result, they would appeal to the emperor directly by kneeling before the palace gate or along an imperial procession route—an act that extended beyond the legally-recognized boundaries of the system.[14] Nonetheless, the petitioners' belief in the emperor's righteousness prompted them to risk violating the law in pursuit of imperial justice.

The current petition system, *xinfang* (信访),[15] maintains many of the original Confucian tenets, although it differs markedly in form and in some cases, purpose. When the Chinese Communist Party (CCP) officially established *xinfang* in the early 1950s, its central purpose was to overcome bureaucratic problems and create a close connection between the Party and the people.[16] *Xinfang* differed in form from earlier petition systems, however, in that it was not just a way in which individuals could express grievance against corrupt officials. Rather, the CCP also intended that the system be used as a means by which individuals could expose counterrevolutionary actions and malfeasant behavior (*jubao*) on the part of government officials[17] or as a means by which citizens could make suggestions for improving governance.[18] Thus, the regime viewed *xinfang* as a governing tool that it could use to gauge public opinion and monitor grassroots conditions.

Although the regime viewed *xinfang* as serving an expressly political purpose, the system's complex mandate has created some uncertainty as to what exactly *xinfang* is and perhaps more importantly, how it functions within the Chinese state. Some scholars characterize *xinfang* as a form of political participation, specifically a contacting institution, with established rules and procedures where individuals approach government officials or other people in power in order to solicit help on behalf of themselves, their families or friends or a larger group. In a state where few modes of political participation exist, government officials actively "promote participation through contacting channels" in order to generate support for the government and localize expressions of discontent.[19] By promoting at least some measure of efficacy, the regime can avoid citizens turning to more contentious forms of political action, such as protests and rioting.[20]

Other scholars argue that in spite of central government intentions *xinfang* does not fully exist in "regime-defined limits,"[21] and thus it cannot and does not fully function in the way the regime intended. Rather than generating support for the government and localizing expressions of discontent, *xinfang* has actually facilitated expressions of dissatisfaction that have filtered up through the system to the central government and negatively impacted petitioners' trust in the justice offered by Beijing.[22] In order to understand how it is possible that a system geared toward promoting regime legitimacy and social stability may actually be having the opposite effect, it is important to discuss both the regulations that govern *xinfang*, as well as its institutional design.

Over the years, the CCP has continually refined and reshaped the framework with which it manages both petitioners and the petitioning process. While this process has improved some aspects of the system, it has also created conflicting incentives for both petitioners and government officials. This is perhaps most clearly demonstrated in changes that have occurred within the petition regulations. The 1994 Beijing Petition Regulations created a system that both punished officials for threatening petitioners *and* punished petitioners for repeatedly pressing their claims. The regulations state that government officials who engage in "petitioner threats, intimidation, repression or retaliation . . . shall be investigated for criminal responsibility."[23] Petitioners shall be likewise investigated for criminal responsibly if they engage in disruptive action, damage property, and threaten staff, among other activities. However, petitioners will also be subject to prosecution if they are "deliberately provocative and incorrigible."[24] In other words, those petitioners who repeatedly petition will be held liable. Furthermore, the regulations also direct local governments to take measures to ensure that petitioners will not continuously appeal to higher authorities.[25] So while the regulations forbid intimidation and repression, they also state that local governments should prevent petitioners from repeatedly appealing to higher-level authorities. Not only does this create a perverse incentive for local officials, but it also detracts from *xinfang*'s capacity to link individuals with higher-level authorities.

The 2005 Letters and Visits Regulations attempted to amend some of the problematic provisions, as well as to reiterate the purpose of *xinfang* as a means of monitoring grassroots conditions. For example, the language regarding repeat petitioners was removed and once again, the regulations stressed that intimidation and coercion should not be used against petitioners. The regulations also direct all levels of government to establish *xinfang* bureaus, and they also state that petition statistics are to be reported to higher-level authorities. The purpose of these regulations is, according to Article 7, to investigate "individuals who are responsible for malfeasance or dereliction of duty committed in the work regarding letters and visits . . ."[26] Hence, the regulations clearly restate that a major function of *xinfang* is to communicate problems in governance. According to Minzner (2006):

> Rather than emphasizing the egalitarian protection of individual rights under a well-defined system of law, the *xinfang* regulations aim at a smooth transfer of information between officials and citizens who cooperate in the process of improving the governance of society.[27]

Although the 2005 regulations emphasize "a smooth transfer of information," by their design they still end up creating a number of perverse incentives. For example, Articles 40-44 state that individuals who "shift responsibility onto another organ" shall be subject to censure. Taking a closer look at this, it becomes apparent that those bureaus, which allow petitions to take their complaints to other bureaus (e.g. higher-level bureaus), will be reprimanded. Furthermore, Article 39 states that statistics should be gathered and reported on those bureaus that receive "a relatively larger number of complaints."[28] So although the 2005 regulations clear up some of the problems that the 1994 regulations created, they still embed within them incentives that encourage officials to prevent petitioners from either filing their petitions and especially, contacting other bureaus. Lastly, it should be noted that the language used in the 2005 regulations provides interpreters significant leeway in deciding what does and what does not constitute a legal act. Oft-used terms such as "*other acts*" or "*other matters*" and even phrases like "[petitioners shall not] disrupt public order" can be subject to wide interpretation.[29] As a result, the ambiguous language can provide local officials with the opportunity to "discourage" petitioners from taking their petitions to higher-level authorities without directly violating *xinfang* regulations.

In addition to the regulations that govern *xinfang*, some scholars argue that the system is, by design, "institutionally amphibious."[30] Because the CCP attempted to employ "mass line," where political participation is carried out under centralized control, *xinfang* ends up fulfilling two contradictory purposes.[31] As a result, it becomes "boundary-spanning," as defined by "behavior that crosses the boundary between sanctioned and unsanctioned behavior . . . [and] . . . the boundary between "legal" and "political" action."[32] Indeed, it is neither fully institutionalized nor non-institutionalized. Citizens are legally allowed to bring forward their grievances, but these channels may present opportunities for greater mobilization than is generally permitted.[33] In November 2008, for example, thirty residents of Longnan, Gansu, gathered in front of CCP offices to petition for compensation regarding what they considered was the illegal demolition of their houses. By the evening, their attempts had attracted the attention of thousands of others who wanted to link their own complaints to the original petitioners' cause in hopes that the sheer number of people present would pressure the government into addressing their cases. Unhappy with the progression of the discussions, however, petitioners began to attack officials and police with rocks and metal batons before inflicting serious property damage to the government offices. Only a massive police response quelled the violence.[34]

While the violence in the Longnan case clearly constituted an illegal act, the preceding events were less clearly defined. At what point did the gathering become "illegal"? Was it during the initial stages when the group exceeded the legal limit of five participants or when the event became violent? If the former, why did officials allow people to congregate in such large numbers? In the context of petitioning, what constitutes a legal or illegal action is often dependent upon the perceptions of the participants, as debate over what is contentious is deeply entrenched within Chinese state.[35] Due to its institutional indeterminance and the regulations that govern it, *xinfang* provides a space in which both citizens and government officials can test the boundaries of both legal and illegal action. In the Longnan case, officials gave petitioners significant leeway with the protest while petitioners continued to push the boundaries of what the officials' would allow. Only when the petitioners fully engaged in illegal action did Longnan officials decidedly intervene.

This lack of clarity not only exists between petitioners and officials, but it also exists within the government itself. In response to repeated protests, for example, the city government of Shenzhen made limited concessions to petitioners, including allowing for limited demonstrations and protests—a tactic commonly used by mass petitioners when trying to call attention to petitions that have previously been ignored. Lower-level officials, however, believed that the city government was too lenient on the petitioners and that their tactics were actually encouraging the demonstrations. They placed pressure on the city government to change its strategy. The resulting strain between the lower level and the city officials eventually forced the city government to alter its policies and adopt a harsher stance towards mass petitioners.[36] In this case, intergovernmental contention played a pivotal role in determining how Shenzhen authorities would handle disaffected petitioners, and as a result, the boundaries of *xinfang*—at least in Shenzhen—were reconstituted to reflect a more restrictive interpretation of what represented a rightful act.

While the Shenzhen and Longnan cases demonstrate that what constitutes a rightful or an illegal act is at least partly determined by how actors interact within the context of the system, they tell us little of why they interact in the way that they do. In order to better understand this, it is necessary to take a deeper look at the institutional indeterminance of *xinfang*. Indeed, *xinfang* is not merely boundary-spanning, but it is also legitimating.

Xinfang and Legitimation

Why regimes are considered legitimate (or illegitimate) is one of the important questions of political science. Yet there is wide disagreement over what legitimacy means, how it is measured and how it is maintained. While it is beyond the scope of this chapter to try and provide a broad conceptualization of the term, this section hopes to provide a better understanding as to how authoritarian regimes maintain legitimacy. Given that understandings of legitimacy hinge, in some way, on political support that concern assessments of the regime from a "common good" perspective,[37] the ambiguity surrounding how people in authoritarian regimes "identify with the political order" is highly problematic.[38]

Using a definition of legitimacy that is based on Gilley (2006) and Beetham (1991), I identify the term as follows: legitimacy is a dynamic process where the system of power and people's values and expectations of legality that justify the system correspond in such as way as to deem the exercise of political power as rightful.[39] In this case rightful is further understood to be in accordance with accepted moral and legal behavior.[40] Because legitimacy rests upon a dynamic process—meaning that the regime and society interact in a variety of ways to create the basis for the regime's legitimacy (e.g. through acts of consent such as voting, provision of stability, symbolism, or how actors understand and conform to legality)—it is entirely possible that, in some cases, there exists a disconnection between how the regime views its justification of power and how citizens view it. This is certainly not to say that there is a complete disconnection (obviously, if that were the case then the regime would no longer be considered legitimate), but rather there can be points in the system where citizen and regime conceptions of the justification of power are at odds.

Because channels of citizen-regime interaction are more limited in authoritarian regimes, there is greater risk of disconnection. In liberal democratic societies, elections, free news media, and civil society, etc. all serve to communicate failures in governance, including voter disaffection due to unpopular policies, ineffectiveness, and possible threats to the social order. Conversely, the modes of political participation in these societies do not simply serve as a mandate for the justification of government power; they also serve as means of communication and an articulation of citizen values and expectations. In authoritarian regimes, however, fewer modes of citizen-regime communication exist. Thus, regimes are more likely to make mistakes by either overestimating or underestimating popular support. In other words, the regime "has less means to see a crisis coming its way and is likely to misinterpret symptoms either by treating them too leniently or vastly exaggerating threats to the political order."[41] Thus, the citizen-regime dynamic that supports regime legitimacy is impeded by the paucity of reliable, clear channels of communication. This, of course, is not to say that authoritarian regimes are illegitimate. Rather, authoritarian regimes tend to more actively engage in legitimation processes, which are continually "constructed and reconstructed"[42] in response to changing goals, expectations, values and conditions.

Although the CCP employs numerous "top-down efforts" to convince the masses that their rule is justified,[43] it also places considerable importance on fostering some measure of communication between itself and its citizens in order to garner support for the regime. As this chapter has already noted, *xinfang* fulfills this purpose through its multifaceted mandate of allowing people to report on grievances and the malfeasant behavior of local officials, as well as making suggestions for improvements in governance. Viewed in a broader sense, these activities "give a voice [however, minimal] to the masses,"[44] and ultimately, support the stability and legitimacy of the regime. In 1996, the Fourth National Complaint Bureau Conference clearly stated the importance of *xinfang* in regards to this purpose:

> Complaint bureau work is important not only for our relations between the party, government, and the masses, for fostering a clean government, and promoting legal construction, but even more so to persist in the life and death struggle of our party and government.[45]

In order to understand exactly how *xinfang* is tied into legitimation processes and why the CCP deems it so important for this purpose, it is necessary to examine how *xinfang*'s mandates, particularly reporting grievances and informing on officials' malfeasance, impact public support for the regime.

Reporting Grievances

The act of reporting a grievance is rooted in a legalistic claim, where a citizen or group of citizens either seek to receive redress for a perceived wrong committed against them, or they report on local government failures to implement the law. In either situation, the citizen is making a claim based in some measure on the laws of the state. Indeed, China's constitution guarantees that every citizen has the legal right to appeal to higher-officials and report on any offenses or illegal action committed by government bureaus or officials, and for those citizens who have had a wrong committed against them, they are legally entitled to compensation.[46] Minzner (2006) argues that the "fundamental nature" of "popular appeals for justice [is best described] as *requests* for assistance from higher authorities rather than *assertions* of clearly defined rights."[47] However, requests and appeals are clearly defined as *rights* within the Chinese constitution, and many petitioners base their claims upon concepts of both traditional and legal concepts of justice. So it is not surprising that petitioners often use the court system first before turning to *xinfang*—roughly 70 percent of petitioners according to one survey.[48]

For many petitioners, the issue of legality is of clear importance, as the following quotes indicate:

> We will absolutely never do anything anti-party or anti-socialist. Most of us are communist party members who have the mission of defending national laws and the socialist system. We have never demanded anything without legal basis . . . whenever we do something, including writing letters, I would like to look up such stuff as the Law of Marching and demonstration, and Regulations on Public security management —*Unnamed petitioner.*[49]

> . . .We do not support radical behavior that violates principles. Such actions are not right, and also provide them [the government] with a chance to seize our queue. We need to act within the boundary of the law –*Unnamed Petitioner.*[50]

> . . . Sometimes we found that local government had not implemented the national policies and laws, and felt it necessary to report such problems to upper-level government . . . —*Unnamed Petitioner.*[51]

Furthermore, most petitioners' claims tend to focus on rights violations including: violation of homeowners' rights, such as land seizures and housing demolition, and worker's rights, including failure to pay wages/pensions and inadequate compensation for lay-offs, as well as police abuse, civil disputes, and failures in the judicial system. The following quotes illustrate some of the various rights-based claims to justice:

> I was just petitioning to get back some money that the police had stolen from me. —*Du Minrong, petitioner.*[52]

> I've met a builder whose wages were never paid, a man engaged in a long-running land dispute, and a father who sobbed as he explained his campaign for an investigation into his only son's death. —*James Reynolds, journalist.*[53]

> Using courts, petitions and appeals to officials at all levels, Shishan's peasants have fought in vain for a decade to get compensation for 200 acres of rich

farmland they maintain was unfairly confiscated by local authorities and sold for development. —*Edward Cody, journalist.*[54]

In the first six months of 2002, 28 percent of the 4,820 letter petitions and 70 percent of the 1,730 in-person petitions received by the Ministry of Construction were about housing demolition.[55] In most of these cases, petitioners complained about the lack of satisfactory compensation, resulting in part from the significant leeway local governments had in implementing and expanding central policies on homeowners' rights.[56]

Given that many petitions stem from rights violations or local government violations of national law, petitioners often use these claims to justice as a way to garner public support for their cause. In order to achieve this, many petitioners choose to escalate their tactics to draw attention to both violations of the law and the failure of government officials to respond to their claims. In late summer of 2003, for example, a man lit himself on fire in front of government buildings in Nanjing in protest of the demolition of his house and what he believed was unfair compensation. A few weeks later, a man from Anhui attempted to do the same thing in the Tiananmen Square, but police were able to stop him. Both of these acts drew the public's attention to the petitioners' plight and generated enough public outrage that the central government felt compelled to respond and improve the position of the homeowners.[57] In late 2003, the central government created new policies, which raised the amount of compensation for homeowners and stated that all "compulsory demolition needs to go through public hearings."[58]

Not all petitioners resort to such extreme measures to achieve their goals, however. On April 13, 2010 over 1,000 residents from two villages in Zhuanghe, Liaoning kneeled in front of the government headquarters demanding an audience with the mayor in order to bring his attention to questionable land seizures. *Shanghai Daily* later called this act a "show of deepest respect." However, the newspaper also noted that the process of kneeling is "an archaic and somewhat undignified means of seeking justice" that has resurfaced in response to failures in the petition system.[59] The act generated widespread public sympathy, with "netizens" (internet-users) being the primary impetus for the negative public reaction.[60] The title of the *Shanghai Daily* article even suggested that "Officials Should Heed Kneeling Petitioners."[61] In response, higher-level authorities removed the mayor from office, with the Shanghai government website stating that the mayor had mishandled the incident and "was responsible for the negative effect it caused." Dalian officials, who oversee Zhuanghe's administration, stated: officials "must attach great importance to the reasonable demands of the masses" and "respond with enthusiasm."[62]

In each of these cases, people's expectations of the law and their belief in the fundamental rightness of their claim led them to challenge perceived legal violations and/or discontinuities. Petitioners were able to call attention to local government violations of the law through a combination of petitioning and the escalation of tactics ranging from the extreme and clearly illegal (e.g. self-immolation, rioting, and destruction of property) to acts that challenged the boundaries of what the government will and will not allow (e.g. kneeling, lighting candles, public gatherings and holding up signs). One petitioner went so far as to argue that collective action was both "rightful and lawful," then justified his comment by stating: "If our action was not legal, you [the government] violated the law before we did, since you have not fulfilled the obligation stipulated by the law."[63]

By providing a legal means of seeking redress for what is often a legally based claim,[64] *xinfang* allows petitioners to link their grievances to broader issues regarding government obligations to its citizens. In other words, *xinfang* presents citizens with an opportunity to challenge the regime's commitment to rule of law and by extension, some measure of its "*right* to rule." Thus, it is not surprising that petitioner-generated collective action often draws sympathetic public attention to their claims. On June 21, 2010, for example, a petitioner from Zhangjiagang City opened a blog in order to draw attention to the January 29, 2010 demolition of her home. The blogger stated that the police failed to produce "any legal procedures for the case" and then proceeded to steal items from hers' and others' homes. She stated that the family was homeless and forced to live off of the assistance of relatives. In the blog, she also provided a detailed list of stolen items, including furniture, appliances, jewelry and bedding. By June 22, dozens of people had responded. Several questioned how society could continue like this, expressing concern and even outrage at the injustice. One blogger responded with a single word: "angry . . ." Another stated: "Such a thing is too much! Why is there no control?" Still another said: "at the people's awakening, corrupt officials will tremble with fear!"[65]

Although not all public disclosures of injustice lead to redress, recent work suggests that some citizens have been able to achieve some success by staging resistance and bringing public attention to their case, effectively forcing higher-level authorities to respond, as public opinion can put pressure on the regime.[66] According to the Chinese Academy of Social Sciences, this seems to be a commonly held perception, as 85.5 percent of 632 petitioners surveyed in Beijing stated that "they will publicize policies and laws in order to mobilize the public to support their rights."[67] Indeed, both the 2003 cases and the Zhuanghe case demonstrate that the mobilization of public support pressured the central government into responding. In the 2003 cases, the central government responded with a more favorable policy. In the Zhuanghe case, higher-level authorities removed a corrupt official. As both of these cases show, however, *xinfang* also presents the regime with an opportunity to correct the challenges to its authority by alerting it to "simmering" public discontent. Hence, *xinfang* embodies relational processes, where the public can challenge certain aspects of the regime's right to rule and the regime can respond in a variety of ways. When the regime responds in a way that satisfies public demands, its legitimacy is necessarily enhanced. As this chapter will demonstrate later on, however, repeated failures to respond can also lead to an erosion of public confidence in the regime.

Malfeasant Behavior of Local Officials

In political systems where government officials are appointed rather than elected, there are fewer sources of direct accountability, particularly at the lower levels of government. In China, the central government is often constrained by its own ideological rhetoric, particularly through its tendency to promote itself as a "servant of the people." Hence, repeated failures to live up to expectations could potentially jeopardize one of its (many) claims to power. Local governments, on the other hand, face few such constraints.[68] Thus, the lack of both direct and symbolic accountability leads to a typical principal-agent problem, where the concentration of power in the hands of the few allows for both control over information channels and increased isolation of lower level officials from accountability to either citizens or the central government.

Although some scholars claim that local agents are far more accountable to the central government than is sometimes argued,[69] others state that the central government actually has a very difficult time monitoring and enforcing the compliance of local officials.[70] In 2007, President Hu Jintao acknowledged this problem when he ordered local officials to "solemnly implement" policies formulated by the center and recognize the latter's "absolute authority." He noted several incidents where "headstrong local officials" ignored instructions from Beijing.[71] Recent scholarship has attempted to explain the lack of local government accountability in several ways. Referring to the principle-agent problem, some scholars argue that the political system itself provides incentives and opportunities for local deviation from central policies, while others state that the incompleteness of power devolution creates opportunities for local malfeasance.[72] Whatever the cause, the effects of formal institutional weakness and their failure to hold government officials accountable are not always clear and can range from corruption—including bribery and nepotism—to those effects that are constrained by institutional, political and economic conditions. Such constraints might lead to irresponsible decision-making[73] or decision-making that must take place amidst difficult conditions, but not necessarily to outright corruption, as defined by the use of public office for illegitimate private gain. Nonetheless, the effects can be extremely problematic for the regime, as failures at the local level can result in difficulties regarding the provision of public goods, inconsistencies in the application of law, corruption and uneven patterns of growth and development, all of which can lead to social discontent.

The central government has long recognized that problems exist at the local level and has publicly stated that these failures could have serious implications for the stability of the country and of the regime. Sub-national public officials and workers have also had similar concerns. Indeed, 54 percent of 1,000 police officers surveyed in Fujian province in 2005 reported that incidents of collective action were primarily triggered by the malfeasance of local governments.[74] As a result, combating 'corruption' has become a major tenant of the regime's domestic governance strategy. As Premier Wen Jiabao noted in an online discussion with "netizens" on February 28, 2009, fostering a "clean government" is the most important "pillar of social stability" and without it, the regimes' "image among the masses could be seriously compromised, and the country's social stability shattered due to the lack of public support for the government."[75] Two years earlier President Hu Jintao expressed the same concern regarding corruption:

> Resolutely punishing and effectively preventing corruption bears on the popular support for the Party and on its very survival, and is therefore a major political task the Party must attend to at all times.[76]

In order to address the issue, the central government has established various legal codes regarding corruption in particular and has brought numerous corrupt officials to trial (passing down death sentences in some cases). As this chapter has already noted, however, difficulties in using official channels to monitor local officials and enforce compliance with central mandates makes the task of rooting out corruption extremely difficult. As a result, both citizens and the central government employ a variety of other methods to increase local government accountability. These include the strengthening of local solidarity groups and the establishment of the Organic Law on Villager's Committees and the Administrative Litigation Law. Regarding the former, the failures in formal institutions can prompt a community's social institutions—such as lineages and temples—to fill the gap. Using informal norms and practices, they can pressure local governments into better fulfilling their obligations to the community.[77] The latter two laws are also aimed at providing some measure of accountability at the local level, with the Organic Law on Villagers' Committees allowing for the election of committees, which serve as a governing body designed to handle everyday village affairs, and the Administrative Litigation Law, which allows citizens limited rights to sue government officials. Similarly, *xinfang* allows individuals an opportunity to report incidents of local government malfeasance and can serve as a link between citizens and higher-level authorities.

While *xinfang*'s ability to improve local government accountability is relatively straightforward, petitioning does serve another purpose regarding local government malfeasance. It can bolster the regime's ability to keep public dissatisfaction aimed primarily at the local level of government. Soviet-scholar Fainsod (1958) argued that complaints waged at the local level direct "bolts of lightening" away from the central government and toward the local government.[78] This statement hinges on the idea that expressions of dissatisfaction can be contained at the local level "before [they] bubble up through the system" and affect public confidence in the regime.[79] Indeed, the CCP adheres to the principle: "Would rather have disturbance in local areas, no disturbance in the center (*ningluan difang, buluan zhongyang*)."[80] In order for this to work, however, citizens have to perceive some measure of distinction between the central and local government—even in a one party state. This distinction is embedded within the petition system itself as it "typically involves visiting higher levels of government to demand sanctions against subordinates for violating laws or central policies," thus necessitating some measure of trust that the central government will arbitrate the case. As a result, petitioning becomes "an act of defiance against targeted local authorities."[81] The Chinese Academy of Social Sciences similarly found that 90.5 percent of 632 petitioners surveyed wanted to bring central attention to their case and 88.5 percent wanted to "apply pressure on local government to get the problems resolved."[82] Hence, the very act of petitioning involves playing one level of government off against the other. Yet this also implies that citizens view the levels of government differently: one level is often the source of their problems, while the other can present the solution. Of course, this naturally begs the question: Is this really the case? Do citizens view the central and local governments differently?

National surveys suggest that citizens do make at least some distinction between the central and local government when it comes to who is engaging in malfeasant behavior and which levels can be "trusted." This is, of course, not to say that people do not realize that the CCP controls all levels of government. Rather, it suggests that people believe that the central and local governments might have different motives, opportunities and means of accountability. According to the 2002 East Asian Barometer Survey, only 14.8 percent of 1,431 respondents believed that most officials in the central government were corrupt, whereas 46.3 percent of 2,514 respondents believed that most officials in the local government were corrupt.[83] In 2008, 38.9 percent of 3,111 respondents agreed with the statement "most officials [at the local level] are corrupt," while 13.3 percent of 2,005 respondents agreed that most officials at the central level are corrupt.[84] While fewer people indicated that they believed most local officials were corrupt in 2008 than they had in 2002, more people indicated that they had lost trust in the local government. In 2002, 17.6 percent of 3,006 respondents stated that they had "not very much trust [in the local government]," while in 2008, 38.1 percent of 4,719 respondents agreed with the same statement. Trust in the central government changed slightly, with 63.3 percent of 3,031 respondents stating that they had "a great deal of trust" in 2002 and 69.3 of 4,709 respondents agreeing with the same statement in 2008. However, in 2002 only 1.1 percent of respondents stated that they had "not very much trust" in the central government, while in 2008 those respondents had increased to 5 percent.[85] Recent discussions with non-petitioners in Beijing similarly suggest that people tend to make a distinction between central and local governments. Out of the eighteen individuals with whom I spoke, thirteen knew about and were willing to discuss the petition system. Out of these, 100 percent stated that the local government was very corrupt and they believed that that is why people came to Beijing to petition, while nearly 70 percent of them stated that they believed the central government is willing to help the petitioners.[86]

Over the past several years, problems with social unrest and corruption have forced the center to more openly acknowledge that there are problems within the government. Several high-profile cases, including the 2009 arrest of the former vice-president of the Supreme People's Court,[87] have drawn attention to the fact that corruption can and does permeate all levels of government. Nonetheless, the majority of the prosecutions for corruption occur at the village, municipal and county-levels. Prosecutions at the provincial level, which are generally touted as high profile, are still considered part of the local government—albeit the highest level. Thus, official malfeasance is more often framed as a local or individual phenomenon rather than a problem that occurs equally within the central government or originates from problems with central policies. In an analysis of 38 Chinese newspaper articles on government officials' malfeasance written between 2007 and 2010, nearly 40 percent of the articles drew a clear distinction between central policy and local failures to implement that policy. Nearly 53 percent of the articles called attention to corrupt local officials, cadres or corruption at the local level, while 24 percent of them made mention of corruption at higher levels of government (e.g. central ministerial positions). Roughly 29 percent of the articles explicitly blamed corruption on lower-level officials. Almost 79 percent of the articles called attention to a central government corrective measure aimed at curbing corruption, in general, but only 8 percent of the articles actually criticized failures in central policy.[88] Indeed, many of the newspaper headlines that I examined tended to reflect a strong regime commitment to fighting corruption:

1. *China hardens line on corruption*
2. *China shows no mercy at corruption*
3. *A miserable year for corrupt officials in China*
4. *China's army issues five-year plan on fighting corruption*
5. *China strives to weed out judicial corruption*
6. *President Hu charts path in anti-corruption drive*
7. *China establishes corruption prevention bureau*
8. *All-out corruption fight*
9. *Hu Jintao: No tolerance to corruption*
10. *China vows to intensify anti-corruption efforts in 2009*[89]

Given that China is a one-party state, framing malfeasance as mostly a local phenomenon may seem ultimately, self-defeating. But as the central government is able to concomitantly frame itself as the "arbiter of justice" and the spearhead in the fight against corruption, as the above headlines indicate, it creates a dynamic that allows the least ideologically vital part of the regime to deflect criticism away from the center. As the aforementioned survey data suggests, to some degree this seems to hold true, as there is greater perception that malfeasant behavior is primarily a local phenomenon rather than a problem that is endemic to the regime itself. However, this perception is not simply supported by political rhetoric. By its very design *xinfang* helps to reinforce a distinction between central action and local behavior, as it allows citizens an opportunity to express their dissatisfaction with failures at the local level (e.g. lack of compensation for land seizure, botched police investigation, illegal housing demolition, etc.) by encouraging the belief that higher-level authorities will intervene on their behalf.

In July 2007, for example, hundreds of people in Xiantang village used a combination of petitioning and collective action to draw attention to official corruption and land seizures. Even after driving local officials from their offices and effectively laying siege to the building, the villagers continued to send delegations to higher levels of government—from Longjiang Town, to Shunde District, to Foshan City, to the province of Guangdong and finally to the national petitioning office in Beijing—believing that they would intervene on their behalf.[90] Although the collective action had the potential to generate media coverage, it was the appeals to higher authorities that the villagers were hoping would elicit a sympathetic government response. Further linking their case to central interests, the villagers even put up a twenty-meter long banner reading: "Support General Secretary Hu Jintao's spirit of anti-corruption. Build a harmonious society together. Fight to end the corrupt officials who violate the people's benefits." In spite of threats and intimidation made by local officials and their families and repeated failures to receive redress from higher-levels, the villagers of Xiantang still harbored a belief in the beneficence of higher-level authorities. By October, they were still hoping that "'wiser, higher officials' would grant them justice."[91]

As the Xiantang case demonstrates, by furthering the distinction between local malfeasance and central government intervention, *xinfang* can help to localize discontent and generate confidence in the regime. Indeed, even after four months of unsuccessful appeals, the villagers still held out hope that the central government would help them. As the final section of the chapter will demonstrate, however, this is not always the case, as both petitioners and non-petitioners alike are increasingly seeing failures in *xinfang* as failures on the part of the central government.

The Limitations of *Xinfang*

Although individuals generally begin petitioning in order to receive redress for a perceived wrong committed them or the laws of the state, the experience of *xinfang* often has more profound consequences than the grievance itself. According to a 2005 survey conducted by the Chinese Academy of Social Sciences, only two in 1,000 personal visits and only three out of 1,000 combined letter petitions *and* personal visits achieve some kind of redress.[92] In March 2010, the *China Daily* reported that only around 17 percent of the ten million petitions filed in 2009 had received redress.[93] Thus, most petitions are never resolved and petitioners often spend years petitioning both local and central level officials for some definitive answer regarding their case. According to Dong Da, a forty-three-year-old petitioner from Hebei, "the departments in Beijing simply kick the cases back and forth. Nobody takes responsibility."[94] As a result, many petitioners have resorted to collective action in order to draw attention to their case, believing that drastic action results in a government response.[95] One official from Liaoning province estimated that 80 percent of collective petitions involved "drastic action."[96] Indeed, 74 percent of the 827 instances of social unrest that took place in 1999 in Fujian province stemmed from collective petitioning, as did 63 percent of 297 instances of unrest that occurred in Qinghai. In the early 2000s, 53 percent of the 108 collective petitions in Zhejiang generated "disruptive action."[97] Indeed, an oft-used slogan reads: "no trouble, no solution; small trouble, small solution; big trouble, generous solution."[98] Given *xinfang*'s importance to the regime—indeed, Chen (2008) calls it "the primary institution the regime uses to handle state-society relations"—why is a system designed to diffuse social unrest actually facilitating it?[99] And what consequences does this have beyond the lack of resolution for the petitions?

While part of the problem lies in the overwhelming numbers of petitions that *xinfang* offices receive and a general weakness in its capacity or authority to handle them, the primary issue lies in *xinfang*'s institutional indeterminance, as it provides actors with both the incentive and the opportunity to pursue different, and often conflicting, courses of action. As a result, *xinfang* is not only a system that "the regime uses to handle state-society relations,"[100] but it is also a system where state-society relations can collide. In other words, *xinfang* has both "bottom-up" and "top-down" properties that—as this chapter has already discussed—allow it to function as both a tool the regime uses to gauge grassroots behavior and bolster its own image and as a tool that citizens use to challenge the regime's commitment to the rule of law and its obligations to society. Thus, *xinfang* means different things to different people and as a result, it has great difficulty fulfilling any of its mandates.

Local Government Incentives, Opportunities, and Responses

By its very design, *xinfang* constitutes a potential threat to the position of local authorities. Because petitioning provides individuals with the opportunity to report on local government malfeasance, it both undermines the legitimacy of local governments[101] and provides perverse incentives that in some circumstances may "encourage" local governments to either ignore or repress petitioners. Indeed, local officials' positions, including promotions and salary, are dependent upon evaluations from higher-level authorities. These evaluations are often tied into local officials' ability to meet specific targets, including the numbers of petitioners who seek redress from higher-level authorities.[102] In some cases, local authorities are openly criticized for having failed to prevent petitioners from traveling to the provincial or central level. In 1997, for instance, Hunan province party secretary circulated an announcement criticizing Baojing county officials because they had not prevented forty migrants from petitioning provincial officials on two separate occasions. On another occasion, Yiyang city officials openly criticized the Heshan district government because the officials they sent to Yiyang lacked the authority to remove petitioners who had protesting there.[103] The risks are widely understood by lower level officials. Indeed, Zhang

Dejiang, party secretary of Guangdong province, expressed this sentiment clearly in a speech delivered in December 2005. He told lower-level officials to pay attention to the concerns of peasants—though not because it was their duty as government officials, but because of the negative impact peasant resistance could have on their careers.[104]

In order to prevent such criticism and the effects it has on local officials' position and salaries, authorities will sometimes engage in "harsh and repressive measures," including the detention of petitioners[105] and the forcible removal of petitioners from political centers (e.g. Beijing or provincial capitals). While not all local officials engage in acts of intimidation or reprisals against petitioners, those that do have had a dramatic impact on petitioners and on the act of petitioning. According to the Chinese Academy of Social Sciences, roughly 71 percent of 560 surveyed petitioners reported that local government reprisals had gotten worse since the 2005 regulations were put in place.[106] Roughly 53.6 percent of petitioners have stated "they will do something that will scare the cadres."[107] Thus, both *xinfang* and the regulations that support *xinfang* create pressure for local governments to act against petitioners rather than support them in their efforts to get redress. By ignoring and/or repressing petitioners, the petitioners themselves become disaffected and often use more disruptive tactics in order to generate public outcry and place pressure on higher-level authorities to address their case. So it is not surprising that, in 2001, Zhu Rongji, the former Vice-Premier, admitted that unresponsive local officials were to be blamed for mass protests.[108]

Central Government Incentives, Opportunities, and Responses

For the center, *xinfang* is a tool of governance that serves as a way to gauge grassroots activity, bolster regime support and provide an "early warning system" so that the government can respond should problems at the local level begin to threaten China as a whole. To the regime, *xinfang* "represent[s] the rule of man (or Party), not the rule of law."[109] Thus, the legalistic aspects of *xinfang*—such as redressing grievances—are less important to the regime than is its political purpose. As a result, the center's response to both the petitioners and local government hinges on its perception of *xinfang* as being related to both state stability and regime legitimacy. Perhaps nowhere is this dynamic more clearly demonstrated than with how the center handles petitioners who come to Beijing to seek redress.

For the center, petitioners who travel to political centers en masse undermine *xinfang*'s ability to localize expressions of discontent. Often petitioners gather in front of government buildings, officials' homes and in public places, such as Tiananmen, in order to draw attention to their case and force central officials to respond. In January 2009, for example, roughly seventy to eighty petitioners gathered outside of the State Council press office in Beijing holding up their petitions.[110] In the summer of 2009, around twenty or so petitioners from the north of China gathered in front of a central official's home near Tiananmen before being arrested by police and forced to return to their villages.[111] In March of 2009, several petitioners released their grievances into the air near a downtown shopping center in Beijing. The leaflets contained reports and photographs of the alleged injuries committed against the petitioners, which were quickly scooped-up by the police. The petitioners disappeared into the crowd before they could be arrested.[112] Incidents such as these not only draw public attention to the petitioners' plight, but by staging them in highly visible political centers, the petitioners are publicly challenging the central government to fulfill its obligations to them. Hence, *xinfang* is not actually containing problems at the local level. Rather, it is generating problems that are filtering up through the system.

In response to petitioners' demonstrations in Beijing, the central government has attempted to push petitioners back to the local levels in an attempt to prevent local disturbances from affecting the political system as a whole. In preparation for the 2008 Olympics, for example, Beijing demolished its "petition village," a collection of homes where thousands of petitioners lived waiting for someone to hear their case.[113] In 2009, Beijing ordered that all petitions were to be addressed at the local level and that petitioners, who came to Beijing, might have their cases dismissed without review.[114] Although Beijing has committed to better monitor lower-level officials and it has set-up a website where people can make complaints online, the incentives that prompted local governments to ignore or repress petitioners in the first place remain effectively the same. Thus, recent reforms may exacerbate, rather than correct, the conflicting incentives associated with *xinfang*.[115] Furthermore, Li argues that Beijing has "so far been two-faced in dealing with petitioners," as internal communications indicate Beijing's distrust of petitioners' motives and has, in many cases, authorized "crackdowns" on them.[116]

For Beijing, however, petitioning is something of a "Catch-22," where if they remove the petitioners from the capital and/or allow the local governments some leeway in how they treat petitioners, they further undermine petitioners' trust in the center by damaging the petitioners' belief that the center will arbitrate their case. Given the increasing numbers of disaffected petitioners, the risks to social stability are greatly amplified. By both allowing petitioners to stay in Beijing and allowing them to repeatedly petition, however, the center risks drawing non-petitioners into what originally began as individual grievances. As this chapter has already noted, the increased publicity and public pressure could also have a negative impact on public trust in the regime.

Petitioner Incentives, Opportunities, and Responses

As this chapter has previously discussed, individuals generally become petitioners when they perceive that some wrong has been committed against them or when they believe that an action threatens their livelihood, their community or the integrity of the state (even if it is the government doing the violating). However, petitioners' understanding of the purpose of *xinfang* is markedly different from that of the regimes. According to Minzner (2009):

> . . . the main function of *xinfang* institutions is not to resolve all grievances equally, according to law. Rather, *xinfang* institutions are an information channel for higher authorities and a means to prompt the intervention of key Party or government officials in the resolution of particular disputes that might result in social instability.[117]

Consequently, there is an inherent disconnection between how petitioners view *xinfang* and how the regime views it. As a result, petitioners' grievances can become entangled in both central and local government political interests, resulting in a general lack of resolution for most petitioners' claims. However, the regime does tend to take interest in those disputes that are potentially destabilizing, suggesting that larger, more disruptive petitions are more likely to attract the attention of higher authorities.[118] Thus, petitioners often try to link their cause to other petitioners' claims or to broader issues in general. Petitioner Qin Xinan, for example, demonstrates this dynamic when he states that he is attempting to "ask the government for justice, to right a wrong," but then says: "I strongly ask Hu Jintao and the Chinese Communist Party Central Committee to punish corruption. Save Chinese people, ordinary people, and the weak in society. Save China."[119] Petitioner Du Mingrong goes even further stating: "I have given up trying to get justice for myself. I just want the world to know what the party and the government have done. We want political reform."[120]

While some petitioners choose to politicize their grievances, others are careful not to; aware that the central leadership may be less likely to respond sympathetically if the petitioners' actions clearly violate the law or threaten the position of the regime as a whole. According to one petitioner:

> We Yiyang people should go [to upper level government] by ourselves, they Changde people should go by themselves. On this issue we should not go together. Going together would violate the party's policies. Establishing ties (chuanlian) would give our action a political nature, and our petition would become a political event. We disabled people live close to the boundary of the law. We should be careful so as not to violate laws. *–Unnamed Petitioner*[121]

Even though many petitioners choose not to overtly politicize their grievances, the experience of *xinfang* can negatively affect petitioners' perceptions of the regime and thus, lead to a situation that may become de facto political. Recent research indicates that the experience of petitioning tends to erode petitioners' trust in the central leadership, particularly for those petitioners who petition Beijing directly.[122] According to Li, "petitioning Beijing, therefore, often becomes a moment of truth, when petitioners have to reflect upon their beliefs about the center."[123] Thus, claims that begin as essentially legalistic can become politicized—directly or indirectly—through the experience of *xinfang*.

Petitioning affords actors with both the incentive and opportunity to use *xinfang* as they see fit, but ultimately each actor is basing their usage of the system on some fundamental claim to the regime's legitimacy—whether that claim comes in the form of a challenge, in the form of a defense, or in the form of a belief about the nature of the political system itself. When these competing perceptions of *xinfang* collide, however, *xinfang* has great difficulty fulfilling any of its mandates. Thus, a paradox emerges. Although *xinfang* is designed to support regime legitimacy and maintain social stability, when actors actually engage in it, petitioners' confidence in the regime often becomes eroded and incidents of instability increase.

Conclusions

Xinfang is a medium through which actors can challenge rules and existing practices, and as such, it can "become [an] engine for change."[124] As this chapter has demonstrated, the interplay between petitioners, local government, central government, and even the general public determine not simply the boundaries of *xinfang* but also how competing perceptions of *xinfang* serve to bolster or undermine regime legitimacy. Whether or not the problems that *xinfang* poses to regime legitimacy extend beyond petitioners to non-petitioners, however, are less clear. Although this chapter has demonstrated that petitioners have been able to generate public pressure that can challenge the regime's legitimacy and as such, persuade it to alter policies or remove a corrupt official, this does not necessarily mean that the broader public is losing confidence in the regime itself. An in-depth analysis of this issue would require extensive fieldwork and years of research and is, thus, beyond the scope of this chapter. Nonetheless, the central leadership has publicly acknowledged the importance of complaint bureau work to the Party's survival, implying that problems with *xinfang* could extend beyond disaffected petitioners. By examining the system of *xinfang* this chapter hopes to have shed some light on our understanding of not only how legitimating processes unfold in authoritarian regimes, but also how various actors interact to create the impetus for regime legitimation.

Notes

1. Laura Luehrmann, "Facing Citizen Complaints in China: 1951–1996," *Asian Survey* 43, no. 5 (September/October 2003), 845–6.

2. Laura M. Luehrmann, "Officials Face the Masses: Citizen Contacting in Modern China" PhD diss., Ohio State University, 2000, 2.

3. China's petitioning is by no means the only one. In the former Soviet Union, officials used a similar system to report on the deviant behavior of grassroots officials in areas where the central government had difficulty in administrative oversight. See Sheila

Fitzpatrick , *Stalin's Peasants: Resistance and Survival in the Russian Village After Collectivization* (Oxford: Oxford University Press, 1994), 15.

4. Figures taken from Carl Minzner, "Social Instability in China: Causes, Consequences and Implications," Council on Foreign Relations (2006).

5. Kevin J. O'Brien, "Rightful Resistance," *World Politics* 49, no. 1 (October 1996): 31–55.

6. For a discussion of everyday forms of protest see: James C. Scott, *Weapons of the Weak: Everyday Forms of Peasant Protest* (New Haven: Yale University Press, 1987).

7. Jayshree Bajoria, "Access to Justice in China," Council on Foreign Relations (USA), (April 16, 2008).

8. Yongshun Cai, "Social Conflict and Modes of Action in China," *The China Journal* no. 59 (January 2008): 90–109.

9. Yongshun Cai, *Collective Resistance in China* (Stanford: Stanford University Press, 2010), 23–4, 30 and 32.

10. Lianjiang Li, "Political Trust and Petitioning in the Chinese Countryside," *Comparative Politics* 40, no. 2 (July 2007): 209–226.

11. Wuyan Han, "Zhongnanhai qinxi yiwan renmin" [Zhongnanhai is affectionately linked with millions upon millions of people], *Liaowang* [Outlook] 11 (1996), 7.

12. Qin Shao, "Bridge under Water: The Dilemma of the Chinese Petition System," *China Currents* 7, no. 1 (Winter 2008), 1; Suzanne Ogden, *Inklings of Democracy in China* (Cambridge: Harvard University Press, 2002), 43.

13. Ogden, *Inklings*, 43.

14 Jonathan K. Ocko, "I'll Take It All the Way to Beijing: Capital Appeals in the Qing," *The Journal of Asian Studies* 47, no. 2 (May 1988), 294.

15. The primary means of communication was through letter-writing and written proposals, which individuals could submit to various higher levels of authority (e.g., local, provincial, or central). However, *xinfang* also included a more traditional means of appeals: *shangfang* (上访), which literally means "going up to visit." In this case, individuals attempt to contact higher-level officials in person in order to seek redress.

16. Kuan Zou, "The Right to Petition in China: New Developments and Prospects," *EAI Background Brief*, no. 285 (May 10, 2006), 2.

17. According to Minzner (2006), the use of petitions many help higher-level officials in determining both the existence of and the extent to which lower-level malfeasance occurs within a given area or administrative region. The practice of *jubao* is present in a variety of official documents and regulations. For example, Article 41 of the Chinese Constitution guarantees the right of informing on official malfeasance, and other related terms (e.g., *jianju*, or revealing mistakes or wrongdoing) can be found in other legal documents and institutional mandates. The Supreme People's Procuracy, for example, has a *Jubao* Center. See: http://jubao.spp.gov.cn. As described in: Carl F. Minzner, "*Xinfang*: An Alternative to Formal Chinese Legal Institutions," *Stanford Journal of International Law*, 42, no. 103 (2006): 109 and 118.

18. Luehrmann, *Officials Face*, 2.

19. Luehrmann, *Officials Face*, 8.

20. Luehrmann, *Officials Face*, 8.

21. Luehrmann, *Facing Citizen Complaints*, 865.

22. See: Li, *Political Trust* and Minzner, *Xinfang An Alternative*.

23. Tenth People's Congress, Twelfth Meeting, *Beijing Petition Regulations*, September 8, 1994, http://www.gjxfj.gov.cn/2006-03/07/content_6399309.htm (accessed November 14, 2010).

24. *Beijing Petition Regulations*, September 8, 1994.

25. Minzner, *Xinfang An Alternative*, 133.
26. State Council of the People's Republic of China, *Regulations on Letters and Visits*, January 10, 2005, http://www.gjxfj.gov.cn/2006-03/07/content_6399309.htm (accessed November 11, 2010).
27. Minzner, *Xinfang An Alternative*, 136.
28. *2005 Letters and Visits Regulations.*
29. The 2005 Letters and Visits Regulations reads in part: "[Petitioners] . . . shall not harm the interests of the State, society or the collective or infringe upon the lawful rights of other citizens, shall conscientiously maintain public order and the order in handling letters and visits, and shall not commit any of the following acts:" a) illegally gather in public places, interfere in state organs, public service vehicles or block traffic, b) carry hazardous materials, c) insult or threaten government workers or restrict the personal freedom of others . . . (g) "committing *other acts* that disrupt public order or impair national or public security" [emphasis added]. See: *2005 Regulations on Letters and Visits.*
30. Xi Chen, "Collective Petitioning and Institutional Conversion," in *Popular Protest in China*, ed. Kevin J. O'Brien (Cambridge: Harvard University Press, 2008), 56.
31. Chen, *Collective Petitioning*, 64–5.
32. Minzner, *Xinfang: An Alternative*, 141.
33. Li, *Political Trust*, 210.
34. "Thousands Battle Police in China's Northwest" *New York Times*, November 18, 2008, http://www.nytimes.com/2008/11/19/world/asia/19china.html (accessed July 2, 2010).
35. O'Brien, *Boundary-Spanning*, 51.
36. As described in: Cai, *Collective Resistance*, 193.
37. David Easton, *A System's Analysis of Political Life* (Chicago: University of Chicago Press, 1965), 278 and 312.
38. Anna Matveeva, "Legitimating Central Asian Authoritarianism," Paper presented at the annual meeting for the American Political Science Association, Boston, Massachusetts, August 28, 2008.
39. David Beetham, *The Legitimation of Power* (Atlantic Highlands: Humanities Press International, Inc., 1991); Bruce Gilley, "The Determinants of State Legitimacy: the Results of 72 Countries," *International Political Science Review* 27, no. 5 (January 2006): 47–71.
40. Gilley, *The Determinants*, 48.
41. Mateeva, *Legitimating Authoritarianism*, 3.
42. Mateeva, *Legitimating Authoritarianism*, 3.
43. For example: Guo (2003) notes that the regime uses a combination of new policies and symbolic rhetoric to promote a more open, friendlier self-image (e.g. simplifying procedures for permits, urging unionization and the promotion of workers' rights). The regime has also publicly emphasized adherence to the rule of law and begun the arduous process of codifying and/or transforming practices into legally based institutions. In what Guo (2003) notes is its weakest tactic, the regime also attempt to present itself in a paternalistic manner, where it attempts to frame itself as a "servant of the people" that professes to know what is best rather than what people want. See Baogang Guo, "Political Legitimacy and China's Transition," *Journal of Chinese Political Science* 8, no. 1–2 (Fall 2003): 1–25.
44. Luehrmann, *Officials Face*, 2.
45. As quoted in Han, *Zhongnanhai*, 7.

46. Article 41 reads: **"Citizens of the People's Republic of China have the right to criticize and make suggestions to any state organ or functionary**. Citizens have the right to make to relevant state organs complaints and charges against, or exposures of, violation of the law or dereliction of duty by any state organ or functionary; but fabrication or distortion of facts with the intention of libel or frame-up is prohibited. In case of complaints, charges or exposures made by citizens, the state organ concerned must deal with them in a responsible manner after ascertaining the facts. No one may suppress such complaints, charges and exposures, or retaliate against the citizens making them. Citizens who have suffered losses through infringement of their civil rights by any state organ or functionary have the right to compensation in accordance with the law" [original bold]. People's Republic of China. *Constitution of the People's Republic of China*. December 2, 1982. See: http://english.peopledaily.com.cn/constitution/constitution.html.

47. Minzner, *Xinfang: An Alternative*, 109.

48. Zhijiang Zhou, "Ren da fu mi shu zhang: duo shu xin fang shi yin ji ceng shi zhi shi wu he cuo wu" [National People's Congress Deputy Secretary: The Majority of Xinfang Petitions are a Result of Lower Level Mistakes and Errors], *Xinhua* (August 5, 2004), http://www.chinacourt.org/public/detail.php?id=126299 (accessed November 20, 2010).

49. As quoted in: Xi Chen, "Art of Troublemaking: Chinese Petitioners' Tactics and Their Efficacy." Paper presented at the annual meeting of the American Political Science Association, Chicago, IL, September 2, 2004, 50.

50. As quoted in: Chen, *Art of Troublemaking*, 49.

51. As quoted in: Chen, *Art of Troublemaking*, 48.

52. As quoted in: Jonathan Watts, "China Voices: The Petitioner" China at the Crossroads Series, *The Guardian,* (May 21, 2009), http://www.guardian.co.uk/ (accessed July 6, 2010).

53. James Reynolds, April 9, 2009 (12:09 p.m.) "Petitions in China," *James Reynolds' China on BBC News,* April 9, 2009, http://www.bbc.co.uk/ (accessed July 6, 2010).

54. Edward Cody, "China's Land Grabs Raise Specter of Popular Unrest," *The Washington Post* (October 5, 2004), http://www.washingtonpost.com/ac2/wp-dyn/A6968-2004Oct4?language=printer (accessed July 6, 2010).

55. Cai, *Collective Resistance*, 168.

56. Cai, *Collective Resistance*, 168.

57. Cai, *Collective Resistance*, 169.

58. Cai, *Collective Resistance*, 170.

59. "Officials Should Heed Kneeling Petitioners," *Shanghai Daily* (April 29, 2010) http://www.shanghaidaily.com/sp/article/2010/201004/20100429/article_435581.htm (July 6, 2010).

60. "Mayor Resigns after Online Blast for Ignoring Petitioners," *Xinhua* (April 29, 2010), http://english.cri.cn/6909/2010/04/29/1781s566474.htm (accessed July 6, 2010).

61. *Shanghai Daily* (April 29, 2010).

62. Shanghai Government Official Website, *Cold-Shoulder, Mayor Quits Post.* Shanghai: April 30, 2010, http://www.shanghai.gov.cn/shanghai/ (accessed July 5, 2010).

63. As quoted in: Chen, *Art of Troublemaking*, 48.

64. Zhuanshun Zhao, Director of Department of Calls and Letters, stated that 80 percent of the petitions have merit. See: Jim Yardley, "Chinese Appeal to Beijing to Resolve Local Complaints," *The New York Times* (March 8, 2004).

65. Comments posted to Tianya.cn BBS, "Illiterate old woman, Zhangjiagang City, Sixty houses were dismantled, on-line help!!" (June 21, 2010),

http://www.tianya.cn/new/publicforum/ArticlesList.asp?strItem=free&idWriter=0&Key=0&Part=0 (accessed June 22, 2010).

66. Cai, *Collective Resistance*, 170.

67. "Where Does the Long Road to Petition End?" *Beijing Youth Daily* (January 1, 2005).

68. Cai, *Collective Resistance*, 192.

69. See, for example: Pierre Landry, *Decentralized Authoritarianism in China* (Cambridge: Cambridge University Press, 2008). He argues that the central government has been able to maintain control of the lower levels of government through its system of personnel management. Thus, the central government maintains broad political control while allowing for decision-making autonomy and economic development at the lower levels of government.

70. O'Brien, *Boundary-Spanning*, 51, 60 and Tanner, Murray Scot and Eric Green, "Principals and Secret Agents: Central versus Local Control Over Policing and Obstacles to "Rule of Law" in China," *China Quarterly*, no. 191 (2007), 644, 646–47.

71. "President Hu Charts Path in Anti-corruption Drive," *China Daily* (January 10, 2007), http://www.chinadaily.com.cn/china/2007-01/10/content_779107.htm (accessed June 26, 2010).

72. For a discussion central-local relations and their impact on corruption see: Ting Gong, "Corruption and Local Governance: The Double-Identity of Chinese Local Governments in Market Reform," *The Pacific Review* 19, no. 1 (March 2006): 85–102. For a discussion of the manifestations of irresponsible cadre behavior resulting from the political system see: Yongshun Cai, "Irresponsible State: Local Cadres and Image-Building in China," *Journal of Communist Studies and Transition Politics* 30, no. 4 (December 2004): 20–41.

73. See Cai, *Local Cadres*, for a discussion of irresponsible cadre behavior.

74. Hu Baozeng, Xie Tianchang, Chen Maohua and Li Yanju, "Hexie shehui goujian yu quntixing shijian falü duice yanjiu" (Research on the Legal Measures of Constructing a Harmonious Society and Dealing with Collective Incidents), *Zhongguo renmin gong'an daxue xuebao* (Journal of the Chinese People's University of Public Security), no. 4 (2006): 105–11.

75. "Chinese Lawmakers Urge Amplified Anti-corruption Efforts to Maintain Social Stability," *People's Daily* (March 11, 2009), http://english.peopledaily.com.cn/ (accessed June 25, 2010).

76. "Hu Jintao zai Zhongguo gongchandang di shiqi ci quanguo daibiao dahui shang de baogao" ["Hu Jintao's Report to the 17th Party Congress"], *Xinhua* (October 15, 2007).

77. Lily Tsai, *Accountability without Democracy: Solidarity Groups and Public Good Provision in Rural China* (Cambridge: Cambridge University Press, 2008).

78. Merle Fainsod, *Smolensk under Soviet Rule* (Cambridge: Harvard University Press, 1958).

79. Luehrmann, *Officials Face*, 8.

80. Chen, *Collective Petitioning*, 14–15.

81. Li, *Political Trust*, 211.

82. *Beijing Youth Daily* (January 1, 2005).

83. Academia Sinica and National Taiwan University, East Asian Barometer Survey, Mainland China (2002), http://www.jdsurvey.net/eab/Analize.jsp.

84. Academia Sinica and National Taiwan University East Asian Barometer Survey, Mainland China (2008), http://www.jdsurvey.net/eab/Analize.jsp.

85. East Asian Barometer Survey (2002) and (2008).

86. Author's discussions with non-petitioners in Beijing (July 2010).

87. Amelia Mathias, "China high court ex-vice president to face corruption charges" Jurist Legal News and Research (August 22, 2009), http://jurist.law.pitt.edu/paperchase/2009/08/china-high-court-ex-vice-president-to.php (accessed November 30, 2010).

88. Author's compilation of thirty-eight newspaper articles from *People's Daily, Shanghai Daily, China Daily, China News Net, Xinhua* and *Southern News Net*, written between 2007–2010.

89. Titles taken from *People's Daily, China Daily, Xinhua,* written between 2007–2010.

90. Bill Schiller, "It Takes an Angry Village to Revolt in Rural China," *The Star* (October 11, 2007).

91. Schiller, *It Takes an Angry Village.*

92. Minxin Pei and Yu Jianrong, "Seeking Justice: Is China's Administrative System Broken?" *Carnegie Endowment for International Peace* (April 5, 2006),http://www.carnegieendowment.org/events/index.cfm?fa=eventDetail&id=870 (accessed November 11, 2010).

93. Yanfeng Qian, and Ma Chao, "Petitioners Travel Miles to Be Heard at Sessions," *China Daily* (March 10, 2010), http://www.chinadaily.com.cn/china/2010-03/13/content_9584293.htm (accessed July 6, 2010).

94. As quoted in: Yardley, *Chinese Appeal.*

95. Jae Ho Chung, Hongyi Lai and Ming Xia, "Mounting Challenges to Governance in China: Surveying Collective Protestors, Religious Sects and Criminal Organizations," *The China Journal*, no. 56 (July 2006), 9.

96. Cai, *Collective Resistance*, 32.

97. Cai, *Collective Resistance*, 32.

98. Chung, Lai and Xia, *Mounting Challenges*, 9.

99. Chen, *Collective Petitioning*, 56.

100. Chen, *Collective Petitioning*, 56.

101. Cai, *Social Conflict*, 109.

102. Carl Minzner, "China's Citizen Complaint System," Statement Prepared for the Congressional-Executive Commission on China (December 4, 2009): 2; also see 2005 Letters and Visits Regulations.

103. Cases reported in Chen, *Collective Petitioning*, 15.

104. Cai, *Collective Resistance*, 192.

105. Minzner, *China's Citizen Complaint*, 2.

106. Shanghai Academy of Social Sciences (March 4, 2009), http://www.sass.org.cn/shkxb/articleshow.jsp?dinji=231&artid=59341&sortid=492 (Accessed July 15, 2010).

107. *Beijing Youth Daily,* (January 1, 2005).

108. As noted in: Chung, Lai and Xia, *Mounting Challenges*, 9.

109. Minzner, *China's Citizen Complaint*, 2

110. James Reynolds, January 14, 2009 (8:36 a.m.) "Petitioners Protest in Beijing" *James Reynolds' China on BBC News,* January 14, 2009, http://www.bbc.co.uk/blogs/thereporters/jamesreynolds/2009/01/one_thing_worries_the_governme.html (accessed July 6, 2010).

111. Author's conversation with non-petitioner in Beijing, July 2010.

112. "Upset China Petitioners Stage Risky Protest," *MSNBC* (March 11, 2009) http://www.msnbc.msn.com/id/29639623/ (Accessed July 17, 2010).

113. "Beijing Petition Village Demolished," *Deutsche Welle* (September 19, 2007).

114. Shirong Chen, "China Bans Petitioners in Beijing," *BBC News* (August 19, 2009), http://news.bbc.co.uk/2/hi/8210047.stm (accessed November 11, 2010).

115. Minzner, *China's Citizen Complaint*, 4.

116. Li, *Political Trust*, 218.

117. Minzner, *China's Citizen Complaint*, 3.

118. Minzner, *China's Citizen Complaint*, 3.

119. As quoted in: "Chinese Dissidents Committed to Mental Hospitals," *PBS News Hour*, (September 11, 2009), http://www.pbs.org/newshour/bb/asia/july-dec09/china_09-11.html (accessed July 6, 2010).

120. As quoted in: Watts, *China Voices.*

121. As quoted in: Chen, *Art of Troublemaking*, 44–45.

122. Li, *Political Trust*, 218 and 221.

123. Li, *Political Trust*, 219.

124. O'Brien, *Boundary-Spanning*, 58.

Chapter 9
Globalization and Transformation of China's Welfare Regime

Huisheng Shou

For many observers, China is different from the rest of the world in almost every aspect. The Maoist socialist welfare system, for instance, was considered to be one of the best models in the world. This once highly-acclaimed system, however, seems to be collapsing almost overnight as the country began integrating into the world market, leaving many observers concerned about the negative consequences of economic and social reforms, particularly to the wellbeing of the ordinary citizens.[1] For both its establishment and alleged collapse, the Chinese welfare system has been puzzling and an easy answer is: "China is exceptional!" A more sophisticated explanation would draw our attention to its political regime that successfully suppressed its labor in order to pursue globalization.[2] For others, China's approach has had a larger impact—it is defining a new "bottom" in a way that forces other countries to drive down their social protection even further.[3]

Such claims, however, are unfounded. The Maoist socialist welfare system is not collapsing for two reasons. First, it *was* not a strong welfare state as we commonly believe; second, it *is* not following a so-called "race to the bottom," in which governments lower their labor standards and give up social agendas in order to compete for the "footloose" foreign capital.[4] As for the past, the Chinese government only mandated urban work units and rural communes to provide welfare protection to their employees and members but the state itself took little financial responsibility. As evidence, the share of government spending on social security and welfare in total government expenditures was considerably lower than that in most developing countries—whereas the spending level in China was 1.7 percent in 1978, the average spending level in developing countries was 11.5 percent. In addition, as discussed later in detail, only a very small portion of China's populace, mostly the urban dwellers in formal sectors, enjoyed generous welfare benefits.

Regarding what it is today, the welfare transformation in the post-1978 China is not defining a new bottom. Instead, it is a restructuring of social protection, which does not constitute collapse but, rather, a "move to the middle"—overall spending on welfare is less, more segments of the populace are covered. Whereas pension and employment insurance programs have been targeted for entrenchment, programs such as social assistance and poverty relief that were traditionally downplayed have made significant progress.

This chapter aims to explain the mechanism underpinning this shift of social protection and place China into a broader context of the developing world. China's leaders may have enjoyed a better position than other countries to promote this process of policy adjustment. However, the time and trajectory of China's welfare transition over the past three decades hardly suggest that this process was determined by its particular regime or specific political leaders. The timing of China's reform, in fact, suggests that its post-1978 social welfare transformation follows a general trend of economic and social transformation that took place in the developing world around the late 1980s and early 1990s. That is, governments in the developing world began undertaking policy adjustments to accommodate the new developments in the context of globalization. More specifically, economic integration into the world market in these countries has fundamentally reshaped their industrial structure in a way that narrows the risk gap between different social groups. As the structure of social preferences with regard to state protection has been fundamentally changed, the government is able to readjust its strategy for maximizing political support by protecting its citizens with a more balanced structure, thus a "move to the middle."

The remainder of this chapter is organized as follows. Section 2 will first present empirical evidence to demonstrate that a similar trend of social protection that has happened in China is taking place in most developing countries, around almost the same period since the late 1980s, suggesting that China has been following an overall historical movement influenced by the world economy. It then provides a theoretical model to explain the mechanism underpinning this trend. Sections 3–5 demonstrate that this model applies in China's specific context. Section 3 introduces the pre-1978 social protection system and describes the overall social and welfare spending since 1978. Section 4 analyzes the interaction between globalization and industrial structure and the impact on the structure of social preferences regarding state protection among major social groups. Section 5 describes the resulting new social protection regime in a globalizing economy. Section 6 concludes with a discussion of the future change of China's social protection system.

Changing Trend of Government Spending in the Developing World

Across the globe, government expenditures have experienced significant change in the past decades. Figure 9.1 below shows the changing trend of the average social spending in fifty-three developing countries from the early 1970s to the late 1990s, a critical period when globalization began emerging. Three categories of social spending are presented in this figure: social security and welfare, education, and health.

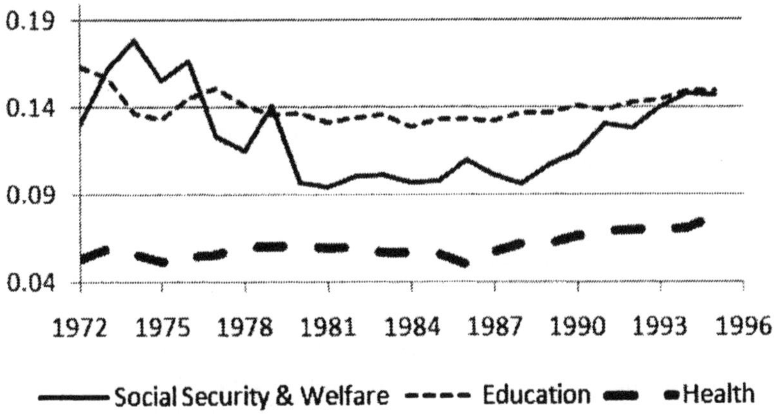

Figure 9.1 Government Spending (%) in the Developing World: 1972–1995

Sources: IMF, various years.
Countries included: Argentina, Bangladesh, Bolivia, Botswana, Brazil, Cameroon, Chile, Colombia, Costa Rica, Cyprus, Dominican Republic, Ecuador, Egypt, El Salvador, Fiji, Ghana, Greece, Guatemala, Guyana, Honduras, India, Indonesia, Iran, Israel, Jordan, Kenya, South Korea, Kuwait, Lesotho, Liberia, Malawi, Malaysia, Mali, Mauritius, Mexico, Morocco, Nepal, Nicaragua, Pakistan, Panama, Paraguay, Philippines, Singapore, Sri Lanka, Syria, Tanzania, Thailand, Trinidad and Tobago, Tunisia, Turkey, Uruguay, Venezuela, and Zimbabwe.[5]

Two things are noticeable. First, the overall trend of social security and welfare spending among developing countries has decreased from the 1970s to the 1990s, despite a slight increase since the late 1980s. The difference between the highest spending (19 percent in 1974) and the lowest (9.4 in 1981) is a significant 31 percent. Second, whereas the spending on social security and welfare has been declining overall during the period, education and health care spending has been largely constant. In fact, health care spending has increased since the late 1980s.

These differences suggest that globalization has multifaceted impacts on government functions, which are reflected in different categories of government expenditures. Spending on social security and welfare—which are commonly used to measure the size of the welfare state—refer to transfers to individual persons and households. In contrast, expenditures on education and health care target the general population. Beneficiaries of these three categories may overlap. Nevertheless, the difference between social security and welfare vs. education and health is significant and reflects the different political weight of social groups in policy choices.

For example, social security and welfare spending in the developing world is considered to be regressive in the sense that it benefits only a narrow group of individuals who can afford social security contributions, because these programs, for instance, pensions and employment insurance, are employment-based and earnings-related. Only a very small amount of the expenditures under this category go to the programs that are non-contributory, such as programs that encourage school attendance and primary health care visits of children. Contrasting to social security and welfare, education and health care programs are less focused on individuals and households but more on the general population, therefore having wider beneficial effects than social security and welfare programs do.[6]

Equalization Effect of Globalization

To explain such different impacts of globalization on government spending, the key mechanism is that globalization has an equalization effect on the demand for state protection among major social groups in the developing world. Following the basic logic of the Stolper-Samuelson theorem, since most developing countries are endowed with abundant unskilled labor, workers in low-skilled sectors gain from greater trade openness as a result of their comparative advantages in these economies.[7] In the long-run, international trade induces skilled workers to migrate into low-skill dependent sectors, therefore repressing wage differentials between high-skilled and low-skilled sectors. Since wages are skill premium for social insurance, the wider the wage differentials between different sectors, the more risks are for high-skilled workers. The narrowed wage differentials resulted from international trade therefore diminish risk gaps among different sectors.

To confirm this assumption, Figure 9.2 below shows the average level of trade openness and skill dependence in developing countries during the period from the 1970s to the 1990s. While trade openness increased significantly, the skill dependence level decreased, particularly since the early 1990s. The reduction from 0.29 percent in 1992 to 0.25 percent in 1995—a 14 percent drop—is significant, given the low skill level for the most part of the period in the developing world. This change suggests that developing countries in general have strengthened their low-skilled manufacturing sectors, which are more in line with their factor endowments.

As market competition encourages fluid labor markets and represses wage differentials among different sectors, international trade reduces uncertainty for high skilled labor, because job opportunities will increase in low-skilled manufacturing sectors. As a result, the employment losses in high-skilled sectors can be absorbed by low-skilled manufacturing and informal sectors. In principle, this could reduce uncertainty among formal sector workers.[8] The structural change of the economy introduced by globalization therefore alters the structure of social preferences among major social groups with regards to the demand for state protection.

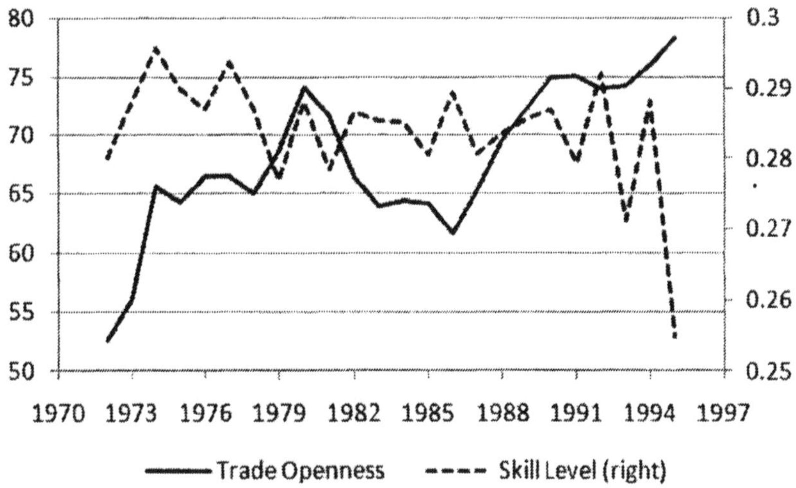

Figure 9.2 Trade Openness and Skill Dependence in the Developing World: 1972–1995

Sources

1. Trade openness from Penn World Table 6.0;
2. Skill level from United Nations Industrial Development Organization (UNIDO), *Database of Industrial Statistics*, various years.
3. Sampled countries are the same for Figure 9.1.

Note:

1. Trade openness is measured by the sum of import and export as the share of GDP;
2. Skill level is measured by the ratio between the number of employees in high-skilled export-manufacturing sectors and the number of employees in low-skilled export-manufacturing sectors.

As globalization reduces the incentives for state protection at the demand side by reducing the risk gap between different sectors, it also discourages incentives of governments—at the supply side—to maintain traditional welfare benefits. The fiscal discipline imposed by market competition makes generous benefits enjoyed by the high-waged workers increasingly unbearable for governments. Most importantly, trade openness and market competition also equalize political support among various social groups. The previously marginalized social groups, such as rural workers, women, urban workers in informal sectors, and those under the poverty line, become increasingly important for a healthy economy and long-term development. Governments have become increasingly aware that leaving any major social groups behind will backfire on their nations' survival in international markets. It therefore becomes increasingly critical for governments to spread benefits around among different social groups.

While traditional social security programs are under retrenchment pressure, globalization induces governments to expand social safety net programs such as minimum wage guarantees, social assistance, poverty relief, education, and health care. These programs previously were downplayed in most developing countries but have become increasingly important for countries to improve human capital infrastructure and pursue sustainable development. In doing so, states that are compelled to remodel their role from "welfare state" to "competition state," in which, welfare effort is refocused toward a more Schumpeterian "competitor" or "work-fare" state.[9]

Thanks to this enabling effect, globalization, rather than producing a "race to the bottom," creates more of a "move to the middle" in which governments pursue a moderate level of spending and a balanced distribution of benefits among their citizens. In most cash-strapped developing countries, this movement to the middle produces a "miserly" social protection system in terms of benefit level, which may have tremendous difficulties fully serving the purposes of protection. However, it nevertheless serves the right purposes of sustainable development.

Social Protection in the Post-Mao China

Prior to 1978, the Chinese welfare system was characterized by the following features. First, it provided comprehensive welfare protection with benefits including social security, education, housing, health care, maternity benefits, elderly care, and childcare.[10] Although socialist strategies of political control reinforced the generosity of welfare protection in terms of comprehensive welfare benefits and rigid labor market institutions, the main dynamic for welfare protection was industrialization beginning in the 1950s, as happened elsewhere in the developing world.[11]

Second, urban work units and rural communes took primary financial responsibilities while the government functioned primarily as a regulator and only used a very small portion of its budget for welfare protection.

Third, the socialist ideology did not obscure the fact that protection was highly stratified and biased in favor of high-skilled labor that took only a very small proportion of the labor force. Firms were classified into three categories of ownership: 1) state-owned enterprises (SOEs), which could be further classified into different levels based on administrative hierarchy across sectors and regions; 2) collective-owned enterprises, where the assets were owned collectively by employees; 3) others, including everything other than state-owned and collectives. The categories of ownership were closely associated with skill levels of these firms. Large SOEs concentrated on heavy industries, which are skill and capital-intensive. Most firms in the non-state sectors were in light industries and non-manufacturing sectors such as construction and agriculture with lower skill and capital inputs. There was a close association between the ownership of firms and welfare benefits. The SOE employers enjoyed much more benefits than those in other sectors. For example, pensions and employment insurance were only available for SOE workers.

Fourth, the price for enjoying such a highly protected welfare system was not trivial. The welfare system was maintained on the basis of a low level of living standards and lack of freedom of mobility. The life-long employment in SOEs, though giving the employees high job stability, made labor mobility across regions and sectors extremely difficult. Once reforms took place, both financial and political freedoms became strong incentives for abandoning the old system.

Figure 9.3 below shows the different trends of government expenditures on two programs—pension insurance and welfare assistance programs—between 1978 and 2005.[12] Pension insurance was the key component of the traditional welfare programs and only covered a small proportion of the labor force; most of which was employers of urban SOEs that were concentrated in high skill dependent sectors. Figure 9.3 shows that 1992 marked a turning point for government spending on pension insurance. Before 1992, the spending trend was upward from 1984, with some minor fluctuation in the early 1980s. Since 1992, the government's spending on pension insurance has experienced a consistent decline in a relatively rapid speed in the entire 1990s, and only increased moderately since 2002.

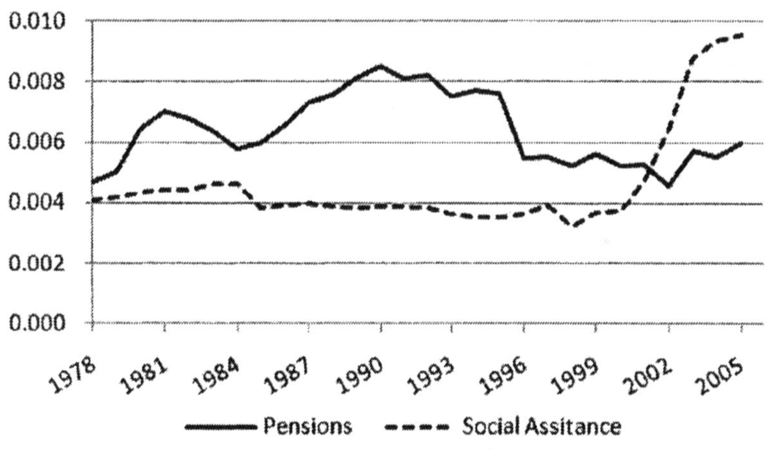

Figure 9.3 Structure of Social Spending (% of Total Government Expenditures): 1978–2005

Source: *China Statistics Yearbook*, various years

The upward trend from 1984 up to 1991 can be partially attributed to the slow reform in urban sectors in the early stage of the reform. As Naughton points out, China did not privatize significant numbers of state firms until the early 1990s. "Indeed, it did not even systematically separate SOEs out from the hierarchical state bureaucracy in which they were embedded."[13] As state firms were still overprotected, the reforms instead attracted more individuals to get into SOEs for shelter and welfare benefits.

The priorities of government spending have been under significant change as well, as shown in the contrast between pension spending and the spending on social assistance programs. Social assistance programs target poor individuals and families that are at the low end of skill distribution. These programs are critical for human capital infrastructure and long-term development, therefore the key component of social safety nets in a market economy. It is striking to see that government spending on the latter category, after the slight decrease for the entire 1980s and the most 1990s, has increased dramatically in the early 2000s. This contrast clearly demonstrates a significant shift of focus from traditional welfare protection to long-term development in a new market environment.

Globalization and Changing Industrial Structure

What mechanisms have underpinned the declining trend of China's welfare regime? Following the discussion in the previous section, this section examines the interaction between China's changing industrial structure and its trade regime. The findings presented below suggest that trade liberalization since the early 1980s, in particular since 1992, has fundamentally reshaped the industrial structure and closed the income gap between low and high skilled workers. That change has had significant impacts on the structure of social preferences among different social groups and has consequently affected the strategies adopted by politicians in policy choices.

Trade Liberalization and Changing Industrial Structure

Figure 9.4 below shows the trend of trade openness and foreign direct investment (FDI) in China since 1978. Before 1978, China's total trade/GDP ratio never significantly exceeded 10 percent. And FDI did not exist. Since 1984 when the government set up export-processing zones in southern China, the new trade regime began taking off. The trade/GDP ratio experienced a steady and rapid increase, then becoming stabilized around 40 percent after 1992, before taking another leap after China entered the WTO in the late 2001.

For most of the period since 1978, China's trade openness has mainly been sustained by foreign direct investment (FDI). However, 1992 was a particularly important moment for China's trade regime. That year, FDI volume jumped from $35 million in the previous year to $110 million, a growth rate of 152 percent. The volume further increased to $275 million in 1993, making China the second largest FDI recipient country next to the United States.[14] The year 2002 marked another significant point, when both FDI volume and trade/GDP ratio increased substantially.

What has made this rapid transition of trade regime possible is China's abundant and low-skilled labor. The labor force in Chinese official statistics is distributed into three sectors based on skill dependence: 1) agriculture as primary enterprises, at the low end of skill distribution; 2) manufacturing the second; and 3) services the third with high skill dependence. At the beginning of the reform, over 70 percent of the total labor force was concentrated in the low skilled primary sector, and that number only decreased to 50 percent in 2000.[15]

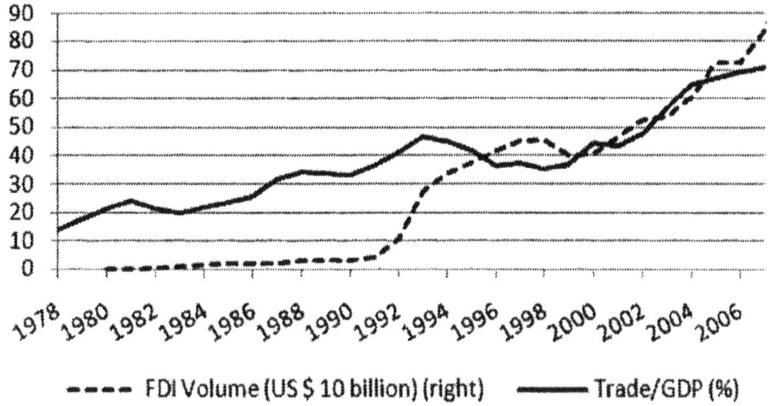

Figure 9.4 Trade Openness and FDI in China: 1978–2007

Sources: Trade openness from Penn World Tables (PWT) 6.3 (current price: 2005 base year); FDI from UNCTAD, *Foreign Direct Investment Database*

Note: Trade openness is measured by trade volume (the sum of imports and exports) as a share of GDP.

It must be noted that the secondary sector are manufacturing industries, most of which are still heavily low-skill and low-capital intensive. Taken together, the primary and secondary sectors took 87.8 percent of total labor force at the beginning of reforms, and still 73.1 percent in 1999, a significant part of which is low-skilled labor. Table 9.1 below further demonstrates that the Chinese export manufacturing since the reforms has become increasingly low-skilled and labor intensive, a shift that is more compatible with China's comparative advantage in abundant low-skilled labor. The values of export manufacturing goods are grouped into three categories of export—labor intensive manufacturing (line 1), capital intensive manufacturing (line 2), and raw material-based (line 3). The first two categories can be further classified according to the level of skill being used.

Most noticeable in this table is the rapid increase of the share of labor-intensive manufacturing goods (line 1), from 33 percent in 1965 to 74 percent in 1990, while the share of capital-intensive manufacturing goods (line 2) decreased from 65 percent to 19 percent during the same period. Notice that while the share of capital intensive manufacturing goods has decreased, the growth

Table 9.1 Export Values (millions in US dollars) of Manufacturing Goods: 1965–1999

Goods	1965		1975		1980		1985		1990		Growth rate (%)	
	Value	%	Value	%	Value	%	Value	%	Value	%	1965–90	1980–90
Total exports	1718	100	6303	100	18237	100	27764	100	80541	100	16.6	16.0
1. Labor-intensive	570	33	2253	36	7168	39	12319	44	59787	74	20.5	23.6
1.1. Non-skill labor-intensive	454	26	1557	25	5254	29	9742	35	41222	51	19.8	22.9
2. Capital-intensive	1113	65	3128	50	6353	35	7984	29	14978	19	10.9	8.9
2.1. Labor intensive	148	9	473	8	1292	7	1708	6	12325	15	19.3	25.3
3. Raw material-based	961	56	3665	58	9116	50	13339	48	5290	21	22.7	2.9
3.1 Coal, oil, natural gap		2		14		22		26		7	--	--

Source: Yin Xiangshuo, *Empirical Analysis of China's Foreign Trade Structural Adjustment* (Taiyuan: Shanxi Economics Press, 2003), 115.

rate of labor-intensive manufacturing goods within both categories (line 1.1 and 2.1) has increased significantly. For example, non-skill intensive manufacturing goods within the category of labor-intensive manufacturing goods (line 1.1) increased from 26 percent to 51 percent, while labor-intensive goods within the category of capital intensive goods (line 2.1) increased from 9 percent to 15 percent. Zhang[16] also confirms this change and further argues that the share of non-skill intensive manufacturing goods is even higher, about 45 percent constantly from 1978 to 1996.

Both studies presented above agree that this shift has become particularly salient since the late 1980s when the export-led trade strategy became a clearer agenda. In the last column of Table 9.1, the growth rates for labor-intensive (line 1), non-skill labor-intensive (line 1.1), as well as labor intensive in capital-intensive (2.1), are all higher in the period between 1980–1990 than in the period between 1965–1990, while the growth rate for capital-intensive (line 2) decreases from the first to the second period, suggesting an accelerating speed of the shift since 1980s.

Table 9.2 Share of Employees by Ownership: 1992–2000

year	SOEs		Non-state Firms*	
	% of total	growth rate (%)	% of total	growth rate (%)
1992	74	2.11	1.9	30.56
1993	74	0.28	4.0	90.07
1994	73	-0.27	5.0	39.37
1995	73	0.60	6.0	17.40
1996	74	-0.05	6.0	7.38
1997	73	-1.67	7	15.28
1998	71	-18.18	13	49.94
1999	71	-5.37	15	9.69
2000	70	-5.50	17	8.35

Sources: Modified from Xiaodong Wu, "Foreign Direct Investment and Dissemination of Job Opening Information in China," in William T. Kosanovich ed., *Improving Labor Market Opportunities and Security for Workers in Developing Countries* (Bureau of International Affairs, U.S. Department of Labor, Washington D.C., 2003), 141–170.

Notes:

* Including all enterprises of domestic funded cooperative units, joint-owned units, collective joint-owned units, limited liability corporations, state-funded corporations, and share holding corporations Ltd. but excluding private enterprises and township and village enterprises, as well as urban collective firms.

The new trade regime centered on low-skilled and labor intensive manufacturing has fundamentally transformed China's industrial structure. The most important indicator is the downsizing of SOEs, which is accompanied by the expansion of non-state sectors that rely on low-skill factors. This change suggests that firms with high-skill dependence have become less suitable to new market structure. Instead, firms with low-skill dependence quickly grasped the opportunity of openness. For instance, township-village enterprises (TVEs) that exclusively depended on labor-intensive manufacturing quickly became the backbone of the new trade regime in the early years, later followed by urban private firms. The growth of TVEs and urban private sectors presented mounting competition for SOEs that relied on high skill and intensive capital inputs. Naughton (2007) notes that "SOE monopoly profits were competed away as aggressive TVEs drove price relationships into line with underlying costs. SOEs had to implement new incentive programs and improve efficiency in order to survive in the face of the TVE competitive onslaught."[17]

Under such pressures, the new "contract system" emerged in 1983 as an effort to change the labor-management relationship in SOEs in order to accommodate the new industrial structure. In 1993, the boom of private sectors following the surge of FDI inflow forced the government to further relax labor market institutions in order to free SOEs from traditional welfare burdens. Laid-off workers became a new phenomenon from 1993. The downsizing of high-skilled SOEs can be seen clearly in comparing the number of employees in SOEs and non-state firms, as shown in Table 9.2. The employees in non-state firms increased by 90 percent from 1992 (1.9 percent of total employees) to 1993 (4.0 percent of total employees). At the same time the growth rate for the employees in SOEs decreased drastically from 2.11 percent in 1992 to 0.28 percent in 1993. Notice that "non-state firms" in this table does not include private enterprises and self-employed. If these categories are taken into account, the non-SOE share can be much higher. In 1998, the number of employees in SOEs and non-state firms experienced another significant change. The share of SOE employees dropped by 18 percent, while that of non-state firms increased by 50 percent.

Changing Structure of Social Preferences—Low Level of Protection as a Social Choice

Diminishing Risks for Skilled Workers

To understand why the new trade regime and industrial structure have helped ease the demand for social protection, it is critical to understand that the new economic structure has narrowed not only the income gap among social groups, but also the risk gap experienced across different sectors. A crucial factor that determines this possibility is the risk exposed to urban workers, particularly urban skilled workers because they had more stakes to loss in the reduction of traditional social welfare benefits. At the early stage of reform, urban SOE workers were the group that felt most strongly the uncertainty from openness.

For example, the breakdown of the "iron rice bowl" since the early 1980s and lay-offs from 1993 produced tremendous pressures on urban workers and managers. Thus it is critical to explain why the risks facing urban skilled workers actually decreased during this period.

First, skilled workers, particularly those at a higher level of the hierarchy, for example, large-scale SOEs and public sectors, were less threatened for the most part of the reform, because the government deliberately avoided putting these sectors at the front line of reforms. The government could afford to do so because employees from this group took a very small portion of entire SOEs. Thus generous protection on them is relatively easy to maintain. Instead, employees from small-scaled SOEs and other urban sectors were the first ones to face the challenge of reform. And yet, since these sectors previously enjoyed a much lower level of protection and fewer benefits, the gains from the new opportunities have far more compensated the new risks they are exposed to them. More importantly, however, the booming private sectors, particularly in the service sector, provided bountiful job opportunities for urban dwellers who, in addition to continuing enjoying at least partial benefits from their work units, could have a so-called "secondary job"—a popular term in the 1980s—outside their regular jobs in formal sectors, and the benefits from their second job could be substantial. As many scholars have noted,[18] the reform in the early stage was the one "without losers" because, as the outcome of a gradualist strategy of transition, state jobs were carefully protected so that marketization began with product markets and only slowly extended to labor markets.[19]

FDI and Decreasing Wage Differentials

Second, openness has decreased wage differentials and the risk gap across sectors. This explains why high-skilled workers find the reforms less threatening to them. This point, however, must be understood within the context of China's particular trade regime, which is sustained by low-skill biased FDI. According to trade theories, FDI has significant impact on income distribution between skilled and unskilled labor because of the technology change induced by FDI. The impact of FDI thus can go either way—increase or decrease income distribution across sectors, depending on whether FDI is relatively labor or skill biased.[20]

Studies have found that China's FDI has been low-skill biased. China's FDI primarily comes from the newly developed East Asian regions such as Hong Kong, Taiwan, Singapore, and South Korea. Huang, Xie and Chen (1994) reported in their survey that 54.1 percent of FDI in the manufacturing sector came from these countries.[21] These findings echo the findings in previous section that the type of FDI from these countries is relatively labor biased rather than skill biased, because industries in these countries are at the lower-end of manufacturing chains in the world market. This type of FDI aims at taking advantage of China's cheap unskilled labor and is mostly concentrated in China's export oriented sectors. Precisely because of this logic, the Chinese government has utilized favorable policies such as tax breaks to attract foreign direct investment with labor biased technology.

Many other empirical studies have confirmed that FDI and trade liberalization in general have had equalizing impacts on wage and skill differentials in China. For instance, based on their analysis of the characteristics of FDI across different provinces, Owen and Yu (2008) found that the effect of FDI on regional differences in wage inequality across industries in China hinges on the type of FDI—whether it is export or import-oriented. Export-oriented FDI tends to raise the wages of workers in industries that rely more on unskilled workers and therefore tends to lower the wages of workers in industries that rely more on skilled workers.[22]

Efficient Allocation of Skills

Third, trade openness not only reduces the wage gap between high-skilled and low-skilled sectors. It also induces efficient allocation of skills. Skilled workers can voluntarily migrate from state sectors to private sectors, while unskilled workers can also find jobs in SOEs which are trying to lower their costs by downgrading the skill level of their products and reducing the proportion of high-skilled workers. Prior to the reform, skilled workers were concentrated in the SOEs. Since FDI inflow increases the job opportunities in the private sector,

Table 9.3 Average Wage of Staff and Workers by Ownership: 1990-2001 (*Yuan*)

Year	National Average	SOE		Private	
		Wage	% of national avg.	Wage	% of SOE
1990	2140	2284	6.73	2987	130.78
1991	2340	2477	5.85	3468	140.01
1992	2711	2878	6.16	3966	137.80
1993	3371	3532	4.78	4966	140.60
1994	4538	4797	5.71	6303	131.39
1995	5500	5625	2.27	7463	132.68
1996	6210	6280	1.13	8261	131.54
1997	6470	6747	4.28	8789	130.27
1998	7479	7668	2.53	8972	117.01
1999	8346	8543	2.36	9829	115.05
2000	9371	9552	1.93	10984	114.99
2001	10870	11178	2.83	12140	108.61

Sources: Modified from Xiaodong Wu. "Foreign Direct Investment and Dissemination of Job Opening Information in China," in William T. Kosanovich, ed., *Improving Labor Market Opportunities and Security for Workers in Developing Countries*, (Bureau of International Affairs, U.S. Department of Labor, Washington D.C., 2003), 141–170.

workers with higher productivity tend to move to private sectors for better wages, even though the social welfare benefits in these firms are much lower and they need to purchase health insurance out of their own pockets. For example, Wu found that since 1994 the percentage of engineers and technicians in non-state sectors has begun surpassing that in state-owned and collective-owned sectors.[23]

To further confirm this trend of efficient allocation of skills, Table 9.3 presents data on average wage of employees by ownership. It demonstrates that the average wage in the non-state sector is higher than that in the state sector, suggesting that workers in the non-state sector, on average, are more productive than those in the state sector. Since 1984, the average wage of employees in the state sector was higher than the national average, but lower than that in private firms. This average wage gap between the state and private sector firms reached its highest peak in 1993 when FDI more than doubled. The trend only began decreasing after SOEs began to increase their productivity and competitiveness since 1998.

In sum, the new trade regime centered on labor-biased FDI has not only increased the size of the pie, but also increases the quality to divide the pie, because the wage and risk gaps between high-skilled and low-skilled workers are narrowed by labor mobility. Many studies demonstrate that there has been a race to the top in terms of income equality because individuals in all areas in China have experienced gains in average income.[24] These findings echo well the argument in this study, which is derived from the standard trade theory: as economic reforms deepen, labor market works more efficiently by balancing the demand and supply of skills. While the skilled labor commands a higher premium to compensate for state protection they previously enjoyed, the low-skilled workers find new opportunities created by openness to substitute for public welfare protection. The free flow of skilled and un-skilled labor across different sectors decreases the attraction of state welfare benefits. That is, the low level of social protection is a social choice made by major social actors.

Changing Strategy for Political Support

The new industrial structure and the changing social preferences that followed provide politicians with opportunities to adjust their strategy to maximize their political support across the social spectrum. Since the reforms began, particularly after 1992, China's political leaders have found their core constituencies under significant change. Previously, the core constituencies for the regime were urban employees from formal sectors, which were critical for maintaining economic autarky. After 1978, however, the shift of the focus on competition in international markets has weakened that sector. When the barriers to labor mobility across sectors are removed as the result of the changing industrial structure, the strategic alliance between formal sectors and skilled labor began to loosen. At the same time, the low-skilled labor that primarily concentrates in non-state sectors became increasingly critical for the economy that relies on low-skilled factors to enhance its comparative advantage. As evidence, by the end of 2004, the urban private sector, without counting foreign-invested firms, employed about twice as many workers as the traditional state sector: 55 million, compared with less than 30 million in SOEs.[25]

The demand for a level playing field between private sectors and SOEs became intensified along with economic reforms since the early 1990s. By the late 1990s, discrimination that had been levied on private sectors largely disappeared. Following Deng's South China tour in 1992, ideological barriers against the growth of private economies were dismantled in the following years, accumulated into the acceptance of private businessmen into the Chinese Communist Party in 2001 and the full legal protection for private property in 2004 Constitution and 2007 Property Rights Law.[26] These changes reflect a far-reaching shift of policy orientation that has significant impact in many areas, in which welfare transformation is part of the broad scheme. New policies since the late 1990s have begun to address issues that are considered to hinder the long-term development, for example, the regional disparity between the western hinterlands and the east coastal regions,[27] policy biases against agriculture and rural residents, and equal rights for rural migrant workers.[28]

It is interesting to note that, despite the rapid policy adjustment since the late 1990s, the political dynamics underlying the relationship between the government and its citizens have remained the same, as the political influence of workers in both state and private sectors has not changed fundamentally since 1978. Similarly, western regions have, if anything, not gained more influence in policy making in Beijing than they were before, due to the strong economic power of the coastal regions. Neither has any new policy given rural residents more political cloud, even though the political control in the countryside has been relaxed.

It is puzzling, therefore, to see that the authoritarian regime has been willingly extending the benefits to those workers, sectors, and regions that still possess less political influence than the traditional constituencies. The leadership transition in 2002, for many observers, motivated the new leaders to drastically depart the previous pro-business approach during the most part of the 1990s and adopted instead a pro-poor approach in order to accumulate their own political capital. This argument, however, fails to explain that the shift of policy had already occurred before 2002. In fact, maintaining a balance between different social groups in terms of distribution of economic benefits and social protection has been the tenet of the reform from the very early stage, as reflected in Deng Xiaoping's grand scheme regarding regional disparity between coastal regions and hinterlands—one region needed to contribute to the development of another region at different stage of development.[29] The idea was expressed by Deng as early as the 1980s and was implemented by both Jiang and Hu administrations.

It is not the political leaders but globalization—intensified since 1992 and further accelerated after 2001—that has determined the shift of economic and industrial structures. The economic integration incurs pressures of sustaining future economic development and maintaining political support for market-oriented reforms. Without fundamental restructure, it would be unimaginable for China to sustain its fragile economy under international competition. In doing so, the government cannot afford leaving any sector behind. By the late 1990s, therefore, in both official rhetoric and academic research, "integration" or "consolidation"—which is similar in Chinese—became a popular term, referring to the need of synergizing domestic institutions, policies, social interests in order to enhance the competiveness of China's economy. Responding to this consensus, the guiding principle for the future development, under the new leadership, is to establish a "harmonious society" based on "balanced and people-oriented development," with an "emphasis on social equity so that entire population can enjoy the fruits of reforms and development."[30]

The "Move to the Middle:" New Welfare Regime under Globalization

As Wang points out, the changing rhetoric reflects the change of policy agenda, which is responding to the reshuffle of social interests.[31] As a result, the concept of "public goods," which was widely discussed in media and academia, entered the official language and began to guide the new social welfare policies. The process of constructing the new social welfare regime as public goods, however, requires two different efforts of policy adjustment, which took place at different stages: the first stage between 1992 and the late 1990s, during which the main task was to reduce the excessive welfare benefits in SOEs and state sectors; the second stage since the late 1990s, in which the policies have targeted the entire population, but with more emphasis on the low-skilled and low-income sectors that are outside the state sector. The balancing of policy adjustment is illustrated by opposite trends of government spending on social security and on social assistance in Figure 9.3. Whereas the spending on social security was reduced considerable after 1996, the rapid increase of government spending on social assistance programs since 2001 suggests more emphasis on the individuals in the low-skilled sectors. In the process of interaction between these two trends, a balanced structure of social welfare spending is emerging to cover the entire population with a low level of government financial burden.

Reducing Welfare Benefits in State Sectors

As the barriers between state and private sectors began breaking down since the early 1990s, it became evident that the costly and inefficient traditional welfare system was no longer sustainable. Laid-off workers became a phenomenon since 1993. By the late 1990s, however, lay-offs became a norm for everyone. Since the early 2000s, "lay-off" and "unemployment"—which is associated with non-state sectors—began to be used interchangeably, suggesting that the line between state and non-state sectors is no longer discernable. As a result, the employees from large-scale SOEs and other public sectors found their benefits shrinking quickly, best illustrated in three categories of traditional welfare benefits: pension, housing, and medical care.

Previously, workers in state sectors did not pay contributions for their pension benefits. The new scheme initiated in the early 1990s required individual contribution for the new pension fund. Since 1994, privatization of housing has begun taking significant steps. A Housing Provident Fund (HPF) with the contribution from both workers and employers was established. In the late 1990s, SOEs were no longer allowed to build housing and had to gradually sell off their apartment blocks. The housing reform disentangled SOEs from social welfare responsibilities and also significantly reduced the financial burden of the government. Between 1981 and 1997, the states' contributions to investment in fixed assets dropped dramatically from 28.1 percent to 2.8 percent.[32] Similar reforms have also taken place in medical care. In 1994 the government announced that a social pooling fund based on an individual accounts replace traditional almost-free medical care benefits.

Expanding Welfare Coverage to Non-state Sectors

As the government reduces traditional welfare benefits in the state sector, it also expands the coverage of these programs to the entire population. Since the late 1990s, government policies towards welfare distribution have become more equity oriented. The government has begun establishing universal schemes in the early and mid-2000s in pension, housing, and medical care that cover all urban residents across sectors, including self-employed and temporary workers. These programs cover all work forces and also standardize the management of funds across regions so that individuals can transfer their welfare benefits across regions.

The more striking policy change, however, has been the establishment of various social assistance programs that target the population who were previously deprived of welfare benefits. These groups include urban informal sectors and, particularly, the rural population. The programs include minimum standard living system, social assistance programs for the urban and rural poor, and poverty relief programs that primarily target poor population in countryside.

In urban areas, the most noticeable new program is unemployment insurance that is designed to cope with the problem of unemployment caused by redundant workers released from the state sector and the huge size of the new labor force. The universal unemployment insurance scheme in 1999 broadened the coverage of the unemployment insurance scheme to employees in all categories of urban firms. Aimed at both unemployment and urban poverty, the Minimum Standard of Living System (MSLS) was introduced in the 1990s. The targeted population includes unemployed workers, low-income and disabled individuals. Initially local governments were expected to bear all expenditure of the MSLS. In 1999, central government resumed its role as the last resort.

In addition, the government has also set up new social assistance programs in education, medical care, housing, and poverty relief, to assist poor families and individuals in urban and rural areas. In education, for example, new initiatives were proposed in 2004 to target poor children in both urban and rural areas, such as free primary and secondary education, education subsidies and exemption. In housing, the Low Rental Housing program (LRH) was implemented in the early 2000s to assist poor households in urban areas. In health care, an area that is widely seen to be neglected by the government in the most part of the 1990s, a New Rural Cooperative Medical Scheme (NRCMS) was initiated in 2002 and established in 2004 to provide financial support for poor families. Public health care programs were reestablished and "all urban and rural residents should be entitled to basic public health services."[33] Finally, the most successful progress in the area of social assistance is the poverty relief program. From 1978 to 2004, the number in poverty reduced from 250 to 29 million, reducing the poverty rate from 64 percent at the beginning of reform to 10 percent in 2004.[34] The amount of investment put into poverty reduction work increased from 9.8 billion in 1994 to 30 billion in 2003.[35]

Market Dependence as the Principle of Welfare Reform

One remaining question is that why the government under the new policy guideline would be able to expand the coverage of welfare programs to the massive low-skilled workers outside the SOEs without incurring the financial burdens on the government. This can be explained by two factors. First is China's low level of skill dependence. Under current industrial structure, the financial pressure for the government is low because the new regime requires individuals to provide the substantial part of the contribution. Although social assistance programs require the government to provide primary financial responsibility, the overall low level of income associated with China's labor force reduces that pressure considerably.

More importantly, however, the pressures from international market competition and from the level playing field at the domestic market make it difficult for the government to use welfare benefits to cater any single social group as the base of political support as it did before. Instead, market competition provides strong incentives for the government to resist the attempt, from both old and new social groups, to make welfare benefits a luxury good rather than a safety net. In reforming the welfare system, the Chinese government strictly follows a principle of market dependence, which ensures that the expansion of the coverage of welfare protection does not impose welfare burdens on the state but instead serves to promote market competition and labor mobility. Efficiency is both the principle that guides the design and implementation of the new welfare system and a goal the new system aims to achieve. This is best illustrated by the "social-pooling-plus-individual-accounts scheme" that has been applied in most welfare programs, such as the old age pension scheme, medical care, unemployment insurance, and Minimum Standard of Living scheme.

The government makes it explicit in its statement that this scheme is an innovation and is suitable to China's particular condition as a low-income society —this approach simultaneously "reflects the merit of traditional welfare scheme as risk-pooling and also emphasizes the mechanism for individual workers' self-reliance and self-motivation." The strength for this scheme, according to the government, is that it not only ensures higher living standards and social stability, but also enhances productivity under varying economic conditions.[36]

In most of these programs, the financial burden essentially is on individuals and firms, while the central and local governments pay only part of the premium. For instance, the government provides only basic pension insurance. Employers and individuals contribute the rest. Medical insurance in urban areas requires that employers contribute 6 percent of their total wage bills while employees pay 2 percent of their wages as premiums. All contributions from workers, together with 30 percent of the premium from their employer, go to the individual account. The remaining 70 percent of the contribution from the employer goes to the social pooling account. In order to address the issue that most programs are underfunded, the government encourages and mobilizes multiple channels and resources to raise the fund and reduce the costs. Local governments, firms, social organizations—such as urban neighborhoods and other non-governmental organizations—and individuals are encouraged to participate in management and contribute to the programs.[37]

Conclusions

China's case has illustrated that globalization has produced a strong detrimental effect on traditional stratified and hierarchical distribution of welfare benefits once the country began opening up. At the same time, globalization has also induced the Chinese government to expand the coverage of social protection to accommodate previously marginalized social groups in non-state sectors. The case demonstrated that this process is not determined by any particular factors that make China exceptional, such as its regime, leadership, or its culture. Instead, it is an active response of the government to the pressures and opportunities introduced by openness. In the new welfare regime, the government finds it in its interests to maintain a balanced welfare structure that compensates more social groups and is nevertheless efficiency-oriented and market-friendly so that aggregate well-being can be sustained in a competitive market. A sustainable economy, in turn, can serve as the base for the government to survive over the long run.

Most importantly, this process of "moving to the middle" is taking place not only in China but also in many other developing countries, even though the variations persist due to various factors.[38] The Chinese welfare regime has been moving toward this balanced structure of welfare distribution in a relatively quick pace and yet without incurring excessive financial burdens on the government. The low skill dependence of the Chinese economy prior to 1978 has played a critical role in this process. The high-skilled sectors were relatively small, concentrated in large-scale SOEs, which are still shrinking as reforms have been deepening. And high-skilled workers now find new better-paying job opportunities. Their resistance to the welfare reforms has, therefore, been minimal. In other countries, such as Brazil, where the size of skilled sectors has been much higher, the process of welfare transformation has been much slower and protracted.[39]

Such an advantage, however, may be undermined. Many signs suggest that China currently is in a critical stage to move towards a more skill-dependent economy in its urban sectors after three decades of development, which will fuel the demand for more government protection. This is illustrated by the shortage of skilled labor and the increasing labor costs in many urban areas in recent years.[40] Given the fact that the current welfare system is still underfunded, it can be predicted that the public social welfare spending will experience an upward trend once the government takes more financial responsibilities and more population is covered in the new welfare system. The strong increase of social assistance expenditures since 2001 and the slight increase of the spending on social security since 2003 in Figure 9.3 indicate that such a trend is undergoing.

At the same time, however, other forces work against this expansionary trend. The industrial structure still remains heavily low-skill based so far. In 2007, the employees in the agricultural sector still counted 40.8 percent and manufacturing 26.8 percent, compared to the service sectors 32.4 percent.[41] China's huge rural labor surplus makes the wage growth largely an urban phenomenon. The loosened rules on rural/urban migration will not only strengthen China's advantage in labor and low-skill-intensive manufacturing, but will also further narrow the wage gap and lower the incentives for welfare expansion. The most important factor, however, is China's integration into the world economy. Joining the WTO has further locked the economy in a competitive market and tied the hands of political leaders. As a result, the principle of market dependence may be strengthened rather than weakened. Though these changes have yet fully developed, it can be speculated that, the expansionary pressures on China's welfare system, though inevitable as the result of skill upgrading, will diminish over the long run under the pressure of globalization.

These two conflicting forces—the demand for low-skilled labor and the demand for high-skilled labor—may produce fluctuation in China's welfare regime in the future. The welfare policy choice will be a delicate game of balancing, highly contingent on politicians' strategic choices. However, as long as China maintains a strong commitment to openness, it is safe to say that China's welfare regime, for a considerable time in the future, will not deviate too far from its equilibrium, in which a low level of welfare expenditures and a balanced structure are maintained to accommodate both social protection and market competition.

Notes

1. For example, see Anita Chan, *China's Workers under Assault: the Exploitation of Labor in a Globalizing Economy* (New York and London: M.E. Sharpe, 2001) and Chak Kwan Chan, King Lun Ngok and David Phillis, *Social Policy in China: Development and Well-being* (Bristol, UK: Policy Press, 2008).

2. Globalization here is narrowly defined to refer to economic integration. The most commonly used indicators are trade openness and capital liberalization. In this study I focus exclusively on trade openness, under the assumption that trade openness and capital liberalization have different impacts on developing countries. Trade openness is measured by the sum of export and import as the share of GDP.

3. William Greider, "A New Giant Sucking Sound," *The Nation* (December 13, 2001).

4. For instance, see William Greider, ibid. Kenichi Ohmae, *The Borderless World* (New York: Harper, 1990).

5. The countries included in the sample were the only developing countries that submitted their data to the International Monetary Fund (IMF) on a regular basis during this period.

6. Quentin Wodon, ed., "Public Spending, Poverty, and Inequality in Latin America" (Washington DC, World Bank, 2003); Kathy Lindert, Emmanuel Skoufias and Joseph Shapiro, "Redistributing Income to the Poor and the Rich: Public Transfers in Latin America and the Caribbean," Discussion Draft (World Bank, October 24, 2005).

7. See e.g., Douglas Irwin, *Free Trade under Fire* (Ewing, NJ: Princeton University Press, 2002); Jagdish Bhagwati, *In Defense of Globalization* (New York: Oxford University Press, 2004) for theoretical discussion. For developing countries, see Jagdish Bhagwati, "The Global Age: From a Skeptical South to a Fearful North," *World Economy* 20, no. 5 (1997): 259–83; Jagdish Bhagwati, "Outward Orientation: Trade Issues," IMF-World Bank Symposium on Growth Oriented Adjustment Strategies, Washington DC, 1987; and David Bigman, "The Pros and Cons of Globalization for Developing Countries," In David Bigman, ed., *Globalization and the Developing Counties: Emerging Strategies for Rural Development and Poverty Alleviation* (Oxfordshire, UK: CABI Publisher, 2002), 27–80.

8. Isabela Mares, "The Great Divergence in Social Protection," Unpublished manuscript, 2006.

9. Bob Jessop, "Towards a Schumpeterian Workfare State? Preliminary Remarks on Post-Fordist Political Economy," *Studies in Political Economy* 40 (Spring 1993): 7–39; Philip Cerney, "Globalization and Changing Logic of Collective Action," *International Organization* 49, no. 4 (1995): 595–625; J. Zysman, "The Myth of a 'Global' Economy: Enduring National Foundations and Emerging Regional Realities," *New Political Economy* 1 (January 1996): 157–184.

10. For early literature review, see Mark Selden and Laiyin You, "The reform of social welfare in China," *World Development* 25, no. 10 (1997): 1657–1668; Xinping Guan, "China's Social Policy: Reform and Development in the Context of Marketization and Globalization," *Social Policy & Administration* 34, no. 1 (2002): 115–130.

11. Ian Little, Tibor Scitovsky and Maurice Scott, *Industry and Trade in Some Developing Countries: a Comparative Study* (London and New York: Oxford University Press, 1970).

12. The data here stop in 2005 because, since 2006, the national Bureau of Statistics of China dramatically changed its measure on social security and welfare expenditures under the section of "government finance." The data in the recent yearbooks are no longer compatible with those prior to 2006.

13. Barry Naughton, *The Chinese Economy Transitions and Growth* (Cambridge, MA: The MIT Press, 2007), 298.

14. United Nations Conference on Trade and Development (UNCTAD), *Foreign Direct Investment database*, Geneva, various years.

15. China Statistics Bureau, *Chinese Statistics Yearbook 2001* (Beijing: China Statistics Press, 2001).

16. Xiaoguang Zhang, *China's Trading Patterns and International Comparative Advantage* (Basingstoke, Hants.: Palgrave Macmillan, 2000).

17. Barry Naughton, *The Chinese Economy Transitions and Growth* (Cambridge, MA: The MIT Press, 2007), 275.

18. Lawrence Lau, Yingyi Qian and Gerard Roland, "Reform without Losers: An Interpretation of China's Dual-Track Approach to Transition," *The Journal of Political Economy* 108, no. 1 (2000): 120–143; Yingyi Qian and Jinglian Wu, "China's Transition to a Market Economy: How Far across the River?" in Nicholas C. Hope, Dennis Tao Yang and Mu Yang Li, eds., *How Far Across the River: Chinese Policy Reform at the Millennium* (Palo Alto, CA: Stanford University Press, 2003), 31–63.

19. Barry Naughton, *The Chinese Economy Transitions and Growth* (Cambridge, MA: The MIT Press, 2007), 183.

20. Robert Feenstram and Gordon Hanson, "Foreign Direct Investment and Relative Wages: Evidence from Mexico's Maquilaoras," *Journal of International Economics*, 42, no. 3–4 (1997), 371–93; Fan Zhang and Jingping Zhang, "The Impact of Multinational Enterprises on Economic Structure and Efficiency in China," working paper, China Center for Economic Research, August 1998.

21. Zhengshen Huang, Wenxia Xie and Xiangjiang Chen, *China 3000 Largest Foreign-Funded Enterprises 1994* (Beijing: China Reform Publishing House, 1994).

22. Ann Owen and Bing Yu, "Regional Differences in Wage Inequality across Industries in China," *Applied Economics Letters* 15 (2008): 113–116.

23. Xiaodong Wu, "Foreign Direct Investment and Dissemination of Job Opening Information in China," in William T. Kosanovich (ed.), *Improving Labor Market Opportunities and Security for Workers in Developing Countries* (Bureau of International Affairs, U.S. Department of Labor, Washington D.C., 2003), 141–170; Xiaodong Wu, "Will Foreign Capital Inflow Alleviate Income Inequality?" *Journal of the Asia Pacific Economy* 10, no. 4 (2005): 528–550.

24. Xubei Luo and Nong Zhu, "Rising Income Inequality in China: A Race to the Top." The World Bank Poverty Reduction and Economic Management Department: Policy Research Working Paper 4700, 2008; Qingbin Wang and Guanming Shi, "Economic Growth and Income Inequality in the Transition toward a Market Economy: China's Experience and Policy Implications," in M. T. Holt and J.–P. Chavas, eds., *Exploring Frontiers in Applied Economics: Essays in Honor of Stanley R. Johnson* (Berkeley, CA: Berkeley Electronic Press, 2006).

25. Barry Naughton, *The Chinese Economy Transitions and Growth* (Cambridge, MA: The MIT Press, 2007), 106.

26. Susan Lawrence, "Jiang Ensures Party Endures," *Far Eastern Economic Review* (Nov. 21, 2002): 34–38.

27. Peiyan Zeng, *In Retrospect of the Strategic Development of the Western Region* (Beijing: Xinhua Press, 2010).

28. Hualou Long, Yansui Liu, Xiubin Li and Yufu Chen, "Building New Countryside in China: A Geographical Perspective," *Land Use Policy* 27, no. 2 (2010): 457–470; Minzi Su, *China's Rural Development Policy: Exploring the "New Socialist Countryside"* (Boulder, CO: First Forum Press, 2009).

29. Peiyan Zeng, *In Retrospect of the Strategic Development of the Western Region* (Beijing: Xinhua Press, 2010).

30. The Central Committee of the Chinese Communist Party, "The Suggestions on Making 11th Five-Year Plan," Beijing, China, 2005.

31. Shaoguang Wang, "The historical Transition from Economic Policies to Social Policies," Unpublished manuscript, the Chinese University of Hong Kong, 2006.

32. Jieming Zhu, "The Changing Mode of Housing Provision in Transitional China," *Urban Affairs Review* 35, no. 4 (2000): 502–519.

33. State Council, "Implementation Plan for the Recent Priorities of the Health Care System Reform (2009–2011)" [*Yiyao weisheng tizhi gaige jinqi zhongdian shishi fangan (2009–2011)*], Beijing, 2009.

34. Martin Ravallion and Shaohua Chen, "China's (Uneven) Progress against Poverty," *Journal of Development Economics* 82, no. 1 (2007): 1–42; Asian Development Bank, *Poverty Profile of the People's Republic of China* (Asian Development Bank, Manila, Philippines, 2004).

35. Chak Kwan Chan, King Lun Ngok and David Phillis, *op cit.*, 86.

36. Ministry of Labor and Social Security, *Policies and Management of China's Medical Insurance System Reforms* (Beijing: China Labor Press, 1999).

37. Chak Kwan Chan, King Lun Ngok and David Phillis, *op cit.*

38. Sarah Brooks, *Social Protection and the Market in Latin America* (Cambridge: Cambridge University Press, 2009); Nita Rudra, *Globalization and the Race to the Bottom in Developing Countries: Who Really Gets Hurt?* (Cambridge, UK: Cambridge University Press, 2008).

39. Sônia Draibe, "The Brazilian Developmental Welfare State: Rise, Decline and Perspectives," in Manuel Riesco and Sonia M. Draibe, eds., *Latin America A New Developmental Welfare State Model in the Making?* (Palgrave Macmillan, 2006); Sarah Brooks, *Social Protection and the Market in Latin America* (Cambridge, UK: Cambridge University Press, 2009); and Raul Madrid, *Retiring the State: The Politics of Pension privatization in Latin America and Beyond* (Palo Alto, CA: Stanford University Press, 2003).

40. Keith Bradsher, "Investors Seek Asian Options to Costly China," *The New York Times*, June 18, 2008; "The Climb in Labor Costs," *China Daily*, February 9, 2010.

41. Ministry of Labor and Social Security and National Statistics Bureau, "2007 Labor and Social security Development Report," Beijing, 2008.

Index

About the Contributors

Lacey Bradley-Storey is a PhD student in the Department of Political Science at Northeastern University. She holds a master's degree in international economics and finance from Brandeis University and a bachelor's degree in political science and economics from New College of Florida. Her research interests include central-local government dynamics, identity-based politics and social instability in China and Central Asia.

Xinjun Gao is Senior Researcher & Professor in China Center for Comparative Politics & Economics, China Central Compilation & Translation Bureau, Beijing, China. He is a political scientist specializing in institutional issues, comparative political & economic systems study; comparative study on local governance; grassroots democracy & political reform; agriculture, farmer & countryside issues. Professor Gao has published numerous books and articles, including his recent contribution book, *Local Governance, Finance & Public Budgeting* (China Northwest University Press 2009). He is a frequent recipient of grants from the Ford Foundation, including support for field study on civil society in China. He was the visiting scholar in Kennedy School of Government in Harvard University from 1999 to 2000 and from 2002 to 2003. In 2007, his "*The Model of Crisis Management & Governance after Election: Analysis on the Institution Innovation of Eight Steps Method in Ma Liu Township of Kai Xian County in Chong Qing City*" got the first place prize in China Civil Affairs Ministry. His paper about Progressive Era in the United States was the cover story in *Journal of China Reform* in 2008.

Baogang Guo is Professor of Political Science at Dalton State College, and the past president of the Association of Chinese Political Studies (ACPS. 2008-2010). He was associate editor of the *Journal of Chinese Political Science* (2004-2010) and research associate in China Research Center based in Metro Atlanta, GA. His research interests include comparative public policy, political culture and political legitimacy, and Chinese and Asia politics. He is author of *China's Quest for Political Legitimacy* (Lexington Books, 2010), associate editor of *China Today* (Greenwood Press, 2005), co-editor of *China's Quiet Rise: Peace Through Integration* (Lexington Books, 2011), *Toward better Governance in China* (Lexington Books, 2010), *Dancing with Dragon* (Lexington Books, 2010), *Thirty Years of China-US Relations* (Lexington Books, 2010), *Greater China in an Era of Globalization* (Lexington Books, 2009), *China in Search of a Harmonious Society* (Lexington Books, 2008), *Challenges Facing Chinese Political Development* (Lexington Books, 2007), and author of nine book chapters and eleven peer reviewed journal articles. His recent publications appeared on *Asian Survey, Journal of Chinese Political Science, Modern China Studies, Journal of Comparative Asian Development, Twenty-first Century,* and *American Journal of China Studies.*

Ziying He got his PhD from Sun Yat-Sen University in China. He is currently Lecturer in College of Public Administration at Zhejiang University (ZJU), Hangzhou, China. He is also Research Fellow at Centre for Public Policy Studies at ZJU. His work focuses on state theory, political economics of transitional countries, Chinese state-building and social policy. His most recent book is *Bob Jessop's State Theory* (Hangzhou: Zhejiang University Press, 2010). In 2010, he was a visiting scholar at University of Southampton in UK.

Xiaobo Hu is Professor of Political Science and Director of Center for China Studies at Clemson University. His research and teaching interests include comparative political economy, institutional economics, and China studies. His publications include *China after Jiang* (Stanford University Press, 2003).

Michael Kilburn is Associate Professor of Political Science and holds an M.A. and Ph.D. in Interdisciplinary Studies from Emory University and a B.A. Honors from St. Thomas University in Fredericton, NB, Canada. His doctoral work was in the field of East European politics, history, and culture. He currently teaches courses in political theory and practice, human rights, and cultural studies, and he is the founder of the Endicott Center for Oral History, which supports oral history projects on campus and internationally. Prior to Endicott College, he taught at Emory University, the Atlanta College of Art, and abroad in Canada, Japan, and the Czech Republic. He is a member of the American Political Science Association, the International Studies Association, the World Society of Victimology, the International Human Rights Education Consortium, the Oral History Association, and the International Oral History Association.

Vitaly Kozyrev is an expert on International Relations in East Asia, Russo-Chinese relations, and regional security. In 1991-2007 he taught at the Institute of Asian and African Studies at Moscow State University and was a visiting professor at a number of institutions, including Amherst College, Yale University, University of Delaware, Yunnan University (China), and Feng Chia University (Taiwan). He has intensively published on political and socio-economic transformations in China and Russia, and contributed to the following books: *Russia Embraces Asia* (Monterrey Institute of International Relations, expected in 2011), *China's Energy Strategy: The Impact on Beijing's Maritime Policies* (Naval Academy Press, 2009), *Societies at Wars in the 20th Century* (Russian Academy of Sciences War Research Center, 2009, in Russian), *Normalization of U.S.-China Relations: An International History* (Harvard University Press, 2006). At present he is an Assistant Professor of Political Science and International Relations at Endicott College, Beverly, MA.

He Li is Professor of Political Science at Merrimack College in North Andover, Massachusetts. Li is the author of *From Revolution to Reform: A Comparative Study of China and Mexico* (University Press of America, 2004) and *Sino-Latin American Economic Relations* (Praeger, 1991). Li has published dozens of articles in journals such as *Journal of Strategic Studies, Problems of Post-Communism, The Historian, Policy Studies Journal, Journal of Chinese Political Science, Asian Perspective, American Journal of Chinese Studies, Asian Affairs*, and chapters in several books.

Huisheng Shou is Assistant Professor of Government Department, Christopher Newport University. His research focuses on international political economy, globalization, and public policies. His regional focus is on China, East Asia and developing countries in general. He was a research fellow at the World and China Institute, a Beijing-based research institution. At the World and China Institute, he studied grassroots elections in rural China, and, as a result, co-authored a book titled *Innovation and Development: Reforms of Township Government Elections* (Beijing: Oriental Press, 2001, in Chinese). Huisheng's current research interests include rural governance, corporate violence, and social welfare policies in China and the developing world.

Congsheng Wu is Professor of International Finance at the School of Business of the University of Bridgeport. His research interests include international finance, the relationship between economic freedom and economic growth, new securities offerings, emerging markets, and financial services. He is the co-author of two books and numerous research articles and book chapters. His papers have appeared in *Financial Management, Journal of Banking and Finance, Review of Quantitative Finance and Accounting, Journal of Multinational Financial Management, Journal of Business and Economic Studies, American Review of China Studies, China and World Economy,* among others.

Jianxing Yu is professor of political science, associate dean of the College of Public Administration, and director of the Institute for Civil Society Development of (ICSD) at Zhejiang University. He was a visiting professor at Arizona State University (2006-2008). His work focuses on state theory, social policy, and civil society organizations in contemporary China. His recent books are *Chinese Civil Society Growing in Participation* (Hangzhou: Zhejiang University Press, 2008), and *Governing Business Associations* (Hangzhou: Zhejiang People's Publisher, 2010)

Siyuan Zhou is graduate assistant at the School of Business of the University of Bridgeport. Her research, under the guidance of her supervisor Dr. Congsheng Wu, focuses on the relationship between economic freedom and economic growth and other international issues.

Yiran Zhou is a Research Assistant of Political Science Department, Missouri State University. His research, under the guidance of his advisor Dr. Dennis

Hickey, focuses on US-China relations, China's Politics, Taiwan issues, and China's ethnic and religious policies. He obtained a degree of MPA from the University of Kentucky in May, 2004. Before he came to the US, he worked at a public organization in Beijing, doing research on ethnic and religious policies as well as engaging in international multicultural exchanges (with more than ten countries' government agencies as well as international ethnic and religious NGOs). His forthcoming conference paper is "China Mainland-US-Taiwan Trilateral Relations since 2000: A Perspective of Complex Interdependence."

www.ingramcontent.com/pod-product-compliance
Ingram Content Group UK Ltd.
Pitfield, Milton Keynes, MK11 3LW, UK
UKHW041630031026
15587UKWH00001B/189

9 780739 165751